AND THEY THOUGHT
WE WOULDN'T FIGHT

Honoring
One Hundred
Fifty Years

RR DONNELLEY

Gibbons's title paraphrases this Victory Liberty Loan poster soliciting citizens to buy bonds to support the war.

The Lakeside Classics

AND THEY THOUGHT WE WOULDN'T FIGHT

by Floyd Gibbons

EDITED BY
MICHAEL S. NEIBERG

The Lakeside Press

R. R. DONNELLEY & SONS COMPANY
DECEMBER 2014

The Lakeside Classics is a registered trademark
of
R. R. Donnelley & Sons Company

Copyright © 2014 by R. R. Donnelley & Sons Company
All Rights Reserved
Printed in U.S.A.

Publisher's Preface

This year, the centennial of the beginning of The Great War, seemed the right time for the Lakeside Classics to publish an American memoir of that conflict. Our only previous volume on this subject, *Fighting the Flying Circus*, by Eddie Rickenbacker (1997), covered the air war, not the ground war. Yet, surprisingly, it proved difficult to find an appropriate account.

It may be because America's participation in World War I was brief compared with the long years of bloody conflict endured by the other combatants in the European theater. Their brutal years of trench warfare and costly offensives gave birth to literary masterpieces: Robert Graves's memoir, *Good-Bye to All That*; Rupert Brookes's and Siegfried Sassoon's poetry; Erich Maria Remarque's novel, *All Quiet on the Western Front*. In comparison, many of the accounts published by Americans seemed less frank about what the soldiers endured or were drawn from letters and diaries, making them more personal than historical.

Finally, on the shelves of the Pritzker Military Museum and Library in Chicago, we found *And They Thought We Wouldn't Fight*, by the *Chicago Tribune*'s war correspondent Floyd Gibbons. While not

Publisher's Preface

classical literature, it is good journalism, good history, and a roaring good read.

Gibbons was a new breed of war correspondent who was what today we would refer to as "embedded" with the troops. From the time he left America's shores, he experienced all of the troops' dangers and hardships: his ship was torpedoed in the Atlantic; he rode in freight cars with the artillerymen and their horses; he slogged through mud; he climbed observation posts; he slept in cellars; he ate field rations; and, most dramatically, he was seriously wounded. Gibbons sent his dispatches home so his readers could understand and experience the war. We are pleased to allow you to do so also by presenting as the 112th Lakeside Classic the book that he compiled from his columns. It has been somewhat abridged to fit our format.

We were particularly fortunate to enlist the talents of Michael S. Neiberg, professor of history at the United States Army War College, as the historical editor for this volume. His excellent essay introduces our readers to America's role in the war and also to the fascinating and exciting life of Floyd Gibbons. For those interested in learning more about World War I, we highly recommend Professor Neiberg's book, *Fighting the Great War: A Global History*, published by the Harvard University Press.

Publisher's Preface

"When in the line and Fritz is busy sending over his iron rations of bombs, minnie-woofers, pineapples and whiz-bangs and occasionally a gas shell . . . and one lands on our dugout or close, you can bet that we will be breathing the mud in the bottom of the trench."

"A few days ago, just before going over the top, I was wounded in the throat. It is not much of a wound, but I am laid up in a base hospital waiting for an operation."

Although these lines could have been drawn from Floyd Gibbons's interviews with troops serving in Europe, they were actually taken from letters published in RR Donnelley employee newsletters during 1918. That year, more than two hundred of the company's employees were in uniform. Several others had given the "last full measure of devotion" to their country and perished during the Great War. The Great War is part of our company's history as well.

As the war began, RR Donnelley was preparing to mark its 50th anniversary. This year, we observed our 150th.

As one of the oldest continuously operating companies in the United States, RR Donnelley has witnessed and weathered events such as the waning months of the Civil War, the Great Chicago Fire, two World Wars, the Great Depression, the Great

Publisher's Preface

Recession, and a revolution in how information is processed and distributed. During this time, RR Donnelley has grown from a single-shop family-owned printer in Chicago to become a publicly traded communication services provider with locations worldwide.

RR Donnelley's product and service diversity, technology resources, digital capabilities, and geographic reach would seem like the stuff of science fiction to the generations who have known RR Donnelley throughout its earlier history. Yet they would easily recognize our dedication to serving our customers, spirit of innovation, and commitment to operating with integrity. Consider just a few moments in our rich history and how these qualities were reflected then and today.

In 1871, on a hot, dry October evening, a fire broke out in a barn more than a mile to the southwest of RR Donnelley's facilities. Fanned by intense winds, the blaze quickly engulfed the city, destroying more than 40 percent of its buildings, including RR Donnelley's plants and the Donnelley family's home.

Insurance could not cover the loss, so the company's founder traveled to New York in order to secure loans to restart the business. He had nothing more to use for collateral than the company's sterling reputation for integrity. That proved to be enough, and he was able to begin anew. Today, this

Publisher's Preface

same commitment to integrity is reflected in our governance and transparency practices, as well as by our *Principles of Ethical Business Conduct* and attendant training, which guide the daily actions of our employees worldwide.

In 1886, just a decade after the invention of the telephone, RR Donnelley won a contract to produce what was then a novelty: a telephone directory. This began a relationship with a communications provider that has continued uninterrupted and blossomed in many directions for more than 125 years. We sustain long-term relationships by anticipating our customers' needs and offering solutions that address their emerging requirements. For example, during the 1800s, businesses were looking for new ways to reach potential customers with advertisements. RR Donnelley responded by inventing the business directory, a new vehicle for helping advertisers reach potential customers. To accomplish this same objective, modern advertisers turn to RR Donnelley for targeted direct response produced on our proprietary digital presses, local directories, TransPromo (digitally customized messaging on billing statements), personalized websites, intelligent retail displays that "talk" to shoppers' mobile devices, and more.

The company was founded with a vision of providing customers with comprehensive services, initially under one literal roof and later under a

Publisher's Preface

worldwide virtual one. Today this is reflected by extensive and fast-growing service offerings, which, by the end of 2013, had come to represent nearly 16.5 percent of RR Donnelley's revenues. These services include copywriting, photography, layout, translation and localization resources, design services, online systems for digital asset management, and more. We provide third-party logistics, outsourced fulfillment centers, judgment-based customer service and back-office support, and more.

In 1921, RR Donnelley opened a new operation, its first outside Chicago. That facility, in Crawfordsville, Indiana, is still in operation, though it is equipped today in a way that would awe its original workforce. This expansion was undertaken to provide new resources and better service to our existing customers and to enable the company to take advantage of new opportunities. This theme has been brought to life ever since, through internal expansions and acquisitions that today see RR Donnelley employees going to work in fourteen different time zones around the world. For example, we provide back-office support resources to global clients from our offices in South Asia; packaging solutions, procurement services, and product assembly resources in Latin America, North America, Europe, and Asia; and translation services across the world.

The year was 1927, and speculation ran rampant in the business and consumer press about what

Publisher's Preface

Ford's first new car offering since the Model T would look like. When it came to this closely guarded secret, RR Donnelley was in the know. Our employees were producing the launch materials that would equip dealerships with the materials they would use to introduce the new Model A. Today, customers continue to trust RR Donnelley with their most important—and in many instances, *regulated*—secrets. Our systems and processes are designed to move new product launches, IPO communications, financial-compliance reports, and more through our facilities and computer network behind firewalls and without compromise.

In 1934, something unusual was afoot at RR Donnelley's flagship facility. A team of engineers was at work, retrofitting a press. They were affixing what would look today like pizza ovens through which the paper would pass. In reality, these were dryers, which would enable ink to set more quickly, to enhance both quality and throughput. As RR Donnelley tested and perfected this innovation, an influential publisher was planning to relaunch a magazine called *LIFE*. His goal was to bring out a news weekly featuring superb photography. Doing so would require levels of speed and quality heretofore unseen. The magazine, produced on RR Donnelley's unique heat-set presses, debuted in 1936 and set a new standard for photojournalism. Innovation continues to fuel the company's new-product pipe-

Publisher's Preface

line, as RR Donnelley's imaging scientists, engineers, software designers, and programmers bring out game-changing capabilities. Printed electronics, our high-speed digital ProteusJet™ presses, ActiveDisclosure, CustomPoint™, VENUE®, and other innovations are expanding and transforming the range of communication services that the company provides.

In 2010, drawing on a range of our capabilities, we undertook to help the United States Census count the country's population. In a project that involved consultative services, printing, variable imaging and personalization, logistics, and more, RR Donnelley prepared communications to 120 million American households. That distribution went to three times more addresses than there were people living in the United States when our company was founded.

When RR Donnelley began, people passing down the bustling street on which its building stood would have noted the large sign that spanned its exterior. It read in part STEAM PRINTERS. During the past 150 years, the company has evolved to become a comprehensive *communication services* provider. These communications may be exclusively digital, come to life in print, be displayed on packaging or signage that you see in stores, arrive in your mailbox, or reach you in a variety of other ways.

Publisher's Preface

Each, though, brings with it a tradition of quality that spans more than 150 years.

At our Annual Meeting in May of this year, Lee Chaden and Stephen M. Wolf retired as members of the RR Donnelley Board of Directors. Mr. Chaden has served as a Director since 2008. Mr. Wolf was elected to the Board in 1996 and became its Chairman in 2004. We are grateful for their wise counsel and guidance. During 2014, a number of employees retired. We are thankful for their service. This preface has recited just some of our company's history. All of the employees who went before *lived* a portion of it.

RR Donnelley has achieved a number of firsts. Two of which we are particularly proud involve safety. In 1998, one of RR Donnelley's operations became the first printing plant in the U.S. to be recognized with OSHA's Voluntary Protection Program Star status, awarded only to facilities that demonstrate exceptional safety processes and performance. It was followed by another RR Donnelley site that became the first gravure facility to be recognized with VPP Star status.

We believe that safety is the first and most important measure of operational excellence. Our statistics worldwide continue to far outpace our industry's performance, but *statistics* do not work around the complex and fast-moving equipment

Publisher's Preface

that enables us to serve our customers. Our *people* do. That is why we will never be satisfied until we achieve 100 percent safety 100 percent of the time.

We are especially mindful of and grateful to our customers. Since RR Donnelley's founding, we have offered many unique resources, but there has never been a time when our customers have not been presented with a wide variety of competitive choices. Their confidence in selecting RR Donnelley to provide integrated communication services allows us to begin a new chapter in our history, as we embark on the next 150 years.

As 2014 comes to a close, we are delighted to wish you a safe and peaceful holiday season and the best for the new year.

THE PUBLISHER
December 2014

Contents

Illustrations xvi

Historical Introduction. xix

The Sinking of the *Laconia* 3

Pershing's Arrival in Europe 31

The Landing of the First American
  Contingent in France 49

Through the School of War 65

Frontward Ho 79

Into the Line 93

The First American Sector 117

The Night Our Guns Cut Loose 143

Into Picardy to Meet the German Push 155

Before Cantigny 181

The Rush of the Raiders 195

On Leave in Paris 213

Château-Thierry and the Bois de Belleau 223

Wounded—How It Feels to Be Shot 243

"Good Morning, Nurse" 267

Groans, Laughs, and Sobs in the Hospital 283

"July 18"—The Turn of the Tide 301

The Dawn of Victory 319

Index 339

Image Credits 347

Illustrations

Victory Liberty Loan poster ii
The dust jacket from the original edition xviii
Pancho Villa. xxviii
Robert R. and Amy Adams McCormick xxxii
Generals Pétain and Pershing. xxxviii
"Over There," sheet music xlii
Floyd Gibbons broadcasting for NBC in 1930 xlviii
American Troops Advancing through Northern France . .2
RMS *Franconia* and *Laconia*, postcard 6
Seamen and civilians from a torpedoed British ship 19
A German U-10 submarine 22
Map of Western Europe 38-39
General Pershing at Lafayette's tomb 46
The first American troops landing in France 52
French officers training U.S. Marines 67
An American soldier writing a letter home. 70
Map of Lorraine 80
American troops marching from training camp 84
Loading Field Artillery, postcard 87
French children cheering U.S. troops. 96
Field kitchen of the U.S. Army, 1st Division. 102
American artillerymen firing the first shot 114
German Observation Balloon, postcard 120
An American convoy in France 122

Illustrations

U.S. soldiers in a trench putting on gas masks	129
A listening post in the advanced French line	139
German Observation Post, postcard	146
U.S. Marines on a troop train in France	157
Map of Picardy	160
U.S. soldiers relaxing in their billet	164
Three Soldiers with a Horse	168
A French *poilu*, or footsoldier	185
A first aid station	188
Over the Top, stereo card	202
U.S. Infantry charging an enemy line	208
Souvenir postcard of Paris	215
Le Théâtre Français, postcard	220
Women walking through the rubble of Château-Thierry	232
Gibbons's helmet with shrapnel damage	256
Americans advancing at Belleau Wood, postcard	258
An ambulance taking away the wounded	270
An army field hospital inside the ruins of a church	273
An American volunteer writing a letter for a wounded soldier	289
A military hospital ward	293
Gibbons recovering from his wounds	298
An American soldier guarding German prisoners	315
African American soldiers marching in France	328
U.S. 64th Regiment celebrating the armistice	337

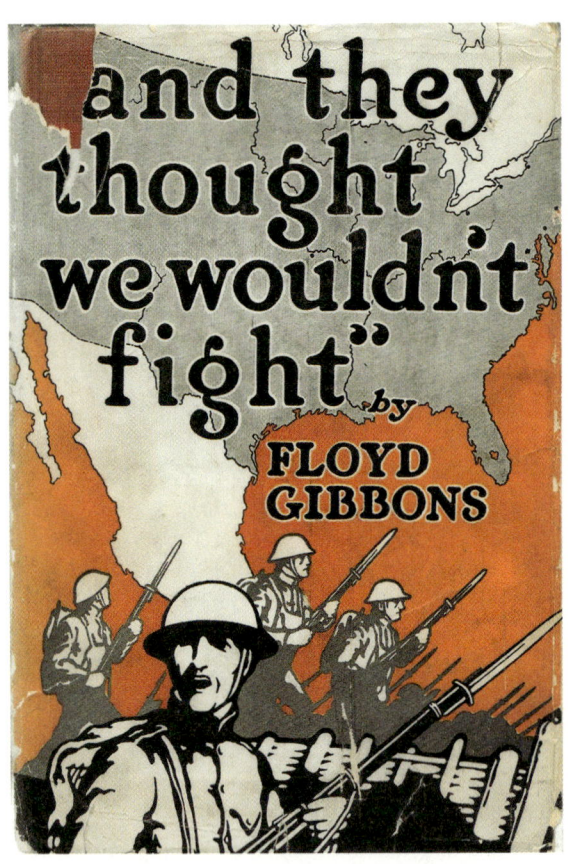

The dust jacket from the original edition, interestingly, shows troops superimposed over Mexico rather than Europe.

Historical Introduction

The outbreak of the First World War in 1914 caught Americans completely by surprise. The war began so quickly that thousands of Americans on vacation or on business found themselves trapped overseas in the middle of a major crisis with no access to European banks and all shipping temporarily under the control of the militaries of the warring powers. The United States government dispatched a battleship with enough gold on board to pay for passage home once shipping became available again. American students studying overseas volunteered to help both stranded Americans and the thousands of Europeans living in foreign countries now deemed to be enemy aliens. London alone had an estimated 100,000 German residents.

Back home, President Woodrow Wilson[1] asked Americans to remain neutral in thought and deed. He hoped both to avoid any actions that might pull the United States into the war and to keep the passions of Europe away from America's shores. Like many native-born Americans, Wilson was afraid that the millions of immigrants from the belligerent countries might either cause trouble in the United States on behalf of their mother countries or fight among themselves on American streets. For the most part those fears were ungrounded, but Ameri-

Historical Introduction

cans remained constantly on guard, afraid that the sparks of Europe might engulf them in flames sooner or later.

Wilson's call for neutrality notwithstanding, most Americans not of German heritage sympathized with the Allies. Wilson himself had strong pro-British sentiments. For some, France and Great Britain (although not their ally, Russia) seemed to be fighting a life-or-death war for democracy against the militarist autocracies of Germany and Austria-Hungary. Other Americans recognized that their nation's economic success was intimately linked to that of Britain, on whose ships more than half of all American commerce traveled.

The behavior of the German army also placed Germany on the defensive from the start. American defenders of the German position claimed that the mobilization of the Russian army in late July had forced a peaceful Germany into fighting a war it had not wanted. But the German war plan, written long before the war, called for seven of its eight field armies to sweep into Belgium and France in an attempt to win a rapid victory in the west before turning east and facing the Russians. German atrocities committed in Belgium and France, both real and those exaggerated by an eager press, made it difficult for Americans to sympathize with the German position.

Americans watched as the war degenerated into one of trenches, poison gas, machine guns, and ar-

Historical Introduction

tillery. Some Americans saw the western front for themselves; most of them returned horrified by the death and destruction but with a clear sympathy for the democratic states of France and Britain against the autocracies of Germany and Austria-Hungary. Thousands of Americans volunteered to help the Allies by sending money, serving as ambulance drivers, and, in a few notable cases, fighting on the side of the French or the British.

Still, most Americans wanted to stay out of the war. They watched from afar as battles like Verdun and the Somme raged. These battles, fueled by fully industrial and fully mobilized societies, went on for months, while only rarely moving the front lines in any meaningful way and were unprecedented in their size and ability to kill. Whereas Gettysburg, the largest battle ever fought in the United States, went on for three days and resulted in an estimated 46,000 total casualties, Verdun lasted for ten months and resulted in an estimated 970,000 total casualties.

Nevertheless, many Americans feared that they could not maintain neutrality forever. The German navy conducted an aggressive policy of submarine warfare that targeted both British and neutral ships. Because approximately half of all American trade went overseas on British ships, Germany's submarine campaign threatened to pull the United States into the war. The British, too, imposed a blockade, but because they used traditional surface ships, Brit-

Historical Introduction

ish sailors could board commercial vessels, remove contraband cargo headed for Germany, and, most importantly, ensure the safety of any passengers on board. While the United States had problems with the blockade policies of both nations, Germany's policy killed people, including women and children. Great Britain's blockade policy, as Wilson himself said, merely inconvenienced people.

Neutrality also became harder for Americans to sustain when a war that most people expected to be short showed few signs of ending. American industry, in recession when the war began, boomed with orders for artillery shells, uniforms, and all the many articles needed by nations at war. American mining companies sold coal and other raw materials as quickly as they could pull them out of the ground, and American farmers suddenly sold wheat, beef, and pork to export markets as never before.

Most of this economic boom connected the United States even more closely with Great Britain. The British navy controlled the major sea lanes, thus making it difficult for German merchant ships to travel to American ports. The British merchant marine, moreover, carried most American commerce across the Atlantic because the American merchant fleet was not large enough to do the job itself. Americans also had the luxury of trading with Canada, which had entered the war alongside Great Britain in August 1914. Even though most Ameri-

Historical Introduction

cans did not like to think about it, their leap out of recession owed a great deal to British and French war contracts.

To German eyes, these economic links hardly made America seem neutral. German officials argued that America had conveniently defined neutrality in a way designed to maximize profit while essentially putting American industry at Britain's disposal. In 1915 and 1916, American agents uncovered a series of plots to destroy American transportation nodes, place incendiary devices on ships bound for Britain, and foment strikes in American factories. The German government denied any direct connection to these schemes, claiming that they were the work of zealous German-Americans, not German agents. The Wilson administration could not conclusively prove otherwise, although Wilson did order several German diplomats out of the country at the end of 1915 because of evidence connecting them to some of the alleged plotters.

Germany also turned up the heat on the high seas, sinking ships regardless of their nationality or whose citizens were on board. When a German submarine torpedoed the Cunard passenger-liner RMS *Lusitania* in May 1915, 1,200 people died. They included 128 Americans. Some Americans demanded war or at least a rupture of diplomatic relations, but President Wilson contented himself with a promise from the German government to be more circumspect in its submarine policy. The torpedoing of the channel ferry SS *Sussex* in March 1916 led to another period of tension, but Wilson again avoided calls for war. He obtained through diplomacy the Sussex Pledge, whereby the Germans again promised not to sink unarmed commercial ships. Thus could Wilson campaign for re-election that year under the slogan "He kept us out of war."

Germany's announcement of its intention to resume unrestricted submarine warfare (USW) in early February 1917 made American entry into the First World War inevitable. German strategists had hoped that by sinking commercial ships traveling from North America, they could starve Great Britain out of a war that seemed to have no end in sight. In American minds, that decision amounted to a declaration of war against the United States and put the onus for starting hostilities firmly in German hands. It also added to the pressure coming from those, led by former president Theodore Roosevelt,[2] who had been arguing for months that the Wilson administration had done far too little to protect American lives, property, and honor from German aggression.

The Americans, oddly enough, did not really enter into German calculations. The Germans envisioned USW as a weapon against the British, not the Americans. Even if the United States did enter the war on the Allied side as a result of USW, the Germans reasoned, Americans were unlikely to

Historical Introduction

make much of a difference on the battlefields of France. German strategists had watched carefully as the United States had sent a failed "punitive expedition" into northern Mexico to find Pancho Villa,[3] a Mexican rebel leader who had raided Columbus, New Mexico, in March 1916, killing seventeen Americans in the process. The American people demanded a response, and President Woodrow Wilson sent General John Pershing[4] into Mexico with orders to find Villa and bring him to justice.

Enter Floyd Gibbons, a twenty-nine-year-old adventure seeker from a comfortable Midwestern family who became a newspaper reporter against his father's wishes. Gibbons had first broken into journalism after managing to obtain an interview with presidential candidate Theodore Roosevelt in Minneapolis in 1912. Shortly thereafter, Gibbons moved to the much bigger newspaper market of Chicago, arriving in the middle of a printers' strike that had shut down the city's papers. It was an inauspicious start to what would become one of the most remarkable careers in American journalism.[5]

In 1914, Gibbons took a job at the *Chicago Tribune*,[6] whose owners shared Gibbons's daring and his interest in military affairs. Gibbons warned his readers that the brewing civil war in Mexico would sooner or later involve the United States. He further warned that the United States Army was not ready to defend the nation's interests. The *Tribune* sent

Historical Introduction

Gibbons to Mexico in December 1914 to report on the ongoing crisis. It was the first of more than twenty wars that Gibbons covered in an extraordinary career that would cover him with glory, earn him a few medals, and cost him an eye. He soon became one of the best-known correspondents in the world. By the 1920s, his colleagues were saying, only half in jest, that "No war can get started until Floyd Gibbons gets there to cover it."[7]

It all began in Mexico in February 1915 when Gibbons met Hipolito Villa, Pancho's younger brother, at a boxing match in Juarez. Pancho Villa was then one of several Mexican rebel leaders looking to take over from Porfiro Diaz, the dictator who had stepped down after thirty-three years of one-man rule. The United States at this point was still supporting Villa, although in mid-October the Americans changed sides and supported Villa's nemesis Venustiano Carranza.[8]

Gibbons wanted to get an interview with Villa at this crucial time in both the Mexican Revolution and Mexican-American relations. Despite having Hipolito's support, Gibbons was taking a huge gamble, as Pancho Villa had a notorious hatred for reporters; rumor had it that he had recently shot a Mexican journalist who had come to interview him. Nevertheless, Pancho Villa seems to have taken a liking to Gibbons, inviting him to travel with Villa's band for the first half of 1915. Gibbons spent four

Historical Introduction

months in the Mexican interior with Villa, which gave Gibbons a rare insight into the events in Mexico and launched his reputation as a daring reporter capable of covering some of the world's most dangerous situations.

The Mexican situation continued to deteriorate as the United States sent troops to Veracruz and Tampico. There were also rumors of a Japanese-Mexican alliance aimed at the United States and of Japanese naval activity on Cedros Island, off the coast of Baja California. Gibbons went to investigate those rumors and reported that Japanese sailors had in fact come to Cedros to explore building a naval base there. Even without the war in Europe, Americans had plenty of reasons to get edgy about the international situation.

By the end of 1915, Villa's relations with the United States had turned confrontational, and the Mexican leader fatefully decided on his raid into New Mexico. Gibbons, who probably knew Villa and his territory better than any other American, went along with Pershing's expedition. He spent four frustrating months with the Americans as Pershing tried but continually failed to bring Villa to justice. The Germans observed American futility and concluded that an army that could not find Pancho Villa, one of the most famous men in North America, posed little threat to a powerful German army located halfway around the world.

Pancho Villa

Historical Introduction

Mexico remained at the forefront of American minds and on the front pages of their newspapers throughout 1916 and 1917. Shortly after the Germans infuriated Americans with their resumption of unrestricted submarine warfare, Mexico became even more important to American readers. In late February 1917, about a month after the USW announcement, the United States government revealed that it had in its possession an intercepted telegram from the German foreign minister, Arthur Zimmermann, to the German ambassador in Mexico.

The contents of that telegram were explosive on many levels. In it, Zimmermann told his ambassador that he expected the United States to declare war on Germany once USW resumed. He then asked the ambassador to lure Mexico into the war on Germany's side by promising the Mexicans the return of Texas, Arizona, and New Mexico, all territory they had lost to the United States in the 1846-48 Mexican-American War. Zimmermann also asked the ambassador to bring Japan into the conversation in the hopes of forming a Mexican-German-Japanese alliance aimed at tying the United States down in North America while the Germans won the war in Europe.

The Zimmermann Telegram threatened to pull the United States deeper into the civil war in Mexico. After the failure of the Villa expedition and the frustrations of the Tampico and Veracruz opera-

Historical Introduction

tions, few Americans wanted to get more involved in the brewing Mexican quagmire. If Mexico did pursue military operations against the United States, the small American army would have thousands of miles of border to cover while simultaneously trying to prepare for the war in Europe. A Mexican-American War could make Villa's raid into New Mexico look like child's play. The Zimmermann Telegram also threatened the South and West of the United States, exactly those regions that had been the most isolationist from 1914 to 1917. The telegram helped convince some of the biggest skeptics across the nation of the need for war.

Furthermore, the telegram's link to Japan tied into the stories Gibbons and others had written about Japanese intentions to build naval bases in Mexico. If Germany, Mexico, and Japan did work together, then the United States faced possible encirclement on land and sea. If the Germans won the war in Europe, moreover, they might claim as part of their spoils some of Britain's Caribbean islands or even parts of Canada. Getting involved in the war now seemed like the only option open to Wilson and his advisers.

Gibbons's title, *And They Thought We Wouldn't Fight*, was aimed primarily at the Germans, but the cover of at least one edition featured American soldiers superimposed over a map of Mexico. In American minds, the two had become carefully linked by

Historical Introduction

February 1917, even if the Mexican government quickly disavowed any thought of military operations or an alliance with either Germany or Japan. Gibbons, with his experiences with both Pancho Villa and John Pershing, probably knew more about Mexico and its possible links to Germany than any other reporter in America. Therefore, it could have come as no surprise to him when his editors told him in early February 1917 to board the S.S. *Frederick VIII* and head to Europe as the *Tribune*'s correspondent to cover the world war that America now appeared certain to enter.

Gibbons then made a decision that nearly cost him his life, yet at the same time made him an international celebrity. The *Frederick VIII* was to take Germany's ambassador to the United States back home after the United States severed diplomatic relations with his country. The Germans had promised safe passage for the ship carrying its ambassador, which meant that Gibbons, too, could have crossed the Atlantic in perfect safety.

Whether out of anger at the Germans or a heightened sense of patriotism, Gibbons passed up the chance to sail in safety on the *Frederick VIII*, choosing instead to book passage on Cunard's RMS *Laconia* in February 1917. Just over halfway through the *Laconia*'s voyage, a German U-boat torpedoed it, killing thirteen people. After being rescued by British ships and reaching the safety of Ireland, Gib-

Robert R. and Amy Adams McCormick on their honeymoon in Europe in 1915

Historical Introduction

bons sent a dispatch to the United States describing his harrowing experience. That dispatch appears as the first part of *And They Thought We Wouldn't Fight*.

Gibbons and his brother later claimed that his dispatch about the *Laconia* brought the United States into the war. Surely, he must have known that he was exaggerating his own influence, but the *Laconia* incident did grab the attention of Americans nationwide. Gibbons's dispatch was read in both houses of Congress and appeared in newspapers across America, increasing anger at Germany and its campaign of sinking civilian ships on the high seas.

By the time he went to Europe, Gibbons's newspaper, the *Chicago Tribune*, had already done some of the best American reporting on the war. Its publisher, Robert McCormick, had already seen quite a bit of the war in Europe with his own eyes. His father had been a diplomat, once serving as ambassador to Russia. In 1915, McCormick went to Europe and saw fighting on both fronts firsthand. Like Gibbons, he often got too close to the action for his own safety. McCormick also secured interviews with some of the leading figures of the day, including Tsar Nicholas II, Grand Duke Nicholas (the commander of the Russian armies until 1915), British prime minister H. H. Asquith, and Great Britain's first lord of the admiralty, a bombastic and hard-charging politician named Winston Churchill. Notably, he did not interview any German leaders.

Historical Introduction

When the United States entered the war in 1917, McCormick, a cavalryman in the Illinois National Guard, went to France as an intelligence officer before joining the First Infantry Division as an artillerist.[9]

With his experience in Mexico and his acquaintance with Pershing, Gibbons was the perfect war correspondent for 1917. Surviving the *Laconia* sinking made him a national celebrity. Still, most senior American officials tended to look down on reporters as just a level or two better than spies. The job of the reporter, to get information from the military and then publish it, ran counter to the interests of the secrecy-obsessed officers on Pershing's staff. Reporters, many officers assumed, were best herded together and kept as far from the scene of action as possible. Even though the United States was embarking on an enormous effort to win the largest war in human history, the War Department accredited just eighteen war correspondents, most of whom they hoped would stay in London or Paris and await official communiqués on which they would then base their stories.

But sitting comfortably in a hotel did not fit Floyd Gibbons's style. He was able to trade on his familiarity with Pershing from the Mexico expedition to get more access than most other American reporters enjoyed. He could also lean on McCormick's connections inside the army. Gibbons went

Historical Introduction

from London to Liverpool in June 1917 to greet Pershing and the first contingent of American officers. They included future World War II heroes George Marshall and George Patton, whose sister Pershing nearly married. Gibbons also managed to talk Pershing into allowing him to travel with the general's official party from Great Britain to France a few days later.

The Americans entered the war at a crucial time. On the eastern front, the Russians had already deposed the tsar in the so-called February Revolution. The revolution solved one American problem, as the end of the reactionary Romanov dynasty now made it possible for President Wilson to claim the moral high ground and make statements such as his description of the war as "a war to make the world safe for democracy."

But the Americans (and the French and British as well) needed the Russians to stay in the war and tie down as many German units as possible in the east. Alexander Kerensky, a nominally pro-democratic Russian politician, had emerged as the head of a provisional government. He tried to keep Russia in the war by telling Russian soldiers that they now fought for the goals of the Russian people, not those of the monarchy. Kerensky, with massive French and British support, gambled everything on a July 1917 offensive that began just as Pershing was introducing himself to French leaders.

Historical Introduction

That offensive failed, proving to many in the West that Russia was nearing the end of its military power. Within three weeks of the start of the offensive, Russian morale had all but collapsed and the Germans had advanced approximately 150 miles. They might well have advanced even farther had they not run out of supplies. The Russian collapse raised two terrifying possibilities for the West. First, with Kerensky and his moderate approach discredited, the Russian people began to listen to more radical voices, like those of the Bolsheviks. Led by militants like Vladimir Lenin and Leon Trotsky, the Bolsheviks called for an immediate end to the war under their slogan "Bread, Peace, and Land." When they finally did take power in November 1917, the Bolsheviks followed through on their promises, opening negotiations with the Germans that resulted in the brutally pro-German Treaty of Brest-Litovsk. Their communist model also offered a serious challenge to Wilson's own vision of how best to organize the post-war world.

Even if the Russians could hold on, however, the West faced the real possibility that the Germans would begin to transfer men and equipment from the east to the west in sufficient number to tip the scales on the theretofore largely static western front. If they did, then the Americans would have to come across the Atlantic Ocean quickly and with enough soldiers to help the French and British even the

Historical Introduction

odds. Having started from such a small base in 1917, there was no guarantee that the Americans could do so in time.

The western front looked every bit as tenuous as the eastern front in the early summer of 1917. A French offensive in April (just as the United States was entering the war) had failed miserably. Begun with high hopes against German positions atop the Chemin des Dames ridge, the offensive soon degenerated into a series of bloody defeats. Shortly thereafter, thousands of French troops refused orders to resume the attack, although they equally refused to leave their trenches. They told their officers that they would defend France but that they would no longer engage in pointless and costly offensives that killed Frenchmen to no larger purpose.

Historians have since debated whether to call the actions of the French soldiers on the Chemin des Dames mutinies, strikes, or acts of indiscipline. They certainly presented the French military with a serious situation, even if French soldiers managed to keep word of the incidents away from both their German enemies and their British allies. The French government sent the commander of the army and architect of the Chemin des Dames offense, Gen. Robert Nivelle, to Algeria, and replaced him with the more cautious and more popular Gen. Henri-Philippe Pétain.[10] Recognizing the severity of the problem he faced, Pétain made important changes,

Generals Henri-Philippe Pétain and John Joseph Pershing

Historical Introduction

including ordering better food and more leave time for his men, demanding that French officers spend more time in the trenches with their soldiers, and ending the use of piecemeal infantry attacks.

Most notably, Pétain sought to buy time to modernize the French army. Even before the war, he had argued for ending the army's traditional infantry-based tactics in lieu of ones that relied more heavily on modern weapons like artillery. As Pétain was fond of saying, "*le feu tue*" (firepower kills). Now in command of the French army, Pétain wanted to base French tactics around the striking power of long-range artillery, poison gas, tanks, and airplanes. But changing the French army's doctrine so fundamentally would take time, and only the arrival of the Americans could buy him that time.

As Pétain was trying to heal the French army, his British counterpart, Sir Douglas Haig, was taking his own army on the offensive. In July, Haig launched the ill-starred third Ypres offensive, often called Passchendaele after the small Belgian village that was its immediate objective. Haig hoped to break through the German lines and clear the Belgian coast of submarine pens, but the offensive soon bogged down due to poor planning, historically rainy weather, and bad command decisions. By the time it ended, the British army had suffered an estimated 400,000 casualties for little gain.

Gibbons watched as Pershing tried to figure out

Historical Introduction

exactly how his American Expeditionary Forces (AEF) would fit into this increasingly gloomy strategic situation. Pershing had to deal with the entreaties of Haig, Pétain, and a parade of politicians who urged him to adopt a policy known as amalgamation. Under this scheme, American regiments would feed into French and British divisions, both to replace the manpower losses of those two armies and to help the Americans learn how to fight modern war from veteran soldiers.

Pershing, one of the most stubborn men in France, hated the idea of amalgamation with every fiber of his being. On the military level, it would leave him with his men scattered all over the western front and therefore no one to command. Pershing also looked aghast at giving American soldiers to the same European generals that had so badly botched the Chemin des Dames and Passchendaele offensives. President Wilson, too, opposed amalgamation because it would reduce his authority to shape the post-war peace. The United States Army, he argued, had to make an identifiably American contribution to victory first. Thus did Wilson and Secretary of War Newton Baker[11] give Pershing their full support to resist any and all European calls for amalgamation no matter how desperate the military situation became.

Gibbons must have had quite a perch from which to observe Pershing build an American army

Historical Introduction

and at the same time keep it away from his own allies. In the end, the Americans did amalgamate to meet the crisis of the first half of 1918 (see below), but at the much larger divisional level and on the condition that once the western front stabilized, the Allies would consent to the creation of a separate American sector on the western front. That landmark moment came on July 24, 1918, with the formation of the United States First Army. Pershing's stubbornness won him few friends with the French and British, although one friend he did make was Pétain, who recognized that France's future might well rest in Pershing's hands.

Gibbons's reports to American audiences reveal the close links between the United States and France. In 1917, France stood in the minds of many Americans as the home of modern democracy, advanced civilization, and, most importantly, the side of the right in a war begun by the Germans. The United States also had no quarrels with the French because France's interests and America's interests did not come into conflict. Americans volunteered in enormous numbers to become doctors, nurses, soldiers, ambulance drivers, even fighter pilots in service to France. Throughout the war, American relations with France were significantly better than those with Britain, in an inverse of the World War II pattern.

Few of his readers would have needed Gibbons to explain the incident at the end of the second

Historical Introduction

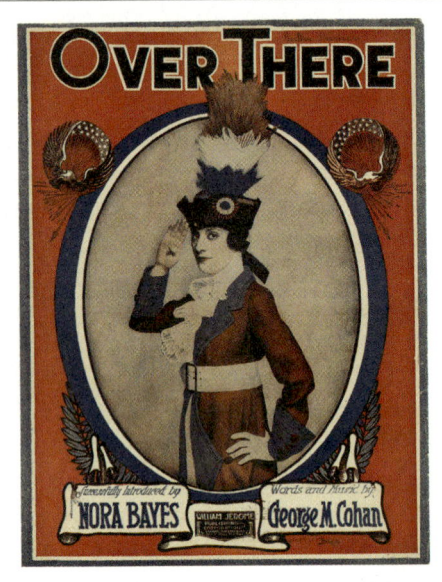

Sheet music for "Over There," the most popular song of World War I, published 1917

chapter. Pershing made international headlines by leading a pilgrimage to the Picpus Cemetery near the Place de la Nation in eastern Paris on July 4, 1917. He went there to lay a wreath at the grave of the Marquis de Lafayette, the young man who had left a life of privilege and wealth in France to fight alongside the Americans in their War of Independence. He and George Washington grew so close that Lafayette named his son George Washington Lafayette. He also gave Washington the key to the

Historical Introduction

Bastille that sits today at Mount Vernon. When Lafayette was wounded at the Battle of Brandywine in 1777, Washington sent his own surgeon to the scene with the admonition to care for Lafayette as if he were Washington's own son. The very soil around Lafayette's casket at Picpus is American, in accord with Lafayette's own wishes.

Thus the words that one of Pershing's senior aides[12] spoke at Picpus, *"Lafayette, nous voici"* ("Lafayette, we are here") carried with them powerful symbolism. The squadron of American volunteer pilots in the French air service had already taken the name "Lafayette Escadrille" to honor the man who, more than any other, stood for the historic links between the United States and France. Pershing's carefully orchestrated and highly publicized visit to Picpus meant that the Americans had come to repay a debt. And, as the songwriter George M. Cohan[13] had already told his countrymen, they wouldn't go back until it was "over, over there."

America's will and spirit were also over there, but her army had a seemingly endless number of problems to solve before it could translate that will into combat power. As Gibbons himself noted, they had first to assemble, train, and transport an army over submarine-infested waters. Then they had to supply that army from an enormous distance. Even if they could achieve those aims, they still had to recruit or conscript men with little to no prewar military

Historical Introduction

training and mold them into a modern fighting force capable of taking on the German army on the most murderous terrain in the world.

Pershing did his own men few favors by designing a way of fighting that proved ill-suited to modern war. Believing that trench warfare was primarily a problem of mindset not materiel, he trained his men in so-called "open warfare" methods. The Pershing system relied on movement and marksmanship even though European armies had long since abandoned such tactics in favor of positional warfare fought mainly from trenches. The Pershing system cost the AEF high casualties and even forced many American commanders to ignore Pershing's doctrine in favor of the more methodical and careful tactics of their French and British allies.

Gibbons might well have had the opportunity to enjoy a safe, comfortable war as a correspondent based in Paris or even at Pershing's headquarters, but he had other plans. He went instead into the front lines with the Marine Corps, then fighting as a brigade attached to the United States Second Division. The marines normally fought in conjunction with the navy, but they went to the western front as regular infantry and fought under army command. Marine Corps leaders worried about that arrangement and dreaded what it might mean for their future and their cherished independence. They did not want their subordination to the army to become permanent.

Historical Introduction

The Marine Corps may well have saved itself from such a fate in a series of small forests known as Belleau Wood. In June 1918, the Germans attacked Belleau Wood as part of their final effort to win the war. The offensives, known collectively as the Ludendorff offensives after the general who designed them, aimed to win the war before the Americans could arrive en masse, the French could complete Pétain's modernization program, and the British blockade could cut even more deeply into rapidly dwindling German food and fuel supplies. Aware that the offensives likely represented Germany's last throw of the dice, the Germans put everything they had into them.

The first two offensives had succeeded spectacularly well, returning movement to the western front and raising the very real specter of Allied defeat. In response to the crisis, Pershing agreed to place American divisions (each about 22,000 men) under French corps and army commands. This way, the French and British could assume responsibility for much of the complex organization and staff work necessary for modern war, but American soldiers would receive their orders from American officers as Pershing had always demanded.

Germany's third Ludendorff offensive brought the Germans to the strategically critical Marne River, the gateway to Paris. German troops took the dominating high ground of Château Thierry and

Historical Introduction

captured the nearby Belleau Wood. The American army rushed to the sector, retaking Château Thierry; although no one knew it at the time, the Germans would not come as close to Paris again in this war. The American Second Division, with the Marine Corps brigade in a prominent role, attacked Belleau Wood with an eye toward recapturing it. The bloody fighting cost the Americans 1,811 dead and 8,000 wounded, but the bravery of those American soldiers and marines soon became legendary. Today the wood is officially known in France as the *Bois de la Brigade de Marine* to honor the courage and the sacrifice of the Americans who fought there.

Of course, the marines were not alone in Belleau Wood. The larger Second Division also contained thousands of soldiers from the army. But army censors were more strict, and the marines, anxious to safeguard their independence, were more eager for publicity. Floyd Gibbons helped to give them that publicity with a stirring account of the battle for Belleau Wood. His dispatch made famous the cry of Sgt. Daniel Daly, who rallied his men with the call "Come on, you sons of bitches! Do you want to live forever?" Daly's exhortation came to stand for the near maniacal level of bravery that the Marine Corps expects its marines to exhibit on the battlefield and in which the corps takes deep martial pride.[14]

Gibbons, who survived the torpedoing of the *Laconia*, had a lucky (or, depending on one's point of

Historical Introduction

view, unlucky) star over him at Belleau Wood. A bullet ricocheted and hit his left eye, producing a gruesome wound that medics on the scene believed would probably kill him. The Marine Corps censors might well have allowed his Belleau Wood report to pass uncorrected because they did not want to change what they assumed would be Gibbons's final dispatch.

Gibbons recovered from his wound with surprising speed. After just ten days of hospitalization in Paris, he was back on the Marne front, his left eye gone, to witness the start of the Second Battle of the Marne. He also met with British prime minister David Lloyd George, joking that one eye would be enough to see the kaiser surrender. Gibbons did not stay in Europe to see the armistice, however. In late July, he decided to return to the United States for more medical treatment and some well-deserved rest. Before leaving, he received one of France's highest awards, the Croix de Guerre. Gibbons had become such a hero to the Marine Corps that it sent an honor guard to receive him in New York City when he stepped off the boat from France.

Back in the United States in late August, Gibbons gave lectures urging his countrymen to give all they could to ensure final victory. He spoke at Carnegie Hall, the New York Public Library, the National Theatre in Washington, D.C., and dozens of lesser-known places in the East and Midwest. He talked with President Wilson, former president Theodore

Historical Introduction

Floyd Gibbons broadcasting for NBC in 1930

Roosevelt, the commandant of the Marine Corps, and numerous congressmen, telling them what he had seen of the war and retelling stories of the American heroism he had witnessed. At the end of the year, Gibbons took a few weeks to rest in Atlantic City, where he wrote *And They Thought We Wouldn't Fight*, probably in less than a month.

Rested, fêted, and perhaps also a bit bored in calm, safe New Jersey, Gibbons soon grew impatient. In January 1919, he headed back to Europe to

Historical Introduction

cover the transition from wartime to peacetime. That fall, the *Tribune* sent him to Ireland to cover the brewing civil war there. From Ireland he went to cover the civil war in Russia, the Russo-Polish War, and, in the years to come, wars from China to Morocco to Nicaragua. He also took part in an expedition across the Sahara, claiming to have planted the first American flag ever put there.

His years covering wars and conflict across the globe turned him into a pacifist. In 1929, he wrote that he was "sick of killing" and that he had developed a "bitter abhorrence for Mars and his bloody harvest." The previous year, he decided to take a break from globetrotting and sat down to write a novel about a war he feared might break out between the United States and the Soviet Union. Dedicated to the "hope that it will not happen," *The Red Napoleon* envisioned a global war that began with a fictitious assassination of Joseph Stalin in 1932. Stalin's successor, the Red Napoleon of the title, then embarked on a war of conquest against the West. By 1936, the Soviets of his novel had conquered most of Europe and taken aim at the United States. At the same time, the Chinese, whom Gibbons depicted in strongly racist terms, had taken advantage of the war in Europe to kick the European colonizers out of Asia.[15]

Gibbons parlayed his celebrity into a career as a narrator of newsreels and a radio broadcaster, for

Historical Introduction

which he earned a star on the Hollywood Walk of Fame.[16] By the mid-1930s, after another trip to Asia to cover the outbreak of war between China and Japan, he had begun to develop heart problems that forced him to reduce his workload and travel schedule. He nevertheless kept busy by interviewing the leading political figures of the day for radio broadcasts based out of Washington, D.C., and New York. Then, in defiance of his doctor's suggestions, he went to Ethiopia to cover the Italian invasion there and to Spain to cover the start of its civil war. In 1937, he finally decided to slow down and purchased a farm near Stroudsburg, Pennsylvania. Floyd Gibbons died in 1939 at the young age of 52, just as the world was sinking into yet another world war. Had he lived, Gibbons would undoubtedly have been itching to get into the middle of the action once again.

Michael S. Neiberg
Professor of History
United States Army War College
Carlisle, Pennsylvania
June 2014

The views expressed herein are those of the author, not of the Army War College, the U.S. Army, or the Department of Defense.

Historical Introduction

NOTES

1. (Thomas) Woodrow Wilson (1856–1924), twenty-eighth U.S. president (1913–21) (Democrat). Professor of political science and history; president of Princeton University (1902–10). Governor of New Jersey (1911–13). Received the Nobel Peace Prize in 1919.

2. Theodore Roosevelt (1858–1919), twenty-sixth U.S. president (1901–09) (Republican). Also served as a colonel in the Spanish-American War (See Lakeside Classics 2003) and governor of New York (1899–1900), and was a leading environmentalist and author. He left the Republican Party to run for president against President William Howard Taft in 1912 as the candidate of the Bull Moose Party but was unsuccessful. Received the Nobel Peace Prize in 1906.

3. Pancho Villa (1878–1923), born Doroteo Arango, was first a bandit and later a Mexican revolutionary leader.

4. John Joseph Pershing (1860–1948), U.S. army officer. Commanded American Expeditionary Force in World War I. Previously fought in the Spanish-American War in Cuba and the Philippines, where he later held command in Manila. Army chief of staff from 1921 until his retirement in 1924.

5. Much of the biographical information in this introduction comes from Edward Gibbons's book, *Floyd Gibbons, Your Headline Hunter: A Biography* (New York: Exposition Press, 1953). Edward Gibbons was Floyd's brother.

6. The *Chicago Tribune,* now a major multimedia company, published its first edition June 10, 1847. It was privately owned by the Medill-McCormick family until it went public in 1983.

7. Gibbons, *Your Headline Hunter,* 145.

8. Venustiano Carranza (1859–1920), leader in the Mexican civil war and first president of the Mexican Republic.

9. McCormick bequeathed his estate and much of his fortune to create a public place for education and recreation. Cantigny Park, in Wheaton, Illinois, was named for the first American offensive of World War I (May 28, 1918). It contains several museums, including one dedicated to the First Division.

10. Henri-Philippe Pétain (1856–1951), French army general who was a hero in World War I for his victory at Verdun. Honored as a marshal of France in 1918. In 1940, Pétain became chief of state of the Vichy government of occupied France, collaborating with the Germans. After the Normandy landings in 1944, he was transferred

Historical Introduction

to Germany but returned to France after liberation, where he was tried, convicted of treason, and died in prison.

11. Newton Baker (1871–1937), lawyer and government official. Mayor of Cleveland, Ohio (1912–16). Loyal Democrat who served as Wilson's secretary of war (1916–21).

12. Although these words are usually credited to Pershing himself, they were actually uttered by Col. Charles E. Stanton, whose French was better than Pershing's. The misattribution was perhaps first committed by Gibbons himself.

13. George M. Cohan (1878–1942), American performer and songwriter who wrote this most popular song of World War I, "Over There."

14. Gibbons, *Your Headline Hunter*, 93–94. See also Emmet Crozier, *American Reporters on the Western Front* (New York: Oxford University Press, 1959).

15. Floyd Gibbons, *The Red Napoleon* (New York: Cape and Smith, 1929), quotations from pp. 1, 3, and 4.

16. His star is at 1631 Vine Street.

AND THEY THOUGHT
WE WOULDN'T FIGHT

American Troops Advancing through Northern France *by Harold Brett*

The Sinking of the *Laconia*

BETWEEN AMERICA and the firing line, there are three thousand miles of submarine-infested water. Every American soldier, before encountering the dangers of the battlefront, must first overcome the dangers of the deep.

Geographically, America is almost four thousand miles from the war zone, but in fact every American soldier bound for France entered the war zone one hour out of New York Harbor. Germany made an ally out of the dark depths of the Atlantic.

That three-thousand-mile passage represented greater possibilities for the destruction of the United States overseas forces than any strategical operation that Germany's able military leaders could direct in the field.

Germany made use of those three thousand miles of water, just as she developed the use of barbed wire entanglements along the front. Infantry advancing across no man's land were held helpless before the enemy's fire by barbed-wire entanglements. Germany, with her submarine policy of ruthlessness, changed the Atlantic Ocean into another no man's land across which every American soldier had to pass at the mercy of the enemy before he could arrive at the actual battlefront.

A sinking at sea is a nightmare. I have been

through one. I have been on a ship torpedoed in mid-ocean. I have stood on the slanting decks of a doomed liner; I have listened to the lowering of the lifeboats, heard the hiss of escaping steam and the roar of ascending rockets as they tore lurid rents in the black sky and cast their red glare o'er the roaring sea.

I have spent a night in an open boat on the tossing swells. I have been through, in reality, the mad dream of drifting and darkness and bailing and pulling on the oars and straining aching eyes toward an empty, meaningless horizon in search of help. I shall try to tell you how it feels.

I had been assigned by the *Chicago Tribune* to go to London as their correspondent. Almost the same day I received that assignment, the "imperial" government of Germany had invoked its ruthless submarine policy, had drawn a blockade zone about the waters of the British Isles and the coasts of France, and had announced to the world that its U-boats would sink without warning any ship, of any kind, under any flag, that tried to sail the waters that Germany declared prohibitory.

In consideration of my personal safety and, possibly, of my future usefulness, the *Tribune* was desirous of arranging for me a safe passage across the Atlantic. Such an opportunity presented itself in the ordered return of the disgraced and discredited German ambassador to the United States, Count von Bernstorff.[1]

The Sinking of the Laconia

Under the rules of international courtesy, a ship had been provided for the use of von Bernstorff and his diplomatic staff. That ship was to sail under absolute guarantees of safe conduct from all of the nations at war with Germany and, of course, it would also have been safe from attack by German submarines. That ship was the *Frederick VIII*. At considerable expense, the *Tribune* managed to obtain for me a cabin passage on that ship.

I can't say that I was over-impressed with the prospect of travel in such company. I disliked the thought that I, an American citizen, with rights as such to sail the sea, should have to resort to subterfuge and scheming to enjoy those rights. There arose in me a feeling of challenge against Germany's order which forbade American ships to sail the ocean. I canceled my sailing on the *Frederick VIII*.

In New York, I sought passage on the first American ship sailing for England. I made the rounds of the steamship offices and learned that the Cunard liner *Laconia* was the first available boat and was about to sail. She carried a large cargo of munitions and other materials of war. I booked passage aboard her. It was on Saturday, February 17, 1917, that we steamed away from the dock at New York and moved slowly down the East River. We were bound for Liverpool, England. My cabin accommodations were good. The *Laconia* was listed at 18,000 tons and was one of the largest Cunarders in the Atlantic

Postcard of the Cunard sister ships RMS Franconia *and* Laconia

The Sinking of the Laconia

service. The next morning we were out of sight of land.

Submarines had been recently reported in the waters through which we were sailing, but we saw none of them, and apparently they saw none of us. They had sunk many ships, but all of the sinkings had been in the daytime. Consequently, there was a feeling of greater safety at night. The *Laconia* sailed on a constantly zigzagging course. All of our lifeboats were swinging out over the side of the ship so that if we were hit, they could be lowered in a hurry. Every other day the passengers and the crew would be called up on the decks to stand by the lifeboats that had been assigned to them.

On Sunday, after we had been sailing for eight days, we entered the zone that had been prohibited by the kaiser. We sailed into it full steam ahead and nothing happened. That day was February 25. In the afternoon, I was seated in the lounge with two friends. One was an American whose name was Kirby; the other was a Canadian, and his name was Dugan. The latter was an aviator in the British army. In fights with German airplanes high over the western front he had been wounded and brought down twice, and the army had sent him to his home in Canada to get well. He was returning once more to the battlefront "to stop another bullet," as he said.

As we talked, I passed around my cigarette case,

and Dugan held a lighted match while the three of us lighted our cigarettes from it. As Dugan blew out the match and placed the burnt end in an ashtray, he laughed and said, "They say it is bad luck to light three cigarettes with the same match, but I think it is good luck for me. I used to do it frequently with my flying partners in France, and four of them have been killed, but I am still alive."

"That makes it all right for you," said Kirby, "but it makes it look bad for Gibbons and myself. But nothing is going to happen. I don't believe in superstitions."

That night after dinner Kirby and I went to the smoke room on the boat deck well to the stern of the ship. We joined a circle of Britishers who were seated in front of a coal fire in an open hearth.

"What do you think are our chances of being torpedoed?" was the question I put before the circle in front of the fireplace.

The deliberative Mr. Henry Chetham, a London solicitor, was the first to answer. "Well," he drawled, "I should say about four thousand to one."

Lucien J. Jerome of the British Diplomatic Service, returning with an Ecuadorian valet from South America, advanced his opinion.

I was much impressed with his opinion because the speaker himself had impressed me deeply. He was the best monocle juggler I had ever met. In his right eye he carried a monocle without a rim and

The Sinking of the Laconia

without a ribbon or thread to save it, should it ever have fallen from his eye.

Repeatedly during the trip, I had seen Mr. Jerome standing on the hurrideck [hurricane deck] of the *Laconia* facing the wind but holding the glass disk in his eye with a muscular grip that must have been viselike. I had even followed him around the deck several times in a desire to be present when the monocle blew out, but the British diplomatist never for once lost his grip on it. I had come to the opinion that the piece of glass was fixed to his eye and that he slept with it. After the fashion of the British Diplomatic Service, he expressed his opinion most affirmatively.

"Nonsense," he said with reference to Mr. Chetham's estimate. "Utter nonsense. Considering the zone that we are in and the class of the ship, I should put the chances down at 250 to one that we don't meet a 'sub.'"

At that minute the torpedo hit us.

Have you ever stood on the deck of a ferry boat as it arrived in the slip? And have you ever experienced the slight sideward shove when the boat rubs against the piling and comes to a stop? That was the unmistakable lurch we felt, but no one expects to run into pilings in mid-ocean, so everyone knew what it was.

At the same time, there came a muffled noise—not extremely loud nor yet very sharp—just a noise like the slamming of some large oaken door a good distance away. Realizing that we had been torpedoed, my imagination was rather disappointed at the slightness of the shock and the meekness of the report. One or two chairs tipped over, a few glasses crashed from table to floor, and in an instant every man in the room was on his feet.

I looked at my watch; it was 10:30.

Five sharp blasts sounded on the *Laconia*'s whistle. Since that night, I have often marveled at the quick coordination of mind and hand that belonged to the man on the bridge who pulled that whistle rope. Those five blasts constituted the signal to abandon the ship. Everyone recognized them.

We walked hurriedly down the corridor leading from the smoke room in the stern to the lounge, which was amidships. We moved fast, but there was no crowding and no panic. Passing the open door of the gymnasium, I became aware of the list of the vessel. The floor of the gymnasium slanted down on the starboard side, and a medicine ball and dozens of dumbbells and Indian clubs were rolling in that direction.

We entered the lounge—a large drawing room furnished with green upholstered chairs and divans and small tables on which the after-dinner liqueur glasses still rested. In one corner was a grand piano with the top elevated. In the center of the slanting floor of the saloon was a cabinet Victrola [phono-

The Sinking of the Laconia

graph-record player], and from its mahogany bowels there poured the last and dying strains of "Poor Butterfly."

The women and several men who had been in the lounge were hurriedly leaving by the forward door as we entered. We followed them through. The twin winding stairs leading below decks by the forward hatch were dark, and I brought into play a pocket flashlight shaped like a fountain pen. I had purchased it before sailing in view of such an emergency, and I had always carried it fastened with a clip in an upper vest pocket.

My stateroom was B19 on the promenade deck, one deck below the deck on which was located the smoke room, the lounge, and the lifeboats. The corridor was dimly lighted, and the floor had a more perceptible slant as I darted into my stateroom, which was on the starboard and sinking side of the ship. I hurriedly put on a light non-sink garment constructed like a vest, which I had come provided with, and then donned an overcoat.

Responding to the list of the ship, the wardrobe door swung open and crashed against the wall. My typewriter slid off the dressing table and a shower of toilet articles pitched from their places on the washstand. I grabbed the ship's life preserver in my left hand and, with the flashlight in my right hand, started up the hatchway to the upper deck.

In the darkness of the boat deck hatchway, the

rays of my flashlight revealed the chief steward opening the door of a switch closet in the panel wall. He pushed on a number of switches, and instantly the decks of the *Laconia* became bright. From sudden darkness, the exterior of the ship burst into a blaze of light, and it was that illumination that saved many lives.

The *Laconia*'s engines and dynamos had not yet been damaged. The torpedo had hit us well astern on the starboard side, and the bulkheads seemed to be holding back from the engine room the flood of water that rushed in through the gaping hole in the ship's side. I proceeded down the boat deck to my station opposite boat No. 10. I looked over the side and down upon the water sixty feet below. The sudden flashing of the lights on the upper deck made the dark, seething waters seem blacker and angrier. They rose and fell in troubled swells.

Steam began to hiss from some of the pipes leading up from the engine well. It seemed like a dying groan from the very vitals of the stricken ship. Clouds of white and black smoke rolled up from the giant gray funnels that towered above us.

Suddenly there was a roaring swish as a rocket soared upward from the captain's bridge, leaving a comet's tail of fire. I watched it as it described a graceful arc and then with an audible pop, it burst in a flare of brilliant color. Its ascent had torn a lurid

The Sinking of the Laconia

rent in the black sky and had cast a red glare over the roaring sea.

Already boat No. 10 was loading up, and men and boys were busy with the ropes. I started to help near a davit [small crane] that seemed to be giving trouble but was sternly ordered to get out of the way and to get into the boat.

Other passengers and members of the crew and officers of the ship were rushing to and fro along the deck, strapping their life preservers to them as they rushed. There was some shouting of orders but little or no confusion. One woman, a blonde French actress, became hysterical on the deck, but two men lifted her bodily off her feet and placed her in the lifeboat.

We were on the port side of the ship, the higher side. To reach the boats, we had to climb up the slanting deck to the edge of the ship. On the starboard side, it was different. On that side, the decks slanted down toward the water. The ship careened in that direction, and the lifeboats suspended from the davits swung clear of the ship's side.

The list of the ship increased. On the port side, we looked down the slanting side of the ship and noticed that her water line on that side was a number of feet above the waves. The slant was so pronounced that the lifeboats, instead of swinging clear from the davits, rested against the side of the ship.

And They Thought We Wouldn't Fight

From my position in the lifeboat I could see that we were going to have difficulty in the descent to the water.

"Lower away," someone gave the order, and we started downward with a jerk toward the seemingly hungry, rising and falling swells. Then we stopped with another jerk and remained suspended in mid-air while the men at the bow and the stern swore and tussled with the ropes. The stern of the boat was down; the bow up, leaving us at an angle of about forty-five degrees. We clung to the seats to save ourselves from falling out.

"Who's got a knife? A knife! A knife!" shouted a fireman in the bow. He was bare to the waist and perspiration stood out in drops on his face and chest and made streaks through the coal dust with which his skin was grimed.

A hatchet was thrust into my hands, and I forwarded it to the bow. There was a flash of sparks as it was brought down with a clang on the holding pulley. One strand of the rope parted.

Down plunged the bow of the boat too quickly for the men in the stern. We came to a jerky stop, this time with the stern in the air and the bow down, the dangerous angle reversed. One man in the stern let the rope race through his blistered fingers. With hands burnt to the quick, he grabbed the rope and stopped the precipitous descent just in time to bring the stern level with the bow.

The Sinking of the Laconia

Then bow and stern tried to lower away together. The slant of the ship's side had increased, so that our boat instead of sliding down it like a toboggan was held up on one side when the taffrail [stern rail] caught on one of the condenser exhaust pipes projecting slightly from the ship's side.

Thus the starboard side of the lifeboat stuck fast and high while the port side dropped down, and once more we found ourselves clinging on at a new angle and looking straight down into the water.

Many feet and hands pushed the boat from the side of the ship, and we renewed our sagging, scraping, sliding, jerking descent. It ended as the bottom of the lifeboat smacked squarely on the pillowy top of a rising swell. It felt more solid than mid-air at least.

But we were far from being off. The pulleys twice stuck in their fastings, bow and stern, and the one axe was passed forward and back (and with it my flashlight) as the entangling mesh of ropes that held us to the sinking *Laconia* was cut away.

Some shout from that confusion of sound caused me to look up. Tin funnels enameled white and containing clusters of electric bulbs hung over the side from one of the upper decks. I looked up into the cone of one of these lights, and a bulky object shot suddenly out of the darkness into the scope of the electric rays.

It was a man. His arms were bent up at the el-

And They Thought We Wouldn't Fight

bows; his legs at the knees. He was jumping, with the intention, I feared, of landing in our boat, and I prepared to avoid the impact. But he had judged his distance well. He plunged beyond us and into the water three feet from the edge of the boat. He sank from sight, leaving a white patch of bubbles and foam on the black water. He bobbed to the surface almost immediately.

"It's Dugan," shouted a man next to me.

I flashed a light on the ruddy, smiling face and water-plastered hair of the little Canadian aviator, our fellow saloon passenger. We pulled him over the side and into the boat. He spluttered out a mouthful of water.

"I wonder if there is anything to that lighting three matches off the same match," he said. "I was trying to loosen the bow rope in this boat. I loosened it and then got tangled up in it. When the boat descended, I was jerked up back on the deck. Then I jumped for it. Holy Moses, but this water is cold."

As we pulled away from the side of the ship, its receding terraces of glowing portholes and deck lights towered above us. The ship was slowly turning over.

We were directly opposite the engine room section of the *Laconia*. There was a tangle of oars, spars, and rigging on the seats in our boat, and considerable confusion resulted before we could

The Sinking of the Laconia

manage to place in operation some of the big oars on either side.

"Get away from her. My Gawd, get away from her," a stoker kept repeating. "When the water hits her hot boilers, she'll blow up the whole ocean, and there's just tons and tons of shrapnel in her hold."

His excitement spread to other members of the crew in our boat. The ship's baker, designated by his pantry headgear of white linen, became a competing alarmist and a fireman, whose blasphemy was nothing short of profound, added to the confusion by cursing everyone. It was the tension of the minute—it was the give way of overwrought nerves—it was bedlam and nightmare.

I sought to establish some authority in our boat, which was about to break out into full mutiny. I made my way to the stern. There, huddled up in a great overcoat and almost muffled in a ship's life preserver, I came upon an old white-haired man, and I remembered him.

He was a sea captain of the old sailing days. He had been a second-cabin passenger with whom I had talked before. Earlier in the year he had sailed out of Nova Scotia with a cargo of codfish. His schooner, the *Secret*, had broken in two in mid-ocean, but he and his crew had been picked up by a tramp [unscheduled commercial vessel] and taken back to New York.

From there he had sailed on another ship bound for Europe, but this ship, a Holland-American Liner, the *Ryndam*, had never reached the other side. In mid-Atlantic her captain had lost courage over the U-boat threats. He had turned the ship about and returned to America. Thus, the *Laconia* represented the third unsuccessful attempt of this gray-haired mariner to get back to his home in England. His name was Captain Dear.

"Our boat's rudder is gone, but we can steer with an oar," he said, in a weak-quavering voice—the thin high-pitched treble of age. "I will take charge, if you want me to, but my voice is gone. I can tell you what to do, but you will have to shout the orders. They won't listen to me."

There was only one way to get the attention of the crew, and that was by an overpowering blast of profanity. I called to my assistance every ear-splitting, soul-sizzling oath that I could think of. I recited the lurid litany of the army mule skinner to his gentle charges and embellished it with excerpts from the remarks of a Chicago taxi chauffeur while he changed tires on the road with the temperature ten below. It proved to be an effective combination, this brimstoned oration of mine, because it was rewarded by silence.

"Is there a ship's officer in this boat?" I shouted. There was no answer. "Is there a sailor or a seaman on board?" I inquired, and again there was silence

The Sinking of the Laconia

Seamen and civilians from a British ship torpedoed by the Germans, by George Hand Wright

from our group of passengers, firemen, stokers, and deck swabs.

They appeared to be listening to me, and I wished to keep my hold on them. I racked my mind for some other query to make or some order to direct. Before the spell was broken, I found one. "We will now find out how many of us there are in this boat," I announced in the best tones of authority that I could assume. "The first man in the bow will count 'one' and the next man to him will count

And They Thought We Wouldn't Fight

'two.' We will count from the bow back to the stern, each man taking a number. Begin."

"One," came the quick response from a passenger who happened to be the first man in the bow. The enumeration continued sharply toward the stern. I spoke the last number.

"There are twenty-three of us here," I repeated. "There's not a ship's officer or seaman among us, but we are extremely fortunate to have with us an old sea captain who has consented to take charge of the boat and save our lives. His voice is weak, but I will repeat the orders for him so that all of you can hear. Are you ready to obey his orders?"

There was an almost unanimous acknowledgment of assent, and order was restored.

"The first thing to be done," I announced upon Captain Dear's instructions, "is to get the same number of oars pulling on each side of the boat; to seat ourselves so as to keep on an even keel, and then to keep the boat's head up into the wind so that we won't be swamped by the waves."

With some little difficulty, this rearrangement was accomplished, and then we rested on our oars with all eyes turned on the still-lighted *Laconia*. The torpedo had hit at about 10:30 P.M. according to our ship's time. Though listing far over on one side, the *Laconia* was still afloat.

It must have been twenty minutes after that first shot that we heard another dull thud, which was

The Sinking of the Laconia

accompanied by a noticeable drop in the hulk. The German submarine had dispatched a second torpedo through the engine room and the boat's vitals from a distance of two hundred yards.

We watched silently during the next minute as the tiers of lights dimmed slowly from white to yellow, then to red, and then nothing was left but the murky mourning of the night which hung over all like a pall.

A mean, cheese-colored crescent of a moon revealed one horn above a rag bundle of clouds low in the distance. A rim of blackness settled around our little world, relieved only by a few leering stars in the zenith, and, where the *Laconia*'s lights had shown, there remained only the dim outlines of a blacker hulk standing out above the water like a jagged headland, silhouetted against the overcast sky.

The ship sank rapidly at the stern until at last its nose rose out of the water and stood straight up in the air. Then it slid silently down and out of sight like a piece of scenery in a panorama spectacle.

Boat No. 3 stood closest to the place where the ship had gone down. As a result of the after suction, the small lifeboat rocked about in a perilous sea of clashing spars and wreckage.

As the boat's crew steadied its head into the wind, a black hulk, glistening wet and standing about eight feet above the surface of the water, approached slowly. It came to a stop opposite the boat

A German U-10 submarine

The Sinking of the Laconia

and not ten feet from the side of it. It was the submarine.

"Vot ship vass dot?" were the first words of throaty guttural English that came from a figure which projected from the conning tower.

"The *Laconia,* Cunard Line," answered the chief steward Ballyn, who commanded the lifeboat.

"Vot did she weigh?" was the next question from the submarine.

"Eighteen thousand tons."

"Any passengers?"

"Seventy-three," replied Ballyn, "many of them women and children—some of them in this boat. She had over two hundred in the crew."

"Did she carry cargo?"

"Yes."

"Iss der captain in dot boat?"

"No," Ballyn answered.

"Well, I guess you'll be all right. A patrol will pick you up some time soon." Without further sound save for the almost silent fixing of the conning tower lid, the submarine moved off.

There was no assurance of an early pickup, so we made preparations for a siege with the elements. The weather was a great factor. That black rim of clouds looked ominous. There was a good promise of rain. February has a reputation for nasty weather in the north Atlantic. The wind was cold and seemed to be rising. Our boat bobbed about like a cork on the swells, which fortunately were not choppy.

How much rougher seas could the boat weather? This question and conditions were debated pro and con.

Had our rockets been seen? Did the first torpedo put the wireless out of commission? If it had been able to operate, had anybody heard our SOS? Was there enough food and drinking water in the boat to last?

This brought us to an inventory of our small craft. After considerable difficulty, we found the lamp, a can of powder flares, the tin of ship's biscuit, matches, and spare oil.

The lamp was lighted. Other lights were now visible. As we drifted in the darkness, we could see them every time we mounted the crest of the swells. The boats carrying these lights remained quite close together at first.

One boat came within sound, and I recognized the Harry Lauder[2]–like voice of the second assistant purser whom I had last heard on Wednesday at the ship's concert. Now he was singing "I Want to Marry 'arry" and "I Love to Be a Sailor."

Hours passed. The swells slopped over the sides of our boat and filled the bottom with water. We bailed it continually. Most of us were wet to the knees and shivering from the weakening effects of the icy water. Our hands were blistered from pulling

The Sinking of the Laconia

at the oars. Our boat, bobbing about like a cork, produced terrific nausea, and our stomachs ached from vain wrenching.

And then we saw the first light—the first sign of help coming—the first searching glow of white radiance deep down the somber sides of the black pot of night that hung over us. I don't know what direction it came from—none of us knew north from south—there was nothing but water and sky. But the light—it just came from over there where we pointed. We nudged dumb, sick boat mates and directed their gaze and aroused them to an appreciation of the sight that gave us new life.

It was way over there—first a trembling quiver of silver against the blackness, then drawing closer, it defined itself as a beckoning finger, although still too far away to see our feeble efforts to attract it.

Nevertheless, we wasted valuable flares, and the ship's baker, self-ordained custodian of the biscuit, did the honors handsomely to the extent of a biscuit apiece to each of the twenty-three occupants of the boat.

"Pull starboard, sonnies," sang out old Captain Dear, his gray chin whiskers bristling with joy in the light of the round lantern which he held aloft.

We pulled—pulled lustily, forgetting the strain and pain of innards torn and racked with violent vomiting, and oblivious of blistered palms and wet, half-frozen feet.

Then a nodding of that finger of light—a happy, snapping, crap-shooting finger that seemed to say: "Come on, you men," like a dice player wooing the bones—led us to believe that our lights had been seen.

This was the fact, for immediately the oncoming vessel flashed on its green and red sidelights, and we saw it was headed for our position. We floated off its stern for a while as it maneuvered for the best position in which it could take us on with a sea that was running higher and higher.

The risk of that rescuing ship was great, because there was every reason to believe that the submarine that had destroyed the *Laconia* still lurked in the darkness nearby, but those on board took the risk and stood by for the work of rescue.

"Come alongside port!" was megaphoned to us. As fast as we could, we swung under the stern and felt our way broadside toward the ship's side.

Out of the darkness above, a dozen small pocket flashlights blinked down on us, and orders began to be shouted fast and thick.

When I look back on the night, I don't know which was the more hazardous, going down the slanting side of the sinking *Laconia* or going up the side of the rescuing vessel.

One minute the swells would lift us almost level with the rail of the low-built patrol boat and mine sweeper, but the next receding wave would swirl us

The Sinking of the Laconia

down into a darksome gulf over which the ship's side glowered like a slimy, dripping cliff.

A score of hands reached out, and we were suspended in the husky, tattooed arms of those doughty British Jack Tars, looking up into their weather-beaten youthful faces, mumbling our thankfulness and reading in the gold lettering on their pancake hats the legend, "HMS *Laburnum*." We had been six hours in the open boat.

The others began coming alongside one by one. Wet and bedraggled survivors were lifted aboard. Women and children first was the rule.

The scenes of reunion were heart-gripping. Men who had remained strangers to one another aboard the *Laconia* now wrung each other by the hand or embraced without shame the frail little wife of a Canadian chaplain who had found one of her missing children delivered up from another boat. She smothered the child with ravenous mother kisses while tears of gladness streamed down her face.

Boat after boat came alongside. The water-logged craft containing the captain came last. A rousing cheer went up as he stepped on the deck, one mangled hand hanging limp at his side. The sailors divested themselves of outer clothing and passed the garments over to the shivering members of the *Laconia*'s crew.

The cramped officers' quarters down under the quarter deck were turned over to the women and children. Two of the *Laconia*'s stewardesses passed boiling basins of navy cocoa and aided in the disentangling of wet and matted tresses. The men grouped themselves near steam pipes in the petty officers' quarters or over the grating of the engine rooms, where new life was to be had from the upward blasts of heated air that brought with them the smell of bilge water and oil and sulfur from the bowels of the vessel. The injured—all minor cases, sprained backs, wrenched legs, or mashed hands—were put away in bunks under the care of the ship's doctor.

Dawn was melting the eastern ocean gray to pink when the task was finished. In the officers' quarters, which had now been invaded by the men, the roll of the vessel was most perceptible. Each time the floor of the room slanted, bottles and cups and plates rolled and slid back and forth. On the tables and chairs and benches the women rested. Seasick mothers, trembling from the aftereffects of the terrifying experience of the night, sought to soothe their crying children.

Then somebody happened to touch a key on the small wooden organ that stood against one wall. This was enough to send some callous seafaring fingers over the ivory keys in a rhythm unquestionably religious and so irresistible under the circumstances that, although no one seemed to know the words,

The Sinking of the Laconia

the air was taken up in a reverent, humming chant by all in the room.

At the last note of the amen, little Father Warring, his black garb snaggled in places and badly soiled, stood before the center table and lifted back his head until the morning light, filtering through the opened hatch above him, shown down on his kindly, weary face. He recited the Lord's Prayer, and all present joined. The simple, impressive service of thanksgiving ended as simply as it had begun.

A survey and cruise of the nearby waters revealed no more occupied boats, and our mine sweeper, with its load of survivors numbering 267, steamed away to the east. A half an hour steaming, and the vessel stopped within hailing distance of two sister ships, toward one of which an open boat manned by jackies [sailors] was being pulled.

I saw the hysterical French actress, her blonde hair wet and bedraggled, lifted out of the boat and carried up the companionway. Then a little boy, his fresh pink face and golden hair shining in the morning sun, was passed upward, followed by some other survivors, numbering fourteen in all, who had been found half-drowned and almost dead from exposure in a partially wrecked boat that was picked up just as it was sinking. It was in that boat that one American woman and her daughter died.

With exchanges of experiences pathetic and humorous, we steamed into Queenstown Harbor shortly after ten o'clock that night. We had been attacked at a point two hundred miles off the Irish coast, and of our passengers and crew, thirteen had been lost.

As I stepped ashore, a Britisher, a fellow passenger aboard the *Laconia*, who knew me as an American, stepped up to me. During the voyage, we had had many conversations concerning the possibility of America entering the war. Now he slapped me on the back with this question, "Well, old Casus Belli,"[3] he said, "is this your blooming overt act?"

I did not answer him, but thirty minutes afterward I was pounding out on a typewriter the introduction to a four-thousand-word newspaper article which I cabled that night and which put the question up to the American public for an answer.

Five weeks later the United States entered the war.

NOTES

1. Johann-Heinrich, count von Bernstorff (1862–1939), diplomat who represented Germany in London and Cairo and as ambassador to the United States from 1908–17.

2. Sir Henry "Harry" Lauder (1870–1950), Scottish comedian and music-hall singer.

3. Casus Belli: act justifying war.

Pershing's Arrival in Europe

Lean, clean, keen—that's the way they looked—that first trim little band of American fighting men who made their historic landing on the shores of England, June 8, 1917.

I went down from London to meet them at the port of arrival. In my dispatches of that date, I, nor none of the other correspondents, was permitted to mention the name of the port. This was supposed to be the secret that was to be religiously kept, and the British censor was on the job religiously.

The name of the port was excluded from all American dispatches, but the British censor saw no reason to withhold transmission of the following sentence—"Pershing landed today at an English port and was given a hearty welcome by the Mayor of Liverpool."

So I am presuming at this late date of writing that it would serve no further purpose to refrain from announcing flatly that General John J. Pershing, commander in chief of the American Expeditionary Forces overseas, and his staff landed on the date above mentioned, at Liverpool, England.

The sun was shining brightly on the Mersey when the giant ocean liner, the *Baltic*, came slowly up the harbor in the tow of numerous puffing tugs. The great gray vessel that had safely completed the crossing of the submarine zone was warped to the dockside.

On the quay there were a full brass band and an honorary escort of British soldiers. While the moorings were being fastened, General Pershing, with his staff, appeared on the promenade deck on the shore side of the vessel. His appearance was the signal for a crash of cymbals and drums as the band blared out the "Star-Spangled Banner." The American commander and the officers ranged in line on either side of him stood stiffly at attention, with right hands raised in salute to the visors of their caps.

On the shore the lines of British soldiery brought their arms to the present with a snap. Civilian witnesses of the ceremony bared their heads. The first anthem was followed by the playing of "God Save the King." All present remained at the salute.

As the gangplank was lashed in place, a delegation of British military and civilian officials boarded the ship and were presented to the general. Below, on the dock, every newspaper correspondent and photographer in the British Isles, I think, stood waiting in a group that far outnumbered the other spectators.

Pershing and his staff stepped ashore. *Lean, clean, keen*—those are the words that described their appearance. That was the way they impressed their critical brothers in arms, the all-observing military dignities that presented Britain's hearty, unreserved

Pershing's Arrival in Europe

welcome at the water's edge. That was the way they appeared to the proud American citizens, residents of those islands, who gathered to meet them.

At attention on the dock, facing the sea-stained flanks of the liner *Baltic*, a company of Royal Welsh Fusiliers[1] stood like a frieze of clay models in stainless khaki, polished brass, and shining leather. General Pershing inspected the guard of honor with keen interest. Walking beside the American commander was the considerably stouter and somewhat shorter Lieutenant General Sir William Pitcairn Campbell,[2] K.C.B., chief of the Western Command of the British Home Forces.

The ceremony was followed by a reception in the cabin of the *Baltic*, where General Pershing received the lord mayor of Liverpool, the lady mayoress, and a delegation of civil authorities. The reception ended when General Pershing spoke a few simple words to the assembled representatives of the British and American Press.

"More of us are coming" was the keynote of his modest remarks. Afterward he was escorted to the quay-side station, where a special train of the type labeled Semi-Royal was ready to make the express run to London.

The reception at the dock had had none of the features of a demonstration by reason of the necessity for the ship's arrival being secret, but as soon as the *Baltic* had landed, the word of the American commander's arrival spread through Liverpool like wildfire.

The railroad from the station lay through an industrial section of the city. Through the railroad warehouses the news had preceded the train. Warehousemen, porters, and draymen crowded the tops of the cotton bales and oil barrels on both sides of the track as the train passed through.

Beyond the sheds, the news had spread through the many floors of the flour mills, and when the Pershing train passed, handkerchiefs and caps fluttered from every crowded door and window in the whitened walls.

From his car window, General Pershing returned the greetings of the trousered girls and women who were making England's bread, while their husbands, fathers, brothers, sweethearts, and sons were making German cemeteries.

In London, General Pershing and his staff occupied suites at the Savoy Hotel, and during the four or five days of the American commander's sojourn in the capital of the British Empire, a seemingly endless line of visitors of all the Allied nationalities called to present their compliments.

There was a widespread revival of an old story which the Americans liked to tell in the barrack rooms at night. When the Welsh Fusiliers received our men at the dock of Liverpool, they had with them their historical mascot, a large white goat with

Pershing's Arrival in Europe

horns encased in inscribed silver. The animal wore suspended from its neck a large silver plate, on which was inscribed a partial history of the Welsh Fusiliers.

"It was our regiment—the Welsh Fusiliers," one of them said, "that fought you Yanks at Bunker Hill. And it was at Bunker Hill that our regiment captured the great-great-granddaddy of this same white goat, and his descendants are ever destined to be the mascot of our regiment. You see, we have still got your goat."

"But you will notice," replied one of the Yanks, "we've got the hill."

During the four days in London, General Pershing was received by King George and Queen Mary[3] at Buckingham Palace. The American commander engaged in several long conferences at the British War Office, and then with an exclusion of entertainment that was painful to the Europeans, he made arrangements to leave for his new post in France.

A specially written permission from General Pershing made it possible for me to accompany him on that historic crossing between England and France. Secret orders for the departure were given on the afternoon and evening of June 12. Before four o'clock of the next morning, June 13, I breakfasted in the otherwise deserted dining room of the Savoy with the general and his staff.

In closed automobiles we were whisked away to

And They Thought We Wouldn't Fight

Charing Cross Station. We boarded a special train whose destination was unknown. The entire party was again in the hands of the Intelligence Section of the British Admiralty, and every possible means was taken to suppress all definite information concerning the departure.

The special train containing General Pershing and his staff reached Folkestone at about seven o'clock in the morning. We left the train at the dockside and boarded the swift channel steamer moored there. A small vociferous contingent of English Tommies returning to the front from leave in "Blighty"[4] were crowded on all decks in the stern.

With lifeboats swinging out over the side and everyone wearing life preservers, we steamed out of Folkestone harbor to challenge the submarine dangers of the channel. Our ship was guarded on all sides and above. Swift torpedo destroyers dashed to and fro under our bow and stern and circled us continually. In the air above, hydro-airplanes and dirigible balloons hovered over the waters surrounding us, keeping sharp watch for the first appearance of the dark subsea hulks of destruction.

We did not learn until the next day that while we were making that channel crossing, the German air forces had crossed the channel in a daring daylight raid and were at that very hour dropping bombs on London around the very hotel which General Pershing had just vacated. Some day, after the war, I

Pershing's Arrival in Europe

hope to ascertain whether the commander of that flight of bombing Gothas [German heavy bombers] started on his expedition over London with a special purpose in view and whether that purpose concerned the supposed presence there of the commander in chief of the American millions that were later to change the entire complexion of the war against Germany.

As we drew close to the shore, I noticed an enormous concrete breakwater extending out from the harbor entrance. It was surmounted by a wooden railing, and on the very end of it, straddling the rail, was a small French boy. His legs were bare, and his feet were encased in heavy wooden shoes. On his head he wore a red stocking cap of the liberty type.[5] As we came within hailing distance, he gave to us the first greeting that came from the shores of France to these first-arriving American soldiers.

"*Vive l'Amérique!*" he shouted, cupping his hands to his mouth and sending his shrill voice across the water to us. Pershing on the bridge heard the salutation. He smiled, touched his hand to his hat, and waved to the lad on the railing.

We landed that day at Boulogne [-sur-Mare], June 13, 1917. Military bands massed on the quay blared out the American national anthem as the ship was warped alongside the dock. Other ships in the busy harbor began blowing whistles and ringing bells; loaded troop and hospital ships lying nearby

Gibbons's Locations in France

GERMANY
NETHERLANDS
Essen
Düsseldorf
Brugge
Antwerpen
Cologne
Schelde
Brussels
Bonn
BELGIUM
Rhine
Meuse
LUXEMBOURG
see page160
Luxembourg
Rheims
Marne
Meuse
Château-Thierry
Mountains
St. Mihiel
see page 80
Nancy
Moselle
Strasbourg
Lorraine Region
Vosges
Troyes
Épinal
Rhine
Chaumont
Seine
Auxerre
Mulhouse
Doubs
Dijon
Besançon
Valdahon
Bern
SWITZERLAND

burst forth into cheering. The news spread like contagion along the harbor front.

As the gangplank was lowered, French military dignitaries, in dress uniforms resplendent with gold braid, buttons, and medals, advanced to that part of the deck amidships where the general stood. They saluted respectfully and pronounced elaborate addresses in their native tongue. They were followed by numerous French government officials in civilian dress attire. The city, the department, and the nation were represented in the populous delegations who presented their compliments and conveyed to the American commander the unstinted and heartfelt welcome of the entire people of France.

The docks and train sheds were decorated with French and American flags and yards and yards of the mutually owned red, white, and blue. Thousands of spectators began to gather in the streets near the station, and their continuous cheers sufficed to rapidly augment their own numbers. General Pershing and his staff boarded a special train for Paris. I went with them.

No one in France, with the exception of a select official circle, had been aware that General Pershing was arriving that day until about thirty minutes before his ship was warped into the dock at Boulogne. It has always been a mystery to me how the French managed to decorate the station at Boulogne upon such short notice.

Pershing's Arrival in Europe

Thus it was that the train crawled slowly toward Paris for the purpose of giving the French capital time to throw off the coat of war weariness that it had worn for 3½ years and don gala attire for this occasion. Paris made full use of every minute of that time, as we found when the train arrived at the French capital late in the afternoon. The evening papers in Paris had carried the news of the American commander's landing on the shores of France, and Paris was ready to receive him as Paris had never before received a world's notable.

The sooty girders of the Gare du Nord shook with cheers when the special train pulled in. General Pershing stepped from his private car. Flashlights boomed, and batteries of cameramen maneuvered into positions for the lens barrage. The band of the Garde Républicaine blared forth the strains of the "Star-Spangled Banner," bringing all the military to a halt and a long standing salute. It was followed by the "Marseillaise."

At the conclusion of the train-side greetings and introductions, Marshal Joffre[6] and General Pershing walked down the platform together. The tops of the cars of every train in the station were crowded with workmen. As the tall, slender American commander stepped into view, the privileged observers on the car tops began to cheer. A minute later, there was a terrific roar from beyond the walls of the station. The crowds outside had heard the cheering within.

They took it up with thousands of throats. They made their welcome a ringing one. Paris took Pershing by storm.

General Pershing and M. Painlevé, minister of war, took seats in a large automobile. They were preceded by a motor containing United States ambassador Sharp and former premier Viviani. The procession started to the accompaniment of martial music by massed military bands in the courtyard of the station. There were some fifty automobiles in the line, the rear of which was brought up by an enormous motorbus-load of the first American soldiers from the ranks to pass through the streets of Paris.

The crowds overflowed the sidewalks. They extended from the building walls out beyond the curbs and into the streets, leaving but a narrow lane through which the motors pressed their way slowly and with the exercise of much care. From the crowded balconies and windows overlooking the route, women and children tossed down showers of flowers and bits of colored paper.

Old gray-haired fathers of French fighting men bared their heads and, with tears streaming down their cheeks, shouted greetings to the tall, thin, gray-mustached American commander who was leading new armies to the support of their sons. Women heaped armfuls of roses into the general's car and into the cars of other American officers that

Pershing's Arrival in Europe

followed him. Paris street gamins climbed the lampposts and waved their caps and wooden shoes and shouted shrilly.

American flags and red, white, and blue bunting waved wherever the eye rested. English-speaking Frenchmen proudly explained to the uninformed that "Pershing" was pronounced "Peur-chigne" and not "Pair-shang."

Paris was not backward in displaying its knowledge of English. Gay Parisiennes were eager to make use of all the English at their command, that they might welcome the new arrivals in their native tongue.

Some of these women shouted "Hello," "Heep, heep, hourrah," "Good morning," "How are you, keed?" and "Cocktails for two." Some of the expressions were not so inappropriate as they sounded.

Occasionally there came from the crowds a good old genuine American whoop-em-up yell. This happened when the procession passed groups of American ambulance workers and other sons of Uncle Sam, wearing the uniforms of the French, Canadian, and English Corps.

They joined with Australians and South African soldiers on leave to cheer on the new-coming Americans with such spontaneous expressions as "Come on, you Yanks," "Now let's get 'em," and "Eat 'em up, Uncle Sam."

The busload of enlisted men bringing up the rear

received dozens of bouquets from the girls. The flowers were hurled at them from all directions. Being the passive recipients of this unusual adulation produced only embarrassment on the part of the regulars who simply had to sit there, smiling and taking it.

Through such scenes as these, the procession reached the great Place de la Concorde. In this wide, paved, open space, an enormous crowd had assembled. As the autos appeared, the cheering, the flower throwing, the tumultuous kiss-blowing began. It increased in intensity as the motors stopped in front of the Hôtel de Crillon into which General Pershing disappeared, followed by his staff. Immediately the cheering changed to a tremendous clamorous demand for the general's appearance on the balcony in front of his apartments.

General Pershing stepped forth on the balcony. He stood behind the low marble railing, and between two enormous white-stoned columns. A cluster of the Allied flags was affixed to each column. The American commander surveyed the scene in front of him. There are no trees or shrubbery in the vast Place de la Concorde. Its broad paved surface is interrupted only by artistically placed groups of statuary and fountains.

General Pershing looked down upon the sea of faces turned up toward him, and then it seemed that nature desired to play a part in the ceremony

Pershing's Arrival in Europe

of that great day. A soft breeze from the Champs Élysées touched the cluster of flags on the general's right and from all the Allied emblems fastened there, it selected one flag.

The breeze tenderly caught the folds of this flag and wafted them across the balcony on which the general bowed. He saw and recognized that flag. He extended his hand, caught the flag in his fingers, and pressed it to his lips. All France and all America represented in that vast throng that day cheered to the mighty echo when Pershing kissed the tri-color of France.

It was a tremendous, unforgettable incident. It was exceeded by no other incident during those days of receptions and ceremonies, except one. That was an incident which occurred not in the presence of thousands, but in a lonely old burial ground on the outskirts of Paris. This happened several days after the demonstration in the Place de la Concorde.

On that day of bright sunshine, General Pershing and a small party of officers, French and American, walked through the gravel paths of Picpus Cemetery in the suburbs of Paris, where the bodies of hundreds of those who made the history of France are buried.

Several French women in deep mourning curtsied as General Pershing passed. His party stopped in front of two marble slabs that lay side by side at the foot of a granite monument. From the general's

General Pershing at Lafayette's tomb

Pershing's Arrival in Europe

party a Frenchman stepped forward and, removing his high silk hat, he addressed the small group in quiet, simple tones and well-chosen English words. He was the Marquis de Chambrun.[7] He said:

"On this spot one can say that the historic ties between our nations are not the result of the able schemes of skillful diplomacy. No, the principles of liberty, justice, and independence are the glorious links between our nations.

"We know that our great nations are together with our Allies invincible, and we rejoice to think that the United States and France are reunited in the fight for liberty, and will reconsecrate, in a new victory, their everlasting friendship of which your presence today at this grave is an exquisite and touching token."

General Pershing advanced to the tomb and placed upon the marble slab an enormous wreath of pink and white roses. Then he stepped back. He removed his cap and held it in both hands in front of him. The bright sunlight shone down on his silvery gray hair. Looking down at the grave, he spoke in a quiet, impressive tone four simple, all-meaning words: "Lafayette, we are here."[8]

And They Thought We Wouldn't Fight

NOTES

1. The Royal Welsh Fusiliers was one of the oldest formations in the British Army. Its soldiers included many famous writers like Siegfried Sassoon, Robert Graves, and David Jones.

2. Sir William Pitcairn Campbell (1856–1933), a lieutenant general who commanded the Western Command in Great Britain, centered on Wales and the Midlands.

3. George V (1865–1936), king, and Mary (1867–1953), queen, of Great Britain, Ireland, the British dominions beyond the seas, and emperor and empress of India.

4. Tommies: British slang for rank-and-file soldiers; Blighty: army slang for England.

5. Cap of the liberty type: The liberty cap is a soft conical hat or Phrygian cap that has become a symbol of freedom.

6. Joseph Joffre (1852–1931) commanded the French army from the outbreak of the war until 1916. In 1917, he made a widely celebrated tour of the United States.

7. The Marquis de Chambrun [Pierre Chambrun] (1865–1954) was, through his mother, a descendent of General Lafayette.

8. The Marquis de Lafayette [Gilbert du Motier](1757–1834), a French nobleman who fought alongside George Washington in the American Revolution. Washington thought of him as another son. American place names like Lafayette, Fayette, Fayetteville, etc., testify to his importance to Americans. "Lafayette we are here" signaled that Americans had come to France to repay the debt. See also Historical Introduction.

The Landing of the First American Contingent in France

THE FIRST EXECUTIVE work of the American Expeditionary Forces overseas was performed in a second-floor suite of the Crillon Hotel on the Place de la Concorde in Paris. This suite was the first temporary headquarters of the American commander.

The tall windows of the rooms looked down on the historic Place which was the scene of so many momentous events in French history. The windows were hardly a hundred yards from the very spot where the guillotine dripped red in the days of the Terror. It was here that the heads of Louis XVI and Marie Antoinette dropped into the basket.

During the first week that General Pershing stopped at the hotel, the sidewalk and street beneath his windows were constantly crowded with people. The crowds waited there all day long, just in the hope of catching a glimpse of the American commander if he should happen to be leaving or returning to his quarters.

But the American commander would not permit demonstrations and celebrations to interfere with the important duties that he faced. Two days are all that were devoted to these social ceremonies which the enthusiastic and hospitable French would have made almost endless. Dinners, receptions, and parades were ruthlessly erased from the working-day calendar. The American commander sounded the order "To work" with the same martial precision as though the command had been a sudden call "To arms."

On the morning of the third day after General Pershing's arrival in Paris, the typewriters began clicking incessantly and the telephones began ringing busily in the large building which was occupied on that day as the headquarters of the American Expeditionary Forces in France.

This building was Numbers 27 and 31 Rue de Constantine. It faced the trees and shrubbery bordering the approach to the Seine front of the Invalides. The building was two stories high with gray-white walls and a mansard roof. At that time it could be immediately identified as the one in front of which stood a line of American motor cars, as the one where trim United States regulars walked sentry post past the huge doors through which frequent orderlies dashed with messages.

This was the first workshop in France of the American commander in chief. Adjoining rooms to the left and right were occupied by the general's staff and his aides. And it was in these rooms that the overseas plans for the landing of the first American armed contingent in France were formulated.

The Landing of the First American Contingent in France

* * *

It is safe now to mention that St. Nazaire on the west coast of France was the port at which our first armed forces disembarked. I was in Paris when the information of their coming was whispered to a few chosen correspondents who were to be privileged to witness this historical landing.

This was the first time in the history of our nation that a large force of armed Americans was to cross the seas to Europe. For 5½ months prior to the date of their landing, the ruthless submarine policy of the imperial German government had been in effect, and our troop ships with those initial thousands of American soldiers represented the first large armada to dare the ocean crossing since Germany had instituted her subsea blockade zone in February of that same year.

Thus it was that any conversation concerning the fact that our men were on the seas and at the mercy of the U-boats was conducted with the greatest of care behind closed doors. In spite of the efforts of the French agents of counter-espionage, Paris, and all France, for that matter, housed numerous spies. There were some anxious moments while that first contingent was on the water.

Our little group of correspondents was informed that we should be conducted by American officers to the port of landing, but the name of that port

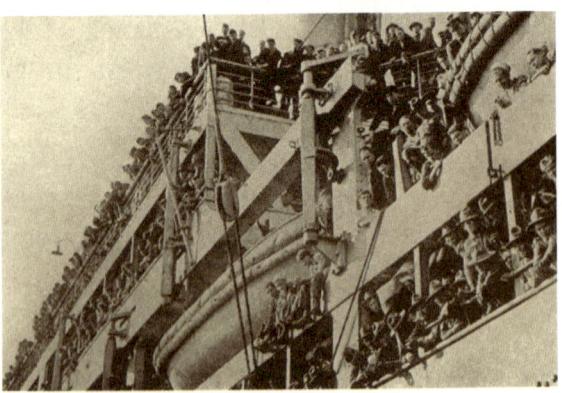

The first American troops landing in France

The Landing of the First American Contingent in France

was withheld from us. By appointment we met at a Paris railroad station, where we were provided with railroad tickets. We took our places in compartments and rode for some ten or twelve hours, arriving early the next morning at St. Nazaire.

This little village on the coast of Brittany was tucked away there in the golden sands of the seashore. Its houses had walls of white stucco and gabled roofs of red tile. In the small rolling hills behind it were green orchards and fields of yellow wheat. The villagers, old women in their starched white headdresses and old men wearing faded blue smocks and wooden shoes, were unmindful of the great event for which history had destined their village.

On the night before the landing, the townspeople had retired with no knowledge of what was to happen on the following day. In the morning they awoke to find strange ships that had come in the night, riding safely at anchor in the harbor. The wooden shutters began to pop open with bangs as excited heads, encased in peaked flannel nightcaps, protruded themselves from bedroom windows and directed anxious queries to those who happened to be abroad at that early hour.

St. Nazaire came to life more quickly that morning than ever before in its history. The mayor of the town was one of the busiest figures on the street. In high hat and full-dress attire, he hurried about trying to assemble the village orchestra of octogenarian fiddlers and flute players to play a welcome for the new arrivals. The townspeople neglected their *café au lait* to rush down to the quay to look at the new ships.

The waters of the harbor sparkled in the early morning sunlight. The dawn had been gray and misty, but now nature seemed to smile. The strange ships from the other side of the world were gray in hulk, but now there were signs of life and color aboard each one of them.

Beyond the troop ships lay the first United States warships, units of that remarkable fighting organization which in the year that was to immediately follow that very day were to escort safely across three thousand miles of submarine-infested water more than a million and a half American soldiers.

When but twenty feet from the quay-side, the successive decks of the first troop ship took on the appearance of mud-colored layers from the khaki uniforms of the stiff-standing ranks of our men. A military band on the forward deck was playing the national anthems of France and America, and every hand was being held at the salute.

As the final bars of the "Star-Spangled Banner" crashed out and every saluting hand came snappily down, one American soldier on an upper deck leaned over the rail and shouted to a comrade on the shore his part of the first exchange of greetings be-

The Landing of the First American Contingent in France

tween our fighting men upon this historic occasion. Holding one hand to his lips, he seriously enquired: "Say, do they let the enlisted men in the saloons here?"

As our men came over the ship's side and down the runways, there was no great reception committee awaiting them. Among the most interested spectators of the event were a group of stolid German prisoners of war and the two French soldiers guarding them. The two Frenchmen talked volubly with a wealth of gesticulation, while the Germans maintained their characteristic glumness.

The German prisoners appeared to be anything but discouraged at the sight. Some of them even wore a smile that approached the supercilious. With some of them that smile seemed to say: "You can't fool us. We know these troops are not Americans. They are either Canadians or Australians coming from England. Our German U-boats won't let Americans cross the ocean." But the stream of khaki continued to pour out of the ship's side. Company after company of our men, loaded down with packs and full field equipment, lined up on the dock and marched past the group of German prisoners.

"We're passing in review for you, Fritzie,"[1] one irrepressible from our ranks shouted, as the marching line passed within touching distance of the prisoner group. The Germans responded only with quizzical little smiles and silence.

And They Thought We Wouldn't Fight

Escorted by our own military bands, the regiments marched through the main street of the village. The bands played "Dixie"—a new air to France. The regiments as a whole did not present the snappy, marching appearance that they might have presented. There was a good reason for this. Sixty percent of them were recruits. It had been wisely decided to replace many of the old regular army men in the ranks with newly enlisted men so that these old veterans could remain in America and train the new drafts.

However, that which impressed the French people was the individual appearance of these samples of American manhood. Our men were tall and broad and brawny. They were young and vigorous. Their eyes were keen and snappy. Their complexions ranged in shade from the swarthy suntanned cheeks of [Mexican] border veterans to the clear pink skins of city youngsters. But most noticeable of all to the French people were the even white rows of teeth which our men displayed when they smiled. Good dentistry and clean mouths are essentially American.

A campsite had been partially prepared for their reception. It was located close to a French barracks. The French soldiers and gangs of German prisoners, who had been engaged in this work, had no knowledge of the fact that they were building the first American cantonment in France. They thought

The Landing of the First American Contingent in France

they were constructing simply an extension of the French encampment.

That first contingent, composed of United States Infantrymen and Marines, made its first camp in France with the smallest amount of confusion, considering the fact that almost three-quarters of them hadn't been in uniform a month. It was but several hours after arriving at the camp that the smoke was rising from the busy camp stoves and the aroma of American coffee, baked beans, and broiled steaks was in the air.

On the afternoon of that first day, some of the men were given permission to visit the town. They began to take their first lessons in French as they went from café to café in futile efforts to connect up with such unknown commodities as cherry pie or ham-and-egg sandwiches. Upon meeting one another in the streets, our men would invariably ask: "Have you come across any of these FROGS that talk American?"

There was nothing disrespectful about the terms "Frogs" or "Froggies" as applied to their French comrades in arms. American officers hastened to explain to French officers that the one piece of information concerning France most popularly known in America was that it was the place where people first learned to eat frog legs and snails.[2]

The Frenchmen, on the other hand, were somewhat inclined to believe that these first Americans didn't live up to the European expectations of Americans. Those European expectations had been founded almost entirely upon the translations of dime novels and moving-picture thrillers of the Wild West and comedy variety.

Although our men wore the high, broad-brimmed felt hats, they didn't seem sufficiently cowboyish. Although the French people waited expectantly, none of these Americans dashed through the main street of the village on bucking broncos, holding their reins in their teeth and at the same time firing revolvers from either hand. Moreover, none of our men seemed to conclude their dinners in the expected American fashion of slapping one another in the face with custard pies.

There was to be seen on the streets of St. Nazaire that day some representative black Americans, who had also landed in that historical first contingent. There was a strange thing about these Negroes.

It will be remembered that in the early stages of our participation in the war it had been found that there was hardly sufficient khaki cloth to provide uniforms for all of our soldiers. That had been the case with these American Negro soldiers.

But somewhere down in Washington, somehow or other, someone resurrected an old, large, heavy iron key, and this, inserted into an ancient rusty lock, had opened some long-forgotten doors in one of the government arsenals. There were revealed old

The Landing of the First American Contingent in France

dust-covered bundles wrapped up in newspapers, yellow with age, and when these wrappings of the past were removed, there were seen the uniforms of old Union blue that had been laid away back in '65—uniforms that had been worn by men who fought and bled and died to free the first black American citizens.

And here on this foreign shore, on this day in June, more than half a century later, the sons and the grandsons of those same freed slaves wore those same uniforms of Union blue as they landed in France to fight for a newer freedom.

Some of these Negroes were stevedores from the lower Mississippi levees. They sang as they worked in their white army undershirts, across the chest of which they had penciled in blue and red, strange mystic devices, religious phrases, and hoodoo signs, calculated to contribute the charm of safety to the running of the submarine blockade.

Our veterans from Mexico and the border campaigns found that their smattering of Spanish did not help them much. But still everyone seemed to manage to get along all right. Our soldiers and the French soldiers in those early days couldn't understand each other's languages, but they could understand each other.

This strange paradox was analyzed for me by a young American lieutenant who said he had made a twelve-hour study of the remarkable camaraderie that had immediately sprung up between the fighting men of France and the fighting men of America. In explaining this relationship, he said: "You see, we think the French are crazy," he said, "and the French know damn well we are."

Those of our men who had not brought small French and English dictionaries with them made hurried purchases of such handy articles and forthwith began to practice. The French people did likewise.

I saw one young American infantryman seated at a table in front of one of the sidewalk cafés on the village square. He was dividing his attention between a fervent admiration of the pretty French waitress, who stood smiling in front of him, and an intense interest in the pages of his small hand dictionary.

She had brought his glass of beer, and he had paid for it, but there seemed to be a mutual urge for further conversation. The American would look first at her, and then he would look through the pages of the book again. Finally, he gave slow and painful enunciation of the following request: "Mad-am-moy-sell, donnie moy oon baysa."*

She laughed prettily as she caught his meaning almost immediately, and she replied: "Doughboy,[3] ware do you get zat stuff?"

---

* Tr: *Mademoiselle, donnez-moi un baiser:* Miss, give me a kiss.

The Landing of the First American Contingent in France

"Aw, hell," said the young infantryman, as he closed the book with a snap. "I knew they'd let those sailors ashore before us."

The attitude of our first arriving American soldiers toward the German prisoners who worked in gangs on construction work in the camps and rough labor along the docks was a curious one. Not having yet encountered in battle the brothers of these same docile-appearing captives, our men were even inclined to treat the prisoners with deference almost approaching admiration.

In a measure, the Germans returned this feeling. The arrival of the Americans was really cheering to them. The prisoners disliked the French because they had been taught to do so from childhood. They hated the English because that was the hate with which they went into battle.

It sounds incongruous now, but, nevertheless, it was a fact then that the German prisoners confined at that first American sea base really seemed to like the American soldiers. Maybe it was because any change of masters or guards was a relief in the uneventful existence which had been theirs since the day of their capture. Perhaps the feeling was one of distinct kindred, based on a familiarity with Americans and American customs—a familiarity which had been produced by thousands of letters which Germans in America had written to their friends in Germany before the war. On the other hand, it may simply have been by reason of America's official disavowal of any animosity toward the German people.

One day I watched some of those prisoners unloading supplies at one of the docks in St. Nazaire, more or less under the eyes of an American sentry who stood nearby. One group of four Germans were engaged in carrying what appeared to be a large wooden packing case. Casually, and as if by accident, the case was dropped to the ground and cracked.

Instantly one of the prisoners' hands began to furtively investigate the packages revealed by the break. The other prisoners busied themselves as if preparing to lift the box again. The first German pulled a spoon from his bootleg, plunged it into the crevice in the broken box and withdrew it heaped with granulated sugar. With a quick movement he conveyed the stolen sweet to his mouth, and that gapping orifice closed quickly on the sugar, while his stoical face immediately assumed its characteristic downcast look. He didn't dare move his lips or jaws for fear of detection.

Of course these Germans had been receiving but a scant ration of sugar, but their lot had been no worse than that of the French soldiers guarding them previously, who got no sugar either. American soldiers then guarding those prisoners reported only

The Landing of the First American Contingent in France

a few of them for confinement for these human thefts.

It should be specially stated that lenience could not and was not extended to the point of fraternization. But the relationship that seemed to exist between the German prisoners and American soldiers at that early date revealed undeniably the absence of any mutual hate.

Around one packing case on the dock I saw, one day, a number of German prisoners who were engaged in unpacking bundles from America and passing them down a line of waiting hands that relayed them to a freight car. One of the Germans leaning over the case straightened up with a rumpled newspaper in his hand. He had removed it from a package. A look of indescribable joy came across his face.

"Deutscher, Deutscher," he cried, pointing to the Gothic type. The paper was a copy of the New York *Staats-Zeitung*.

The lot of those prisoners was not an unhappy one. To me it seemed very doubtful whether even a small percentage of them would have accepted liberty if it carried with it the necessity of returning to German trenches.

The German prison camps at St. Nazaire were inspected by General Pershing on the third day of the American landing when he, with his staff, ar-

And They Thought We Wouldn't Fight

rived from Paris. The general and his party arrived early in the morning in a pouring rain. The American commander in chief then held the rank of a major general. In the harbor was the flagship of Rear Admiral Gleaves.[4]

There was no delay over the niceties of etiquette when the question arose as to whether the rear admiral should call on the major general or the major general should call on the rear admiral.

The major general settled the subject with a sentence. He said, "The point is that I want to see him," and with no further ado about it, General Pershing and his staff visited the admiral on his flagship.

NOTES

1. Fritzie: also Fritz, a nickname for a German soldier, originally used during the First World War.

2. Frogs or Froggies: nickname for French, now considered derogatory. Another explanation of derivation is that it refers to the ornamental fastenings on French military uniforms.

3. Doughboy: slang term for American infantryman. Usually associated with World War I.

4. Rear Admiral Gleaves: Albert Gleaves (1858–1937) commanded the American navy's Transport Service.

Through the School of War

Clip the skyline from the Blue Ridge, arch it over with arboreal vistas from the forests of the Oregon, reflect the two in the placid waters of the Wisconsin—and you will have some conception of the perfect Eden of beauty in which the first contingent of the American Expeditionary Forces trained in France.

The training area was located in the Vosges, in east central France. By train, it was a nine-hour day trip from Paris. It was located about an hour's motor ride behind the front lines, which at that time were close to the north of the cities of Nancy and Toul.

The area had long since been stripped of male civilian population that could be utilized for the French ranks. The war had taken the men and the boys but had left the old people and children to till the fields, tend the cattle, prune the hedges, and trim the roads.

Along the white roads, clay-colored rectangles that moved evenly, like brown caravans, represented the marching units of United States troops. The columns of bluish-gray that passed them with shorter, quicker steps, were companies of those tireless Frenchmen, who after almost three years of the front-line real thing, now played at a mimic war of make-believe, with taller and heavier novitiates.

And They Thought We Wouldn't Fight

Those French troops were Alpine Chasseurs[1]—the famous Blue Devils. They wore dark blue caps, which resemble tam-o'-shanters, but are not. They were proud of the distinction which their uniform gave them. They were proud of their great fighting records. One single battalion of them boasted that of the twenty-six officers who led it into the first fight at the opening of the war, only four of them existed.

It was a great advantage for our men to train under such instructors. Correspondents who had been along the fronts before America's entry into the war had a great respect for the soldierly capacity of these same fighting Frenchmen; not only these sturdy young sons of France who wore the uniform, but the older French soldiers—ranging in age from forty to fifty-five years—who had been away to the fronts since the very beginning of the war.

It was under such veteran instructors as these that our first Americans in France trained, in the province that boasts the birthplace of Jeanne d'Arc.

On the few leave days, many of our men, with permission, would absent themselves from camp and make short pilgrimages over the hills to the little town of Domrémy [-la-Pucelle] to visit the house in which the Maid of Orleans was born.

Our men were eager to learn. I observed them daily at their training tasks. One day when they had progressed as far as the use of the new French auto-

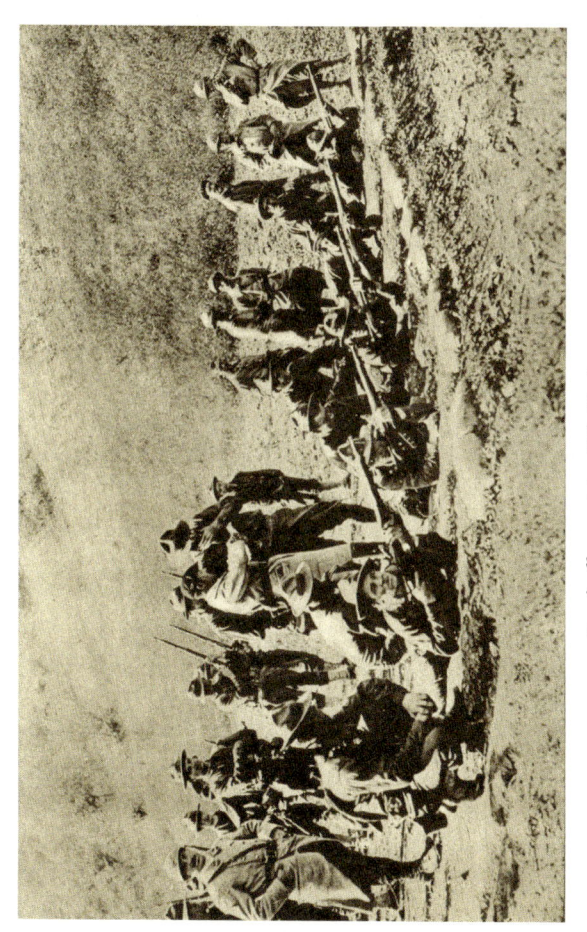

French officers training U.S. Marines

matic rifles, I visited one of the ranges to witness the firing.

At one end of the firing trench a raw American recruit, who admitted that he had never handled an automatic rifle before, flushed to his hat brim and gritted his teeth viciously as his shots, registering ten feet above the targets, brought forth laughter and exclamations from the French soldiers nearby. He rested on his gun long enough to ask an interpreter what the Frenchmen were talking about.

"They say," the interpreter replied, "that you belong to the antiaircraft service."

The recruit tightened his grip on his rifle and lowered his aim, with better results. At the end of his first fifty shots, he was placing one in three on the target, and the others were registering close in.

"Bravo!" came from a group of French officers at the other end of the trench, where another American, older in the service, had signalized his first experiences with the new firearm by landing thirty targets out of thirty-four shots, and four of the targets were bull's-eyes. The French instructors complimented him on the excellence of his marksmanship, considering his acknowledged unfamiliarity with the weapon.

Further along the depression, in another set of opposing trenches and targets, a row of French machine guns manned by young Americans sprayed lead with ear-splitting abandon, sometimes reach-

Through the School of War

ing the rate of five hundred shots a minute. Even with such rapidity, the Americans encountered no difficulties with the new pieces.

One day, in the early part of August 1917, a whirlwind swept through the string of French villages where the first contingent was training. The whirlwind came down the main road in a cloud of dust. It sped on the fleeting tires of a high-powered motor which flew from its dust-gray hood a red flag with two white stars. It blew into the villages and out, through the billets and cook tents, mess halls, and picket lines. The whirlwind was John J. Pershing.

The commander in chief "hit" the training area early in the morning, and his coming was unannounced. Before evening he had completed a stern inspection which had left only one impression in the minds of the inspected, and that impression was to the effect that more snap and pep, more sharpness and keenness were needed. When the Pershing whirlwind sped out of the training area that night, after the first American inspection in France, it left behind it a thorough realization of the sternness of the work which was ahead of our army.

* * *

It might be reassuring at this point to remark that girls in America really have no occasion to fear that many of our soldiers will leave their hearts in France.

An American soldier writing a letter home, by W.T. Benda

Through the School of War

The French women are kind to them, help them in their French lessons, and frequently feed them with home delicacies unknown to the company mess stoves, but every American soldier overseas seems to have that perfectly natural hankering to come back to the girl he left behind.

The soldier mail addressed daily to mothers and sweethearts back in the States ran far into the tons. The men were really homesick for their American womenfolks. I was aware of this even before I witnessed the reception given by our men to the first American nurses to reach the other side.

The hospital unit to which they belonged had been transported into that training area so quickly and so secretly that its presence there was unknown for some time. I happened to locate it by chance.

Several of us correspondents seeking a change of diet from the monotonous menu provided by the hard-working madam of our modest hostelry, motored in a new direction, over roads that opened new vistas in this picture book of the world.

And there in that prettiest of French watering places—Vittel—we came upon those first American nurses attached to the American Expeditionary Forces. They told us that all they knew was the name of the place they were in, that they were without maps and were not even aware of what part of France they were located in.

It developed that the unit's motor transportation

had not arrived and, other automobiles being as scarce as German flags, communication with the nearby camps had been almost nonexistent. Orders had been received from field headquarters and acknowledged, but its relation in distance or direction to their whereabouts were shrouded in mystery. But not for long.

Soon the word spread through the training area that American nurses had a hospital in the same zone, and some of the homesick Yanks began to make threats of self-mutilation in order that they might be sent to that hospital.

The hospital unit was soon followed by the arrival of numerous American auxiliary organizations, and the kindly activities of the workers as well as their numbers became such as to cause the men to wonder what kind of a war they were in.

* * *

While our infantry perfected their training in the Vosges, the first American artillery in France undertook a schedule of studies in an old French artillery post located near the Swiss frontier. This place is called Valdahon and for scores of years had been one of the training places for French artillery. But during the third and fourth years of the war, nearly all of the French artillery units being on the front, all subsequent drafts of French artillerymen received their training under actual war conditions.

Through the School of War

So it was that the French War Department turned over to the Americans this artillery training ground which had been long vacant. Three American artillery regiments, the Fifth, Sixth, and Seventh, comprising the first U.S. Artillery Brigade, began training at this post.

The American officer in command of that post went there as a brigadier general. As I observed him at his work in those early days, I seemed to see in his appearance and disposition some of the characteristics of a Grant. He wore a stubby-pointed beard, and he clamped his teeth tight on the butt end of a cigar. I saw him frequently wearing the $11.50 regulation issue uniform of the enlisted men. I saw him frequently in rubber boots standing hip-deep in the mud of the gun pits, talking to the men like a father—a kindly, yet stern father who knew how to produce discipline and results.

While at the post, he won promotion to a major general's rank, and in less than six months he was elevated to the grade of a full general and was given the highest-ranking military post in the United States. That man who trained our first artillerymen in France was General Peyton C. March,[2] chief of staff of the United States Army.

Finding the right man for the right place was one of General March's hobbies. He believed in military mobilization based on occupational qualifications. In other words, he believed that a man who had been a telephone operator in civilian life would make a better telephone operator in the army than he would make a gunner.

Those first American artillerymen in our overseas forces applied themselves strenuously to their studies. They were there primarily to learn. It became necessary for them at first to make themselves forget a lot of things that they had previously learned by artillery and adapt themselves to new methods and instruments of war.

At Valdahon, American artillery became acquainted with the Seventy-five, the seventy-five millimeter field pieces that stopped the Germans' Paris drive at the Marne. The khaki-clad gun crews called her "some cannon." At seven o'clock every morning, the glass windows in my room at the post would rattle with her opening barks, and from that minute on until noon, the Seventy-fives, battery upon battery of them, would snap and bark away until their seemingly ceaseless fire becomes a volley of sharp cracks which sent the echoes chasing one another through the dark recesses of the forests that conceal them.

The targets, of course, were unseen. Range elevation, deflection, all came to the battery over the signal wires that connected the firing position with some observation point also unseen but located in a position commanding the terrain under fire.

Through the School of War

A signalman sat cross-legged on the ground back of each battery. He received the firing directions from the transmitter clamped to his ears and conveyed them to the firing executive who stood beside him. They were then megaphoned to the sergeants chief of sections.

The corporal gunner, with eye on the sighting instruments at the side of each gun, "laid the piece" for range and deflection. Number one man of the crew opened the block to receive the shell, which was inserted by number two. Number three adjusted the fuse-setter and cut the fuses. Numbers four and five screwed the fuses in the shells and kept the fuse-setter loaded.

The section chiefs, watch in hand, gave the firing command to the gun crews, and number one of each piece jerked the firing lanyard at ten-second intervals or whatever interval the command might call for. The four guns would discharge their projectiles. They whined over the damp wooded ridge to distant imaginary lines of trenches, theoretical crossroads, or designated sections where the enemy was supposed to be massing for attack. Round after round would follow, while telephoned corrections perfected the range, and burst. The course of each shell was closely observed as well as its bursting effect, but no stupendous records were kept of the individual shots. That was "peacetime stuff."

And They Thought We Wouldn't Fight

* * *

It is late on a Saturday afternoon, and I accept the major's offer of a seat in his mud-bespattered "Hunka Tin." The field guns have ceased their roar for the day, and their bores will be allowed to cool over Sunday. It is a long ride to the ancient town, but speed laws and motor traps are unknown, and the hood of the Detroit Dilemma shakes like a wet dog as her sizzling hot cylinders suck juice from a full throttle.

We dine in a room three hundred years old. The presence of our automobile within the inner quadrangle of the ancient building jars on the sense of fitness. It is an old convent, now occupied by irreligious tenants on the upper three floors, restaurants and *estaminets* [small cafés] on the lower floor. These shops open on a broad gallery, level with the courtyard, and separated from it only by the rows of pillars that support the arches. It extends around the four sides of the court.

Consider the company. That freckle-faced youth with the fluffed reddish hair of a bandmaster is a French aviator, and among the row of decorations on his dark blue coat is one that he received by reason of a well-known adventure over the German lines, which cannot be mentioned here. That American colonel whose short gray hair blends into the white wall behind him is a former member of the

Through the School of War

United States war college and one of the most important factors in the legislation that shaped the present military status of his country. That other Frenchman with the unusual gold shoulder straps is not a member of the French army. He is a naval officer, and the daring with which he carried his mapping chart along exposed portions of the line at Verdun and evolved the mathematical data on which the French fired their guns against the German waves has been the pride of both the navy and the army.

There are three American women in the room. One, who is interested in YMCA work and in a number of newspapers, wears a feminine adaptation of the uniform and holds court at the head of a table of five officers. Another, Mrs. Robert R. McCormick,[3] who is engaged in the extension of the canteen work of a Paris organization, is sitting at our table, and she is willing to wager her husband anything from half a dozen gloves to a big donation check that Germany will be ready for any kind of peace before an American offensive in the spring.

The interests of the other American woman are negative. She professes no concern in the fact that war correspondents' life insurances are canceled, but she repeats to me that a dead correspondent is of no use to his paper, and I reply that if madame puts yet another one of her courses on the board, one correspondent will die with a fork in his hand instead of a pencil.

The diners are leaving. Each opening of the salon door brings in a gust of dampness that makes the tablecloths flap. Raincoats swish and rustle in the entry. Rain is falling in sheets in the black courtyard. The moon is gone.

"Great times to be alive," I say to the wife. "This place is saturated with romance. I don't have to be back to the post until tomorrow night. Where will we go? They are singing *Carmen* in the old opera house on the square. What do you say?"

"There's a Charlie Chaplin on the program next to the hotel," the wife replies.

Romance was slapped with a custard pie.

Notes

1. The Chasseurs Alpins, or Alpine Hunters, were light infantry and among the most elite troops in the French army. They originally specialized in mountain warfare.
2. General Peyton Conway March (1864–1955) became chief of staff in 1918. He was thus the senior ranking soldier in the United States.
3. Amy Irwin Adams McCormick (1872–1939), first wife of the publisher of the *Chicago Tribune,* served as a Red Cross nurse during World War I.

Frontward Ho

WHEN THE ARTILLERY training had proceeded to such a point that the French instructors were congratulating our officers upon their proficiency, the rumors spread through the post that the brigade had been ordered to go to the front—that we were to be the first American soldiers to actually go into the line and face the Germans.

The news was received with joy. The men were keen to try out their newly acquired abilities upon the enemy. Harness was polished until it shone. Brass equipment gleamed until you could almost see your face in it. The men groomed the horses until the animals got pains from it. Enlisted men sojourning in the guard house for petty offenses dispatched their guards with scrawled pleadings that the sentences be changed to fines so that they could accompany the outfits to the front.

With one special purpose in view, I made application to General March for an assignment to Battery A of the Sixth Field Artillery. I received the appointment. The Sixth was the first regiment of the brigade, and A was the first battery of the regiment. I knew that we would march out in that order, that Battery A would entrain first, detrain first, go in the line first, and I hoped to be present at the firing of the first American shot in the war.

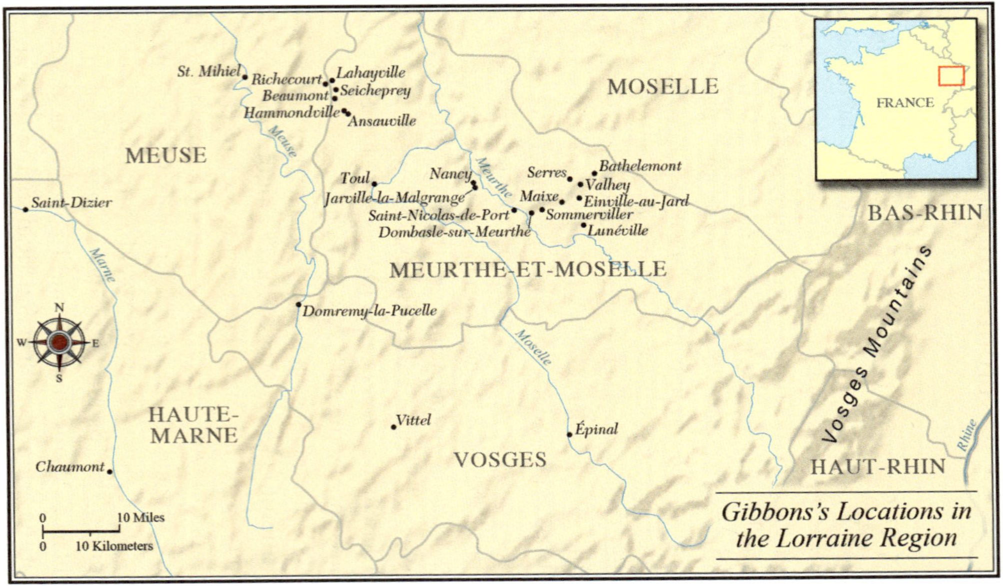

Gibbons's Locations in the Lorraine Region

Frontward Ho

We pulled out of the post on schedule, early in the morning, two days later. Officers and men had been up and dressed since midnight. Ten minutes after their arising, blankets had been rolled and all personal equipment packed ready for departure with the exception of mess kits.

While the stable police details fed the horses, the rest of us "leaned up against" steak, hot biscuits, syrup, and hot coffee. The cook had been on the job all night, and his efforts touched the right spot. It seemed as if it was the coldest hour of the night, and the hot "chow" acted as a primer on the sleepy human machines.

In the darkness, the animals were packed into the gun carriages and caissons down in the gun park, and it was 4 A.M. on the dot when the captain's whistle sounded and we moved off the reserve. As we rattled over the railroad crossing and took the road, the men made facetious goodbyes to the scene of their six weeks' training.

We rode on. Soon, on the left, the sun came up cold out of Switzerland's white-topped ridges miles away, and, smiling frigidly across the snow-clad neutral Alps, dispelled the night mist in our part of the world.

The battery warmed under its glow. Village after village we passed through, returning the polite salutes of early-rising grandsires who uncovered their gray heads, or wrinkled, pink-faced grandmothers, who waved kerchiefs from gabled windows beneath the thatch and smiled the straight and dry-lipped smile of toothless age as they wished us good fortune in the war.

We messed at midday by the roadside, the green fields and hills of France, our table decorations, cold beef and dry bread, our fare, with canteens full to wash it down. When the horses had tossed their nose bags futilely for the last grains of oats, and the captain's watch had timed the rest at three-quarters of the hour, we mounted and resumed the march.

The equipment rode easy on man and beast. Packs had been shifted to positions of maximum comfort. The horses were still fresh enough to need tight rein. The men had made final adjustments to the chin straps on their new steel helmets, and these sat well on heads that never before had been topped with armored covering. In addition to all other equipment, each man carried two gas masks. Our top sergeant had an explanation for me as to this double gas mask equipment.

"I'll tell you about it," he said, as he ruthlessly accepted the next-to-the-last twenty-five centime Egyptian cigarette from my proffered case. I winced as he deliberately tore the paper from that precious fine smoke and inserted the filler in his mouth for a chew.

"You see, England and France and us is all Allies," he said. "Both of them loves us, and we love

Frontward Ho

both of them. We don't know nothing about gas masks, and they knows all there is to know about them. The French say their gas mask is the best. The British say their gas mask is the best.

"Well, you see, they both offer us gas masks. Now Uncle Sam don't want to hurt nobody's feelings, so he says, 'Gentlemen, we won't fight about this here matter. We'll just use both gas masks, and give each of them a tryout.'

"So here we are carrying two of these human nose bags. The first time we get into a mess of this here gas, somebody will send the order around to change masks in the middle of it—just to find out which is the best one."

The sergeant, with seeming malice, spat some of that fine cigarette on a roadside kilometer stone and closed the international prospects of the subject.

Our battery jangled through a tunneled ridge and emerged on the other side just as a storm of rain and hail burst with mountain fury. The hailstones rattled on our metal helmets, and the men laughed at the sound as they donned slickers. The brakes grated on the caisson wheels as we took the steep downgrade. The road hugged the valley wall, which was a rugged granite cliff.

I rode on ahead through the stinging hailstones and watched our battery as it passed through the historic rock-hewn gateway that is the entrance to the medieval town of Besançon. No Roman con-

American troops marching from training camp to the actual fighting

queror at the head of his invading legions ever rode through that triumphal arch with greater pride than rode our little captain at the head of his battery.

Our way led over the stone spanned bridge that crossed the sluggish river through the town, and on to the hilly outskirts, where mounted French guides met and directed us to the railroad loading platform.

The platform was a busy place. The regimental supply company which was preceding us over the road was engaged in forcibly persuading the last of its mules to enter the toy freight cars which bore on the side the printed legend, "*Hommes* [men] 40, *Chevaux* [horses] 8."

Several arc lights and one or two acetylene flares illuminated the scene. It was raining fitfully, but not enough to dampen the spirits of the YMCA workers who wrestled with canvas tarpaulins and foraged materials to construct a makeshift shelter for a free coffee and sandwich counter.

Their stoves were burning brightly, and the hurriedly erected stove pipes, leaning wearily against the stone wall enclosing the quay, topped the wall like a miniature of the skyline of Pittsburgh. The boiling coffeepots gave off a delicious steam.

During it all, the mules brayed and the supply company men swore. Most humans, cognizant of the principles of safety first, are respectful of the rear quarters of a mule. We watched one disrespecter of these principles invite what might have been called "mulecide" with utter contempt for the consequences. He deliberately stood in the dangerous immediate rear of one particularly ornery mule, and kicked the mule.

His name was "Missouri Slim," as he took pains to inform the object of his caress. He further announced to all present, men and mules, that he had been brought up with mules from babyhood and knew mules from the tips of their long ears to the ends of their hard tails.

The obdurate animal in question had refused to enter the door of the car that had been indicated as his Pullman. "Missouri Slim" called three other ex-natives of Champ Clark's state[1] to his assistance. They fearlessly put a shoulder under each of the mule's quarters. Then they grunted a unanimous "heave" and lifted the struggling animal off its feet. As a perfect matter of course, they walked right into the car with him with no more trouble than if he had been an extra-large bale of hay.

The supply company completed loading, and the train moved down the track. Our battery took possession of the platform. A train of empties was shunted into position, and we began loading guns and wagons on the flat cars and putting the animals into the box cars.

Considerable confusion accompanied this operation. The horses seemed to have decided scruples

Frontward Ho

Loading Field Artillery, *postcard*

against entering the cars. It was dark, and the rain came down miserably. The men swore. There was considerable kicking on the part of the men as well as the animals.

By the time our battery had been loaded, another battery was waiting to move onto the platform. Our captain went down the length of the train examining the halter straps in the horse cars and assuring himself of the correct apportionment of men in each car. Then we moved out on what developed to be a wild night ride.

The horse has been described as man's friend, and no one questions that a horse and a man, if placed out in any large open space, are capable of getting along to their mutual comfort. But when army regulations and the requirements of military transportation place eight horses and four men in the same toy French boxcar and then pat all twelve of them figuratively on the neck and tell them to lie down together and sleep through an indefinite night's ride, it is not only probable, but it is certain, that the legendary comradeship of the man and the horse ceases. The described condition does not encompass the best understood relation of the two as traveling companions.

On our military trains in France, the reservations of space for the human and dumb occupants of the same car were something as follows: Four horses occupied the forward half of the car. Four more horses occupied the rear half of the car. Four men occupied the remaining space. The eight four-footed animals are packed in lengthwise with their heads toward the central space between the two side doors. The central space is reserved for the four two-footed animals.

Then the train moves. If the movement is forward and sudden, as it usually is, the four horses in the forward end of the car involuntarily obey the rules of inertia and slide into the central space. If the movement of the train is backward and equally sudden, the four horses in the rear end of the car obey the same rule and plunge forward into the central space. On the whole, night life for the men in the straw on the floor of the central space is a

Frontward Ho

lively existence, while "riding the rattlers with a horse outfit."

Our battery found it so. I rode a number of miles that night sitting with four artillerymen in the central space between the side doors, which had been closed upon orders. From the roof of the car, immediately above our heads, an oil lantern swung and swayed with every jolt of the wheels and cast a feeble light down upon our conference in the straw. We occupied a small square area which we had attempted to particularize by roping it off.

On either side were the blank surfaces of the closed doors. To either end were the heads of four nervous animals, eight ponderous hulks of steel-shod horseflesh, high strung and fidgety, verging almost on panic under the unusual conditions they were enduring, and subject at any minute to new fits of excitement. We sat at their feet as we rattled along.

The horses had been comparatively quiet for some time, but now they seemed to be growing restless. They pricked their ears, and we knew something was bothering them. Above the rattle of the train, there came to us the sound of firing. It seemed to come from the direction in which we were going. With surprising quickness, the explosions grew louder. We were not only speeding toward the sounds of conflict, but the conflict itself seemed to be speeding toward us.

Then came a crash unmistakably near. One of the horses in the forward end reared, and his head thumped the roof of the car. Once again on four feet, he pranced nervously and tossed his blood-wet forelock. Immediately the other horses began stamping.

Another crash!—this time almost directly overhead. In the light of the swinging lantern, I could see the terror in the eyes of the frightened brutes. We clung to their halters and tried to quiet them, but they lifted us off our feet.

The train was slowing down. The brakes shrieked and grated as we came to a jerky stop. Three of us braced ourselves at the heads of the four horses in the rear of the car and prevented them from sliding on top of us. Boyle and Slater were doing their best to quiet the forward four. The explosions overhead increased. Now we heard the report of field pieces so close that they seemed to be almost alongside the track.

There came a sharp bang at one of the side doors, and I thought I recognized the sound of the lead-loaded handle of the captain's riding whip. His voice, coming to us a minute later above the trampling and kicking of the panic-stricken animals, verified my belief.

"Darken that lantern," he shouted. "Keep all lights out, and keep your helmets on. Stay in the

Frontward Ho

cars, and hang on to the horses. There is an air raid on right above us."

"Yes, sir," replied Boyle, and we heard the captain run to the next car. I blew out the light, and we were in complete darkness, with eight tossing, plunging horses that kicked and reared at every crash of the guns nearby or burst of the shells overhead.

We hung on while the air battle went on above. One horse went down on his knees and, in his frantic struggles to regain his feet, almost kicked the feet from under the animal beside him.

At times, thunderous detonations told us that aerial bombs were doing their work near at hand. We supposed correctly that we were near some town not far behind the lines and that the German was paying it a night visit with some of his heaviest visiting cards.

I opened one side door just a crack and looked out. The darkness above blossomed with blinding blotches of fire that flashed on and off. It seemed as though the sky were a canopy of black velvet perforated with hundreds of holes behind which dazzling lights passed back and forth, flashing momentary gleams of brilliance through the punctures. Again, this vision would pass as a luminous dripping mass would poise itself on high and cast a steady white glare that revealed clusters of gray smoke puffs of exploded shrapnel.

We had to close the door because the flashes added to the terror of the horses, but the aerial activity passed almost as suddenly as it had come and left our train untouched. As the raiding planes went down the wind, followed always by the poppings of the antiaircraft guns, the sound of the conflict grew distant. We got control over the horses, although they still trembled with fright.

There came another rap at the door, and I hurriedly accepted the captain's invitation to accompany him forward to a first-class coach, where I spent the remainder of the night stretched out on the cushions. As our train resumed its way into the darkness, I dreamed of racing before a stampede of wild horses.

NOTES

1. James Beauchamp Clark (1850–1921) was a congressman from Missouri who served as Speaker of the House of Representatives.

Into the Line

A DAMP, CHILL morning mist made the dawn even grayer as our battery train slid into a loading platform almost under the walls of a large manufacturing plant engaged in producing war materials.

In spite of the fact that the section chiefs reported that not a man had been injured and not so much as a leg broken in the crowded horse cars, every man in the battery now declared the absence of any doubt but the air raid had been directly aimed at Battery A.

The sign on a station lamppost told us the name of the town. It was Jarville [-la-Malgrange]. But it jarred nothing in our memories. None of us had ever heard of it before. I asked the captain where we were.

"Just about thirty miles behind the front," he replied. "We are moving up to our last billets as soon as we unload and feed."

The horses had made the ride wearing their harness, some of which had become entangled and broken in transit. A number of saddles had slipped from backs and were down behind forelegs.

"We're learning something every minute," the captain exclaimed. "American army regulations call for the removal of all harness from the horses before they are put into the cars, but the French have learned that that is a dangerous practice over here.

"You can't unload unharnessed horses and get them hitched to the guns as quick as you can harnessed horses. The idea is this: We're pretty close behind the lines. A German air party might make this unloading platform a visit at any time, and if any of them are in the air and happen to see us unloading, they'd sure call on us.

"The French have learned that the only way to make the best of such a situation, if it should arise, is to have the horses already harnessed so that they can be run out of the cars quickly, hitched to the guns in a jiffy, and hurried away. If the horses are in the cars unharnessed, and all of the harness is being carried in other cars, confusion is increased, and there is a greater prospect of your losing your train, horses, guns, and everything from an incendiary bomb, not to mention low-flying machine work."

His explanation revealed a promising attitude that I found in almost all American soldiers of all ranks that I had encountered up to that time in France. The foundation of the attitude was a willingness to admit ignorance of new conditions and an eagerness to possess themselves of all knowledge that the French and British had acquired through bitter and costly experience.

Further than that, the American inclination pushed the soldier students to look beyond even

Into the Line

those then-accepted standards. The tendency was to improve beyond the French and British, to apply new American principles of time- or labor-saving to simple operation, to save manpower and horseflesh by sane safety appliances, to increase efficiency, speed, accuracy—in a word, their aim was to make themselves the best fighting men in the Allied cause.

* * *

The unloading had continued under the eyes of smiling French girls in bloomers [loose trousers] who were just departing from their work on the early morning shift in the munitions factory beside the station. These were the first American soldiers they had seen, and they were free to pass comment upon our appearance. So were the men of Battery A, who overlooked the oiled, grimed faces and hands of the bloomered beauties, and announced the general verdict that "they sure were fat little devils."

We moved off the platform, rattled along under a railroad viaduct, and down the main street of Jarville, which was large enough to boast streetcar tracks and a shell-damaged cathedral spire.

The remaining townsfolk had lived with the glare and rumble of the front for three years now, and the passage back and forth of men and horses and guns hardly elicited as much attention as the occasional promenade of a policeman in Evanston, Illinois. But these were different men that rode

French children cheering U.S. troops

Into the Line

through those streets that day. This was the first battery of American artillery that had passed that way. This was an occasion, and the townspeople responded to it. Children, women, and old men chirped "*viva*"s. kissed hands, bared heads, and waved hats and aprons from curb and shop door and windows overhead.

Onward into the zone of war we rode. On through successive battered villages, past houses without roofs, windows with shattered panes, stone walls with gaping shell holes through them, churches without steeples, our battery moved toward the last billeting place before entering the line.

This was the ancient town of Saint-Nicolas-de-Port on the banks of the river Meurthe. Into the Place de la République of the town the battery swung with a clamorous advance guard of schoolchildren and street gamins.

The guns were parked, the horses picketed, and the potato peelers started on their endless task. The absence of fuel for the mess fires demanded immediate correction.

It was a few minutes past noon when the captain and I entered the office of the French town major. It was vacant. The officers were at *déjeuner* [lunch], we learned from an old woman who was sweeping the commandant's rooms. Where?—Ah, she knew not. We accosted the first French officer we met on the street.

"Where does the town major eat?" the captain inquired in his best Indianapolis French. After the customary exchange of salutes, introductions, handshakes, and greetings, the Frenchman informed us that Monsieur le Commandant favored the *pommard* [wine] that Madame Larue served at the Hôtel de la Fontaine.

We hurried to that place, and there in a little back room behind a plate-cluttered table with a red-and-white checkered tablecloth, we found the major. The major said he spoke the English with the fluency. He demonstrated his delusion when we asked for wood.

"Wood! Ah, but it is impossible that it is wood you ask of me. Have I not this morning early seen with my own eyes the wood ordered? By now I believe it has been delivered for you in the Place de la République."

"But it hasn't," remonstrated the captain, "and the fires have not yet been started, and—"

"But it is on the way, probably," said the major. "Maybe it will be there soon. Maybe it is there now."

The captain took another tack.

"Where was the wood bought?" he asked.

"From the wood merchant beyond the river," replied the major. "But it is already on the way, and—"

"How do you go to the wood merchant?" in-

Into the Line

sisted the captain. "We have got to have the wood toot sweet."

"Ah! *tout de suite—tout de suite—tout de suite,*" repeated the major in tones of exasperation. "With you Americans it is always *tout de suite*. Here—"

He took my notebook and drew a plan of streets indicating the way to the place of the wood merchant. We left on the run.

The wood merchant was a big man, elderly, and fat. His face was red, and he had bushy gray eyebrows. He wore a smock of blue cloth that came to his knees. He remonstrated that it was useless for us to buy wood from him because wood had already been bought for us. He spoke only French.

In some remarkable fashion the kindly wood merchant gathered that the captain wanted wood piled in a wagon, drawn by a horse, and wanted it in a hurry. *Tout de suite*, pronounced "toot sweet" by our soldiers, was a term calling for speed that was among the first acquired by our men in France.

The old man shrugged his shoulders, elevated his hand, palm outward, and signified with an expression of his face that it was useless to argue further for the benefit of these Americans. He turned and gave the necessary loading orders to his working force.

That working force consisted of two French girls, each about eighteen years of age. They wore long baggy bloomers of brown corduroy, tight at the ankles, where they flopped about in folds over clumsy wooden shoes. They wore blouses of the same material and tam-o'-shanter hats to match, called berets.

Each one of them had a cigarette hanging from the corner of her mouth. One stood on the ground and tossed up the thirty- or forty-pound logs to her sister who stood above on top of the wagon. The latter caught them in her extended arms and placed them in a pile. To the best of my recollection, neither one of the girls missed a puff.

While the loading proceeded, the wood merchant, speaking slowly in French, made us understand the following: "Many peculiar things happen in the war, monsieur," he said. "Listen, my name is Helois. Ten days ago there came to me one of the washerwomen who clean the clothes on the banks of the Meurthe, and she said to me: 'Ah, monsieur, the wood merchant. You are the sly fox. I have your secret.' And I say to her that I know not of what she speaks.

"'You boast in the town that your two sons are at the front,' she said, 'but I know that one at least of them is not.' And I was dumbfounded. I say to her, 'Woman, it is a lie you tell me. Both of my boys are with their regiments, in the trenches even now, if by the grace of the good God they still live.'

"'No,' she say to me, 'one of your sons hides in the hotel of Madame Larue. How do I know this secret, monsieur, the wood merchant? I know because this day have I washed the shirt, with his name on it, at the river bank. His name, Helois—the Lieutenant Helois—was stamped on the collar, and the shirt came from the hotel La Fontaine.'

"I tell her that it is a mistake—that it is the great injustice to me she speaks, and that night I dressed in my best clothes to penetrate this mystery—to meet this man who disgracefully used the name of my son—to expose this impostor who would bring shame to the name of Helois, the wood merchant, whose two sons have been fighting for France these three long years.

"And so, monsieur, I meet this man at the hotel. She was right. His name was Helois. Here is his card. The Lieutenant Louis F. Helois, and he is a lieutenant in the United States Army."

"So it was a mistake," replied the captain, handing the card back to the wood merchant, whose lobster-red features bore an enigmatical smile.

"No, not the mistake, the truth," replied the wood merchant. "Not my son—but my grandson—the son of my son—the son of my third son, who went to America years ago. And now he comes back in the uniform of liberty to fight again for France. Ah, *Messieurs les Officiers*—the sons of France return from the ends of the world to fight her cause."

We escorted the fuel proudly to the Place de la

Field kitchen of the U.S. Army, 1st Division

République. Soon the fires were burning briskly and the smell of onions and coffee and hot chow was on the air.

The stoves were pitched at the bottom of a stone monument in the center of the square. The monument was topped with a huge cross of stone on which was the sculptured figure of the Christ.

Little Sykoff, the battery mess sergeant, stood over the stove at the bottom of the monument. He held in his hand a frying pan, which he shook back and forth over the fire to prevent the sizzling chips in the pan from burning. His eyes lowered from an

Into the Line

inspection of the monument and met mine. He smiled.

"Mr. Gibbons," he said, "if that brother of mine, who runs the photograph gallery out on Paulina and Madison Streets in Chicago, could only see me now, he sure would tell the rabbi. Can you beat it—a Jew here frying ham in the shadow of the cross."

In the evening, a number of the battery located the *buvette* that carried across its curtained front the gold-lettered sign *bar Parisien*. It was a find. Some thirty American artillerymen crowded around the tables.

Cigarette smoke filled the low-ceilinged room with blue layers, through which the lamplight shone. In one corner stood a mechanical piano which swallowed big copper *sous* [coins] and gave out discord's metallic melody. It was of an American make, and the best number on its printed program was "Aren't You Coming Back to Old Virginia, Molly?" *Sous* followed *sous* into this howitzer of harmony, and it knew no rest that night. Everybody joined in and helped it out on the choruses.

Things were going fine, when the door opened at about nine thirty, and there stood two members of the American Provost Guard. They carried with them two orders. One instructed Madame, the proprietress, to dispense no more red ink or beer to American soldiers that night, and the other was a

And They Thought We Wouldn't Fight

direction to all Americans around the table to get back to their billets for the night.

The bunch left with reluctance but without a grumble. It was warm and comfortable within the *bar Parisien,* and Madame's smiles and red wine and beer and Camembert cheese composed the Broadway of many recent dreams. But they left without complaint.

They made their rollicking departure, returning Madame's parting smiles, gallantly lifting their steel helmets and showering her with vociferous "bong swore"s.* And—well it simply must be told. She kissed the last one out the door and, turning, wiped away a tear with the corner of her apron. Madame had seen youth on the way to the front before.

Early the next morning, our battery pulled out for the front. We were bound for the line. We took the roads out of Saint Nicolas to the east, making our way toward that part of the front that was known as the Lunéville sector. Our way lay through the towns of Dombasle, Sommerviller, Maixe, Einville [-au-Jard], Valhey, Serres, to the remains of the ruined village of Hoeville.

The sector runs almost along the border between France and old Lorraine, occupied by the Germans since 1870. Even the names of the old French towns beyond the border had been changed to German in

---

* Tr: *Bonsoir*: Good evening.

the effort of the Prussians to Germanize the stolen province.[1]

It was in this section during the few days just prior to the outbreak of the war that France made unwise demonstration of her disinclination toward hostilities with Germany. Every soldier in France was under arms, as was every soldier in Europe. France had military patrols along her borders. In the French chamber of deputies, the socialists had rushed through a measure which was calculated to convince the German people that France had no intentions or desire of menacing German territory. By that measure every French soldier was withdrawn from the Franco-German border to a line ten miles inside of France. The German appreciation of this evidence of peacefulness was manifested when the enemy, at the outbreak of the war, moved across the border and occupied that ten-mile strip of France.

France had succeeded in driving the enemy back again in that part of Lorraine, but only at the cost of many lives and the destruction of many French towns and villages. Since the close of the fighting season of 1914, there had been little or no progress on either side at this point. The opposing lines here had been stationary for almost three years, and it was known on both sides as a quiet sector.

Before nine o'clock that morning as we rode on to the front, the horse-drawn traffic, including our battery, was forced to take the side of the road numerous times to permit the passage of long trains of motor trucks loaded down with American infantrymen, bound in the same direction.

Most of the motor vehicles were of the omnibus type. A number of them were worthy old double-deckers that had seen long years of peaceful service on the boulevards of Paris before the war. Slats of wood ran lengthwise across the windows of the lower seating compartment, and through these apertures young, sun-burned American faces topped with steel helmets, peered forth.

The road to the front was a populous one. We passed numerous groups of supply wagons carrying food and fodder up to the front lines. Other wagons were returning empty, and here and there came an ambulance with bulgy blankets outlining the figures of stretcher cases, piled two high and two wide. Occasionally a YMCA runabout [small open auto] loaded down with coffee pots and candy tins and driven by helmeted wearers of the Red Triangle, would pass us carrying its store of extras to the boys up front.

We passed through villages where manufacturing plants were still in operation and, nearer the front, the roads lay through smaller hamlets, shell torn and deserted, save for sentries who stood guard in wooden coops at intersections. Civilians became fewer and fewer, although there was not a village that did not have one or two women or children or old men unfit for uniform.

Finally the road mounted a rolling hill, and here it was bordered by roadside screens consisting of stretched chicken wire to which wisps of straw and grass and bits of green-dyed cloth had been attached. Our men riding behind the screen peered through apertures in it and saw the distant hills forward, from which German glasses could have observed all passage along that road had it not been for the screen.

So we moved into position. It was late in the night of October 22, 1917, that our batteries of artillery and companies of infantry moved through the darkness on the last lap of their trip to the front. The roads were sticky and gummy. A light rain was falling. The guns boomed in front of us, but not with any continued intensity. Through streets paved with slippery cobbles and bordered with the bare skeletons of shell-wrecked houses, our American squads marched four abreast. Their passing in the darkness was accompanied by the sound of the unhastened tread of many hobnailed boots.

At times, the rays of a cautiously flashed electric light would reveal our infantrymen with packs on back and rifles slung over their shoulders. A stiff wind whipped the rain into their faces and tugged the bottoms of their flapping, wet overcoats. Notwithstanding the fact that they had made it on foot a number of miles from the place where they had disembarked from the motor trucks, the men marched along to the soft singing of songs, which were ordered discontinued as the marching columns got closer to the communicating trenches which led into the front line.

In the march were machine gun carts hauled by American mules, and rolling kitchens, which at times dropped on the darkened road swirls of glowing red embers that had to be hurriedly stamped out. Anxious American staff officers consulted their wristwatches frequently in evidence of the concern they felt as to whether the various moving units were reaching designated points upon the scheduled minute.

It was after midnight that our men reached the front line. It was the morning of October 23, 1917, that American infantrymen and Bavarian regiments of *Landwehr* and *Landsturm* faced one another for the first time in front-line positions on the European front. Less than eight hundred yards of slate and drab-colored soft ground, blotched with rust-red expanses of wire entanglements, separated the hostile lines.

There was no moon. A few cloud-veiled stars only seemed to accentuate the blackness of the night. There, in the darkness and the mud, on the slippery firing step of trench walls and in damp, foul-smelling dugouts, young red-blooded Ameri-

Into the Line

cans tingled for the first time with the thrill that they had trained so long and traveled so far to experience.

Through unfortunate management of the press arrangements in connection with this great historical event, American correspondents accredited by the War Department to our forces were prevented from accompanying our men into the front that night. Good fortune, however, favored me as one of the two sole exceptions to this circumstance. Raymond G. Carroll, correspondent of the Philadelphia *Public Ledger*, and myself, representing the *Chicago Tribune* and its associated papers, were the only two newspaper men who went into the line with the men that night. For enjoying this unusual opportunity, we were both arrested several days later, not, however, until after we had obtained the firsthand story of the great event.

A mean drizzle of rain was falling that night, but it felt cool on the pink American cheeks that were hot with excitement. The very wetness of the air impregnated all it touched with the momentousness of the hour. Spirits were high and the mud was deep, but we who were there had the feeling that history was chiseling that night's date into her book of ages.

Occasionally a shell wheezed over through the soggy atmosphere, seeming to leave an unseen arc in the darkness above. It would terminate with a sullen thump in some spongy, water-soaked mound behind us. Then an answering missive of steel would whine away into the populated invisibility in front of us.

French comrades, in half English and half French, gushed their congratulations and shook us by the hand. Some of us were even hugged and kissed on both cheeks. Our men took the places of French platoons that were sent back to rest billets. But other French platoons remained shoulder to shoulder with our men in the front line. The presence of our troops there was in continuation of their training for the purpose of providing a nucleus for the construction of later contingents. Both our infantry and our artillery acted in conjunction with the French infantry and artillery, and the sector remained under French command.

Our men were eager to ask questions, and the French were ever ready to respond. They first told us about the difference in the sound of shells. Now that one that started with a bark in back of us and whined over our heads is a *départ*. It is an Allied shell on its way to the Germans. Now, this one, that whines over first and ends with a distant grunt, like a strong wallop on a wet carpet, is an *arrivée*. It has arrived from Germany. In the dugouts, our men smoked dozens of cigarettes, lighting fresh ones from the half-consumed butts. It is the appetite that

Into the Line

comes with the progressive realization of a long-deferred hope. It is the tension that comes from at last arriving at an object and then finding nothing to do, now that you are there. It is the nervousness that nerveless youth suffers in inactivity.

The men sloshed back and forth through the mud along the narrow confines of the trench. The order is against much movement, but immobility is unbearable. Wet slickers rustle against one another in the narrow traverses, and equipment, principally the French and English gas masks, hanging at either hip become entangled in the darkness.

At times a steel helmet falls from some unaccustomed head and, hitting perhaps a projecting rock in the trench wall, gives forth a clang which is followed by curses from its clumsy owner and an admonition of quiet from some young lieutenant.

"Olson, keep your damn fool head down below the top of that trench or you'll get it blown off." The sergeant is talking, and Olson, who brought from Minnesota a keen desire to see no man's land even at the risk of his life, is forced to repress the yearning.

"Two men over in B Company just got holes drilled through their beans for doing the same thing," continued the sergeant. "There's nothing you can see out there anyhow. It's all darkness."

Either consciously or unconsciously, the sergeant

was lying, for the purpose of saving Olson and others from a fool's fate. There was not a single casualty in any American unit on the line that first night.

"Where is the telephone dugout?" a young lieutenant asked his French colleague. "I want to speak to the battalion commander."

"But you must not speak English over the telephone," replied the Frenchman. "The Germans will hear you with the instruments they use to tap the underground circuit."

"But I was going to use our American code," said the front-line novice; "if the Germans tap in, they won't be able to figure out what it means."

"Ah, no, my friend," replied the Frenchman, smiling. "They won't know what the message means, but your voice and language will mean to them that Americans are occupying the sector in front of them, and we want to give them that information in another way, *n'est-ce pas?*"*

Undoubtedly there was some concern in the German trenches just over the way with regard to what was taking place in our lines. Relief periods are ticklish intervals for the side making them. It is quite possible that some intimation of our presence may have been given.

I believe the Germans did become nervous, because they made repeated attacks on the enveloping

---

* Tr: *N'est-ce pas*: Isn't it so?

Into the Line

darkness with numbers of star [illuminating] shells. These aerial beauties of night warfare released from their exploding encasements high in the air hung from white silk parachutes above the American amateurs.

The numerous company and battery jesters did not refrain from imitative expressions of "Ahs" and "Ohs" and "Ain't it bootiful?" as their laughing upturned faces were illuminated in the white light.

That night one rocket went up shortly before morning. It had a different effect from its predecessors. It reared itself from the darkness somewhere on the left. Its flight was noiseless as it mounted higher and higher on its fiery staff. Then it burst in a shower of green balls of fire.

That meant business. One green rocket was the signal that the Germans were sending over gas shells. It was an alarm that meant the donning of gas masks. On they went quickly. It was the first time this equipment had been adjusted under emergency conditions, yet the men appeared to have mastered the contrivances.

Then the word was passed along the trenches and through the dugouts for the removal of the masks. It had not been a French signal. The green rocket had been sent up by the Germans. The enemy was using green rockets that night as a signal of their own. There had been no gas shells. It was a false alarm.

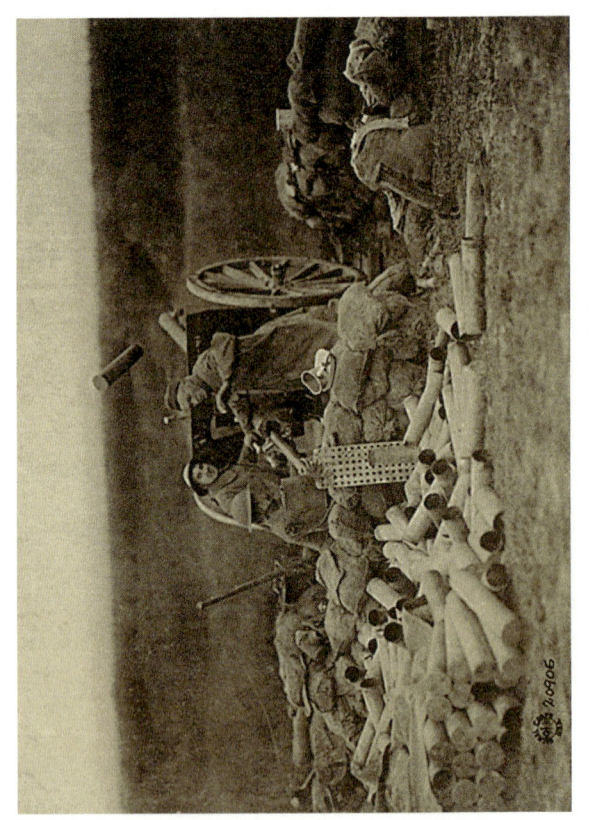

American artillerymen firing the first shot

Into the Line

"The best kind of practice in the world," said one of our battalion commanders; "it's just the stuff we're here for. I hope the Germans happen to do that every night a new bunch of our men get in these trenches."

While the infantry were experiencing these initial thrills in the front line, our gunners were struggling in the mud of the black gun pits to get their pieces into position in the quickest possible time and achieve the honor of firing that first American shot in the war.

Each battery worked feverishly in intense competition with every other battery. Battery A of the 6th Field, to which I had attached myself, lost in the race for the honor. Another battery in the same regiment accomplished the achievement. That was Battery C of the 6th Field Artillery.

By almost superhuman work through the entire previous day and night, details of men from Battery C had pulled one cannon by ropes across a muddy, almost impassable, meadow. So anxious were they to get off the first shot that they did not stop for meals.

They managed to drag the piece into an old abandoned French gun pit. The historical position of that gun was one kilometer due east of the town of Bathelemont and three hundred meters northeast of the Bauzemont-Bathelemont road. The position was located two miles from the old international boundary line between France and German-Lorraine. The position was 1½ kilometers back of the French first line, then occupied by Americans.

The first shot was fired at 6:5:10 A.M., October 23, 1917. The missile fired was a 75-millimeter, or 3-inch, high-explosive shell. The target was a German battery of 150-millimeter or 6-inch guns located two kilometers back of the German first-line trenches, and one kilometer in back of the boundary line between France and German-Lorraine. The position of that enemy battery on the map was in a field 100 meters west of the town which the French still call Xanrey, but which the Germans have called Schenris since they took it from France in 1870. Near that spot—and damn near—fell the first American shell fired in the Great War.

Notes

1. Germany annexed the provinces of Alsace and Lorraine from France after the Franco-Prussian War of 1870–71.

The First American Sector

THE FIRST all-American sector on the western front was located in Lorraine some distance to the east of the Lunéville front. It was north and slightly west of the city of Toul. It was on the east side of the St. Mihiel salient,[1] then occupied by the Germans.

The sector occupied a position in what the French called the Pont-à-Mousson front. Our men were to occupy an eight-mile section of the front-line trenches extending from a point west of the town of Flirey, to a point west of the ruins of the town of Seicheprey. The position was not far from the French stronghold of Verdun to the northwest or the German stronghold of Metz to the northeast and was equidistant from both.

That line changed from French blue to American khaki on the night of January 21. The sector became American at midnight. I watched the men as they marched into the line. In small squads they proceeded silently up the road toward the north, from which direction a raw wind brought occasional sounds resembling the falling of steel plates on the wooden floor of a long corridor.

A half-moon doubly ringed by mist made the hazy night look gray. At intervals, phantom flashes flushed the sky. The mud of the roadway formed a colorless paste that made marching not unlike skating on a platter of glue. This was their departure for the front—this particular battalion—the first battalion of the 16th United States Infantry. I knew, and every man in it knew, what was before them.

For two days the battalion had rested in the mud of the semi-destroyed village of Ansauville, several miles back of the front. A broad, shallow stream, then at the flood, wound through and over most of the village site. Walking anywhere near the border of the water, one pulled about with him pounds of tenacious, black gumbo. Dogs and hogs, ducks and horses, and men—all were painted with nature's handiest camouflage.

Where the stream left the gaping ruins of a stone house on the edge of the village, there was a well-kept French graveyard, clinging to the slope of a small hill. Above the ruins of the hamlet stood the steeple of the old stone church, from which it was customary to ring the alarm when the Germans sent over their shells of poison gas.

Our officers busied themselves with unfinished supply problems. Such matters as rubber boots for the men, duckboards [boardwalks] for the trenches, food for the mules, and ration containers necessary for the conveyance of hot food to the front lines were not permitted to interfere with the battalion's movements. In war, there is always the alternative of doing without or doing with makeshifts, and that

The First American Sector

particular battalion commander, after three years of war, was the kind of soldier who made the best of circumstances no matter how adverse they may have been. That commander was Major Griffiths.[2] He was an American fighting man.

Just before daylight failed that wintry day, three *poilus*[3] walked down the road from the front and into Ansauville. Two of them were helping a third, whose bandaged arm and shoulder explained the mission of the party. As they passed the rolling kitchens where the Americans were receiving their last meal before entering the trenches, there was silence and not even an exchange of greetings or smiles.

The sight of that one wounded man did not make our boys realize more than they already did, what was in front of them. They had already made a forty-mile march over frozen roads up to this place and had incurred discomforts seemingly greater than a shell-shattered arm or a bullet-fractured shoulder. After that grueling hiking experience, it was a pleasant prospect to look forward to a chance of venting one's feelings on the enemy.

At the same time, no chip-on-the-shoulder cockiness marked the disposition of these men about to take first grips with the Germans—no challenging bravado was revealed in the actions or statements of these grim, serious trailblazers of the American front, whose attitude appeared to be one of soldierly

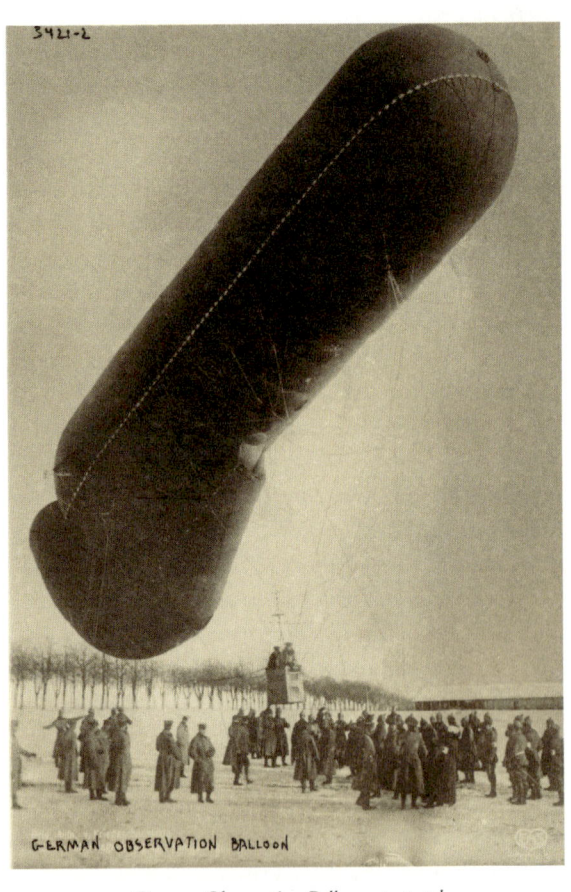

German Observation Balloon, *postcard*

The First American Sector

resignation to the first martial principle "Orders is orders."

As the companies lined up in the village street in full marching order, awaiting the command to move, several half-hearted attempts at jocularity died cold. One irrepressible made a futile attempt at frivolity by announcing that he had Cherokee blood in his veins and was so tough he could "spit battleships." This attempted jocularity drew as much mirth as an undertaker's final invitation to the mourners to take the last, long look at the departed.

While there was still light, an aerial battle took place overhead. For fifteen minutes, the French antiaircraft guns banged away at three German planes which were audaciously sailing over our lines. The Americans rooted like bleacherites for the guns, but the home team failed to score, and the Germans sailed serenely home. They apparently had had time to make adequate observations.

During the entire afternoon, German sausage balloons had hung high in the air back of the hostile line, offering additional advantages for enemy observation. On the highroad leading from Ansauville, a conspicuous sign *L'enemie vous voit** informed newcomers that German eyes were watching their

---
* Tr: *L'enemie vous voit*: The enemy is watching you.

An American convoy in France

The First American Sector

movements and could interfere at any time with a long-range shell. The fact was that the Germans held high ground and their glasses could command almost all of the terrain back of our lines.

Under this seemingly eternal espionage punctuated at intervals by heavy shelling, several old women of the village had remained in their homes, living above the ground on quiet days and moving their knitting to the front yard dugout at times when gas and shell and bomb interfered. Some of these women operated small shops in the front rooms of their damaged homes, and the Americans lined up in front of the window counters and exchanged dirty French paper money for canned *pâté de foie gras* or jars of mustard.

A machine-gun company with mule-drawn carts led the movement from Ansauville into the front. It was followed at fifty-yard intervals by other sections. Progress down that road was executed in small groups—it was better to lose one whole section than an entire company.

That high road to the front, with its border of shell-withered trees, was revealed that night against a bluish-gray horizon occasionally rimmed with red. Against the sky, the moving groups were defined as impersonal black blocks. Young lieutenants marched ahead of each platoon. In the hazy light, it was difficult to distinguish them. The only difference was that their hips seemed bulkier from the heavy sacks, field glasses, map cases, canteens, pistol holsters, and cartridge clips.

Each section, as it marched out of the village, passed under the eye of Major Griffiths, who sat on his horse in the black shadow of a wall. A section passed forward, the moonlight gleaming on the helmets jauntily cocked over one ear and casting black shadows over the faces of the wearers. From these shadows glowed red dots of fire.

"Drop those cigarettes," came the command from the all-watchful, unseen presence mounted on the horse in the shadow of the wall. Automatically, the section spouted red arcs that fell to the road on either side in a shower of sparks.

"It's a damn shame to do that," Major Griffiths spoke to me, standing beside his horse. "You can't see a cigarette light fifty yards away, but if there were no orders against smoking, the men would be lighting matches or dumping pipes, and such flashes can be seen."

There was need for caution. The enemy was always watchful for an interval when one organization was relieving another on the line. That period represented the time when an attack could cause the greatest confusion in the ranks of the defenders. But that night our men accomplished the relief of the French Moroccan division then in the line, without incident.

The First American Sector

* * *

Two nights later, in company with a party of correspondents, I paid a midnight visit to our men in the front-line trenches of that first American sector. With all lights out, cigarettes tabooed, and the siren silenced, our overloaded motor slushed slowly along the shell-pitted roads, carefully skirting groups of marching men and lumbering supply wagons that took shape suddenly out of the mist-laden road in front of us.

We approached an engineers' dump, where the phantoms of fog gradually materialized into helmeted khaki figures that moved in mud knee-deep and carried boxes and planks and bundles of tools. Total silence covered all the activity, and not a ray of light revealed what mysteries had been worked here in surroundings that seemed no part of this world.

An irregular pile of rock loomed gray and sinister before us, and, looking upward, we judged, from its gaping walls, that it was the remains of a church steeple. It was the dominating ruin in the town of Beaumont.

"Turn here to the left," the officer conducting our party whispered into the ear of the driver.

The sudden execution of the command caused the officer's helmet to rasp against that of the driver with a sound that set the cautious whispering to naught.

And They Thought We Wouldn't Fight

"Park here in the shadow," he continued. "Make no noise; show no light. They dropped shells here ten minutes ago. Gentlemen, this is regimental headquarters. Follow me."

In a well-buttressed cellar, surmounted by a pile of ruins, we found the colonel sitting at a wooden table in front of a grandfather's clock of scratched mahogany. He called the roll—five special correspondents; Captain Chandler, American press officer, with a goatee and fur coat to match; Captain Vielcastel, a French press officer, who is a marquis and speaks English; and a lieutenant from brigade headquarters, who already had been named "Whispering Willie."

With two runners in the lead, we started down what had been the main street of the ruined village. Ten minutes' walk through the mud, and the colonel stopped to announce: "Within a hundred yards of you, a number of men are working. Can you hear 'em?"

No one could, so he showed us a long line of sweating Americans stretching off somewhere into the fog. Their job was more of the endless trench digging and improving behind the lines. While one party swung pick and spade in the trenches, relief parties slept on the ground nearby. The colonel explained that these parties arrived after dark, worked all night, and then carefully camouflaged all evidences of new earth and departed before daylight, leaving no trace of their night's work to be discov-

The First American Sector

ered by prying airman. Often the work was carried on under an intermittent shelling, but that night only two shells had landed near them.

An American-manned field gun shattered the silence, so close to us that we could feel its breath and had a greater respect for its bite. The proximity of the gun had not even been guessed by any of our party. A yellow stab of flame seemed to burn the mist through which the shell screeched on its way toward Germany.

The colonel then left us, and with the whispering lieutenant and runners in advance, we continued toward the front.

"Walk in parties of two" was the order of the soft-toned subaltern. "Each party keep ten yards apart. Don't smoke. Don't talk. This road is reached by their field pieces. They also cover it with indirect machine-gun fire. They sniped the brigade commander right along here this morning. He had to get down into the mud. I can afford to lose some of you, but not the entire party. If anything comes over, you are to jump into the communicating trenches on the right side of the road."

His instructions were obeyed, and it was almost with relief that, ten minutes later, we followed him down the slippery side of the muddy bank and landed in front of a dugout.

In the long, narrow, low-ceilinged shelter which completely tunneled the road at a depth of twenty feet, two twenty-year-old Americans were hugging a brazier filled with charcoal. In this dugout was housed a group from a machine-gun battalion, some of whose members were snoring in a double tier of bunks on the side.

Deep trenches at the other end of the dugout led to the gun pits, where this new arm of the service operated at ranges of two miles. These special squads fired over the heads of those in front of them or over the contours of the ground and put down a leaden barrage on the front line of the Germans. The firing not only was indirect but was without correction from the rectifying observation, of which the artillery had the benefit by watching the burst of their missiles.

Regaining the road, we walked on through the ruins on the edge of the village of Seicheprey, where our way led through a drunken colony of leaning walls and brick piles.

Here was the battalion headquarters, located underneath the old stones of a barn which was topped by the barest skeleton of a roof. What had been the first floor of the structure had been weighted down heavily with railroad iron and concrete to form the roof of the commander's dugout. The sides of the decrepit structure bulged outward and were prevented from bursting by timber props radiating on all sides like the legs of a centipede. A mule team stood in front of the dugout.

The First American Sector

U.S. soldiers in a trench putting on gas masks

The battalion commander, Major Griffiths, was so glad to see us that he sent for another bottle of the murky gray water that came from a well on one side of a well-populated graveyard not fifty yards from his post.

"A good night," he said; "haven't seen it so quiet in three years. We have inter-battalion relief on. Some new companies are taking over the lines. Some of them are new to the front trenches, and I'm going out with you and put them up on their toes. Wait till I report in."

He rang the field telephone on the wall and waited for an answer. An oil lamp hung from a low ceiling over the map table. In the hot, smoky air we quietly held our places while the connection was made.

"Hello," the major said, "operator, connect me with Milwaukee." Another wait—

"Hello, Milwaukee, this is Larson. I'm talking from Hamburg. I'm leaving this post with a deck of cards and a runner. If you want me, you can get me at Coney Island or Hinky Dink's. Wurtzburger will sit in here."

"Some code, Major," Lincoln Eyre, [*New York World*] correspondent, said. "What does a pack of cards indicate?"

"Why, anybody who comes out here when he doesn't have to is a funny card," the major replied, "and it looks as if I have a pack of them tonight. Fritz gets quite a few things that go over our wires, and we get lots of his. All are tapped by induction.

"Sometimes the stuff we get is important, and sometimes it isn't. If we heard that the society editor of the *Fliegende Blaetter* and half a dozen pencil strafers were touring the German front line, we'd send 'em over something that would start 'em humming a hymn of hate. If they knew I was joy riding a party of correspondents around the diggin's tonight, they might give you something to write about and cost me a platoon or two. You're not worth it. Come on."

Our party now numbered nine, and we pushed

The First American Sector

off, stumbling through uneven lanes in the center of dimly lit ruins. According to orders, we carried gas masks in a handy position.

This sector had a nasty reputation when it comes to that sample of Teutonic culture. Fritz's poison shells dropped almost noiselessly and, without a report, broke open, liberating to enormous expansion the enclosed gases. These spread in all directions, and, owing to the lowness and dampness of the terrain, the poison clouds were imperceptible both to sight or smell. They clung close to the ground to claim unsuspecting victims.

"How are we to know if we are breathing gas or not?" asked the Philadelphia correspondent [*Philadelphia Evening Ledger*], Mr. Henri Bazin.

"That's just what you DON'T know," replied the major.

"Then when will we know it is time to adjust our masks?" Bazin persisted.

"When you see someone fall who has breathed it," the major said.

"But suppose we breathe it first?"

"Then you won't need a mask," the major replied. "You see, it's quite simple."

"Halt!" The sharp command, coming sternly but not too loud from somewhere in the adjacent mist, brought the party to a standstill in the open on the edge of the village. We remained motionless while the major advanced upon command from the unseen. He rejoined us in several minutes with the remark that the challenge had come from one of his old men, and he only hoped the new companies taking over the line that night were as much on their jobs.

"Relief night always is trying," the major explained. "Fritz always likes to jump the newcomers before they get the lay of the land. He tried it on the last relief, but we burnt him."

While talking, the major was leading the way through the first trench I had ever seen above the surface of the ground. The bottom of the trench was not only on a level with the surrounding terrain, but in some places it was even higher. Its walls, which rose almost to the height of a man's head, were made of large wicker woven cylinders filled with earth and stones.

Our guide informed us that the land which we were traversing was so low that any trench dug in the ground would simply be a ditch brimful of undrainable water, so that, inasmuch as this position was in the first-line system, walls had been built on either side of the path to protect passersby from shell fragments and indirect machine-gun fire. We observed one large break where a shell had entered during the evening.

Farther on, this communicating passage, which was more corridor than trench, reached higher ground and descended into the earth. We reeled

The First American Sector

through its zigzag course, staggering from one slanting corner to another.

The sides were fairly well retained by French wicker work, but every eighth or tenth duckboard was missing, making it necessary for trench travelers to step knee-deep in cold water or to jump the gap. Correspondent Eyre, who was wearing shoes and puttees [knee-length leggings], abhorred these breaks.

We passed the major's post of command, which he used during intense action, and some distance on, entered the front line. With the major leading, we walked up to a place where two Americans were standing on a firing step with their rifles extended across the parapet. They were silently peering into the gray mist over no man's land. One of them looked around as we approached. Apparently he recognized the major's cane as a symbol of rank. He came to attention.

"Well," the major said, "is this the way you let us walk up on you? Why don't you challenge me?"

"I saw you was an officer, sir," the man replied.

"Now, you are absolutely sure I am YOUR officer?" the major said slowly and coldly, with emphasis on the word *your*. "Suppose I tell you I am a German officer and these men behind me are Germans. How do you know?"

With a quick movement the American brought his rifle forward to the challenge, his right hand slapping the wooden butt with an audible whack.

"Advance one, and give the countersign," he said with a changed voice and manner, and the major, moving to within whispering distance, breathed the word over the man's extended bayonet. Upon hearing it, the soldier lowered his gun and stood at attention.

It was difficult to figure whether his relief over the scare was greater than his fears of the censure he knew was coming.

"Next time anybody gets that close to you without being challenged," the major said, "don't be surprised if it is a German. That's the way they do it. They don't march in singing 'Deutschland über alles.'

"If you see them first, you might live through the war. If they see you first, we will have wasted a lot of Liberty Bonds and effort trying to make a soldier out of you. Now, remember; watch yourself."

Arriving at an unmanned firing step large enough to accommodate the party, we mounted and took a first look over the top. We were two hundred yards from the German front lines. Between their trenches and ours, at this point, was low land, so boggy as to be almost impassable. The opposing lines hugged the tops of two small ridges. Fifty yards in front was our wire barely discernible in the fog.

The major appeared to be itching for action, and he got into official swing a hundred yards farther

The First American Sector

on, where a turn in the trench revealed to us the muffled figures of two young Americans, comfortably seated on grenade boxes on the firing step.

From their easy positions they could look over the top and watch all approaches without rising. Each one had a blanket wrapped about his legs and feet. They looked the picture of ease. Without moving, one, with his rifle across his lap, challenged the major, advanced him, and received the countersign. We followed the major in time to hear his first remark:

"Didn't they get the rocking chairs out here yet?" he said with the provoked air that customarily accompanies any condemnation of the quartermaster department.

"No, sir," replied the seated sentry. "They didn't get here. The men we relieved said that they never got anything out here."

The major continued: "You know you are not sitting in a club window in Fifth Avenue and watching the girls go by. You're not looking for chickens out there. There's a hawk over there, and sometimes he carries off precious little lambs. Now, the next time anybody steps around the corner of that trench, you be on your feet with your bayonet and gun ready to mix things."

The lambs saluted as the major moved off with a train of followers, who, by this time, were beginning to feel that these trenches held other lambs, only they carried notebooks instead of cartridge belts.

Stopping in front of a dugout, the major gathered us about to hear the conversation that was going on within. Through the cracks of the door, we looked down a flight of steep stairs, dug deep into this battlefield graveyard. There were lights in the chamber below, and the sound of voices came up to us. One voice was singing softly.

> *Oh, the infantry, the infantry, with the dirt behind their ears,*
> *The infantry, the infantry, they don't get any beers.*
> *The cavalry, the artillery, and the lousy engineers,*
> *They couldn't lick the infantry in a hundred million years.*

The major interrupted by rapping sharply on the door.

"Come in" was the polite and innocent invitation guilelessly spoken from below. The major had his helmet on, so he couldn't tear his hair.

"Come up here, you idiots, every one of you." The major directed his voice down into the hole in an unmistakable and official tone. There was a scurrying of feet, and four men emerged carrying their guns. They were lined up against the trench wall.

"At midnight," the major began, "in your dugout in the front line forty yards from the Germans, with

The First American Sector

no sentry at the door, you hear a knock on the door and you shout, 'Come in.' I commend your politeness, and I know that's what your mothers taught you to say when visitors come, but this isn't any tea fight out here. One German could have wiggled over the top here and stood in this doorway and captured all four of you single-handed, or he could have rolled a couple of bombs down that hole and blown all of you to smithereens. What's your aim in life—hard labor in a German prison camp or a nice little wooden cross out here four thousand miles from Punkinville? Why wasn't there any sentry at that door?"

The question remained unanswered, but the incident had its effect on the quartet. Without orders, all four decided to spend the remainder of the night on the firing step with their eyes glued on the enemy's line. They simply hadn't realized they were really in the war. The major knew this but made a mental reservation of which the commander of this special platoon got full benefit before the night was over.

The front line from here onward followed a small ridge running generally east and west but now bearing slightly to the northward. We were told the German line ran in the same general direction but at this point bore to the southward.

The opposing lines in the direction of our course were converging, and we were approaching the

And They Thought We Wouldn't Fight

place where they were the closest in the sector. If German listening posts heard the progress of our party through the line, only a telephone call back to the artillery was necessary to plant a shell among us, as every point on the system was registered.

As we silently considered various eventualities immaterial to the prosecution of the war but not without personal concern, our progress was brought to a sudden standstill.

"Huh-huh-halt!" came a drawn-out command in a husky, throaty stammer, weaker than a whisper, from an undersized tin-hatted youngster planted in the center of the trench not ten feet in front of us. His left foot was forward, and his bayoneted rifle was held ready for a thrust.

"Huh-huh-huh-halt!" came the nervous, whispering command again, although we had been motionless since the first whisper.

We heard a click as the safety catch on the man's rifle lock was thrown off and the weapon made ready to discharge. The major was watching the nervous hand that rested none too steadily on the trigger stop. He stepped to one side, but the muzzle of the gun followed him.

"Huh-huh-huh-halt! I tuh-tuh-tell you."

This time the whisper vibrated with nervous tension, and there was no mistaking the state of mind of the sentry.

"Take it easy," replied the major with attempted

A listening post in the advanced French line

calm. "I'm waiting for you to challenge me. Don't get excited. This is the commanding officer."

"What's the countersign?" came from the voice in a hard strain.

"Troy," the major said, and the word seemed to bring worlds of reassurance to the rifleman, who sighed with relief but forgot to move his rifle until the major said: "Will you please take that gun off me and put the safety back in?"

The nervous sentry moved the gun six inches to the right, and we correspondents, standing in back of the major, looked into something that seemed as big as the LaSalle Street Tunnel. I jumped out of range behind the major. Eyre plunged knee-deep into water out of range, and [Junius] Wood, [*Chicago Daily News*], with rubber boots on, started to go over the top.

The click of the replaced safety lock sounded unusually like the snap of a trigger, but no report followed, and three hearts resumed their beating.

"There is no occasion to get excited," the major said to the young soldier in a fatherly tone. "I'm glad to see you are wide-awake and on the job. Don't feel any fears for your job, and just remember that with that gun and bayonet in your hands, you are better than any man who turns that trench corner or crosses out there. You've got the advantage of him, and besides that, you are a better man than he is."

The First American Sector

The sentry, now smiling, saluted the major as the latter conducted the party quietly around the trench corner and into a sap[4] leading directly out into no man's land. Twice the trench passed under broad belts of barbed wire, which we were cautioned to avoid with our helmets, because any sound was undesirable for obvious reasons.

After several minutes of this cautious advance, we reached a small listening post that marked the closest point in the sector to the German line. Several silent sentries were crouching on the edge of the pit. Gunny sacks covered the hole and screened it in front and above. We remained silent while the major in the lowest whisper spoke with a corporal and learned that except for two or three occasions, when the watchers thought they heard sounds near our wire, the night had been calm.

We departed as silently as we came. The German line from a distance of forty yards looked no different from its appearance at a greater distance, but since it was closer, it was carried with a constant tingle of anticipation.

Into another communicating trench and through better walled fortifications of splintered forest, the major led us to a place where the recent shelling had changed twenty feet of trench into a gaping gulley almost without sides and waist-deep in water. A working detail was endeavoring to repair the damage. In parties of two, we left the trench and crossed an open space on the level. The forty steps we covered across that forbidden ground were like stolen fruit. Such rapture! Bazin, who was seeking a title for a book, pulled "Eureka!"

"Over the top armed with a pencil," he said. "Not bad, eh?"

Back in Seicheprey, just before the major left us for our long trip back to quarters, he led the way to the entrance of a cemetery, well kept in the midst of surrounding chaos. Graves of French dead ranged row upon row.

"I just wanted to show you some of the fellows that held this line until we took it over," he said simply. "Our own boys that we've lost since we've been here are buried down in the next village."

We silently saluted the spot as we passed it thirty minutes later.

Notes

1. Salient: a "bump" in a military line that projects into the enemy's position.
2. Richard Henry Griffiths (1873–1918). U.S. soldier, served in the Philippines, volunteered with the Australians and the British in the early days of World War I, then transferred to the American forces. He was killed in action April 27, 1918.
3. *Poilus*: a popular, friendly slang nickname for French infantrymen in the First World War.
4. Sap: a covered trench or tunnel dug to a place near or within an enemy position.

The Night Our Guns Cut Loose

On early morning of March 4, it was my privilege to witness from an exceptional vantage point, the first planned and concentrated American artillery action against the enemy. The German lines selected for this sudden downpour of shell comprised two small salients jutting out from the enemy's positions in the vicinity of the ruined village of Lahayville, in the same sector.

In company with an orderly who had been dispatched as my guide, I started from an artillery battalion headquarters shortly before midnight, and together we made our way up the dark, muddy road that led through the dense Bois de la Reine to the battery positions. Half an hour's walk, and O'Neil, the guide, led me off the road into a darker tunnel of overlaced boughs, where we stumbled along on the ties of a narrow-gauge railroad that conveyed heavy shells from the road to the guns. We passed through several gun pits and stopped in front of a huge *abri* [shelter] built entirely aboveground. Its walls and roof must have been between five- and seven-feet thick and were made from layers of logs, sandbags, railroad iron, and slabs of concrete reinforced with steel. It looked impenetrable.

"Battery commander's headquarters," O'Neil said to me as we entered a small, hot room lighted by two oil lamps and a candle. Three officers, at two large map tables, were working on sheets of figures. Two wooden bunks, one above the other, and two posts supporting the low ceiling completed the meager furnishings of the room. A young officer looked up from his work, O'Neil saluted, and addressed him.

"The major sent me up with this correspondent. He said you could let him go wherever he could see the fun and that you are not responsible for his safety." O'Neil caught the captain's smile at the closing remark and withdrew. The captain showed me the map.

"Here we are," he said, indicating a spot with his finger, "and here's what we are aiming at tonight. There are two places you can stay to see the fun. You can stay in this shelter and hear the sound of it, or you can go up a little further front to this point, and mount the platform in our observation tree. In this *abri* you are safe from splinters and shrapnel, but a direct hit would wipe us out. In the tree you are exposed to direct hits and splinters from nearby bursts, but at least you can see the whole show. It's the highest point around here and overlooks the whole sector."

I sensed that the captain expected a busy evening and looked forward with no joy to possible interference from a questioning visitor, so I chose the tree.

"All right," he said, "you've got helmet and gas

The Night Our Guns Cut Loose

masks, I see. Now how's your watch? Take the right time off mine. We have just synchronized ours with headquarters. Zero is one o'clock. You had better start now."

He called for an orderly with a German name, and the two of us left. Before I was out of the room, the captain had returned to his mathematics and was figuring out the latest range variations and making allowances for latest developments in wind, temperature, and barometer. The orderly with the German name and I plunged again into the trees and brought up shortly on the edge of a group of men who were standing in the dark near a large tree trunk. I could hear several other men and some stamping horses off to one side.

The party at the foot of the tree was composed of observers, signal linemen, and runners. All of them were enlisted men. I inquired who were to be my comrades in the treetop, and three presented themselves. One said his name was Pat Guahn, the second gave his as Peter Griffin, and the third acknowledged Mike Stanton. I introduced myself, and Griffin said, "I see we are all from the same part of Italy."

At twenty minutes to one, we started up the tree, mounting by rudely constructed ladders that led from one to the other of the four crudely fashioned platforms. We reached the top breathless and with no false impressions about the stability of our sway-

German Observation Post, *similar to the one Gibbons climbed*, postcard

The Night Our Guns Cut Loose

ing perch. The tree seemed to be the tallest in the forest, and nothing interfered with our forward view. The platform was a bit shaky, and Guahn put my thoughts to words and music by softly singing—

Rock-a-bye baby, in the treetop,
When the shell comes the runners all flop.
When the shell busts, goodbye to our station.
We're up in a tree, bound for damnation.

The compass gives us north, and we locate in the forward darkness an approximate sweep of the front lines. Guahn is looking for the flash of a certain German gun, and it will be his duty to keep his eyes trained through the fork of a certain marked twig within arm's reach.

"If she speaks, we want to know it," Guahn says; "I can see her from here when she flashes, and there's another man who can see her from another place. You see, we get an intersection of angles on her, and then we know where she is just as though she had sent her address. Two minutes later we drop a card on her and keep her warm."

In our treetop all seems quiet, and so is the night. There is no moon, and only a few stars are out. A penetrating dampness takes the place of cold, and there is that in the air that threatens a change of weather.

The illuminated dial of my watch tells me that it is three minutes of one, and I communicate the information to the rest of the Irish quartet. In three minutes, the little world that we look upon from our treetop is due to change with terrific suddenness and untold possibilities.

Somewhere below in the darkness and to one side, I hear the clank of a ponderous breech lock as the mechanism is closed on a shell in one of the heavy guns. Otherwise all remains silent.

Two minutes of one. Each minute seems to drag like an hour. It is impossible to keep one's mind off that unsuspecting group of humans out there in that little section of German trench upon which the heavens are about to fall. Griffin leans over the railing and calls to the runners to stand by the horses' heads until they become accustomed to the coming roar.

One minute of one. We grip the railing and wait.

Two flashes and two reports, the barest distinguishable interval, and the black horizon belches red. From extreme left to extreme right the flattened proscenium in front of us glows with the ghastliness of the Broockon [sic].[1]

Waves of light flush the dark vault above like the night sky over South Chicago's blast furnaces. The heavens reflect the glare. The flashes range in color from blinding yellow to the softest tints of pink. They seem to form themselves from strange combinations of greens and mauves and lavenders.

The sharp shattering crash of the guns reaches our ears almost on the instant. The forest shakes,

The Night Our Guns Cut Loose

and our treetop sways with the slam of the heavies close by. The riven air whimpers with the husky whispering of the rushing load of metal bolts passing above us.

Looking up into that void, we deny the uselessness of the act and seek in vain to follow the trains of those unseen things that make the air electric with their presence. We hear them coming, passing, going, but see not one of them.

Now comes the thunder of the shell arrivals. You know the old covered wooden bridges that are still to be found in the country? Have you ever heard a team of horses and a farm wagon thumping and rumbling over such a bridge on the trot?

Multiply the horse team a thousand times. Lash the animals from the trot to the wild gallop. Imagine the sound of their stampede through the echoing wooden structure, and you approach in volume and effect the rumble and roar of the steel as it rained down on that little German salient that night.

"Listen to them babies bustin'," says Griffin. "I'm betting them groundhogs is sure huntin' their holes right now and trying to dig clear through to China."

That was the sound and sight of that opening salvo from all guns, from the small trench mortars in the line, the lightest field pieces behind them, the heavy field pieces about us, and the ponderous railroad artillery located behind us.

And They Thought We Wouldn't Fight

Its crash has slashed the inkiness in front of us with a lurid red meridian. I don't know how many hands had pulled lanyards on exactly the same instant, but the consequent spread of fire looked like one continuous flame.

Now the "Seventy-fives" are speaking, not in unison, but at various speeds, limited only by the utmost celerity of the sweating gun crews.

But the German front line is not the only locality receiving unsolicited attention. Enemy gun positions far behind the lines are being plastered with high explosives and anesthetized with gas shells.

So effective is the American artillery neutralization of the German batteries, that it is between fifteen and twenty minutes before the first enemy gun replies to the terrific barrage. And though expected momentarily, a German counter-barrage fails to materialize.

In our treetop we wait for the enemy's countershelling, but the retaliation does not develop. When occupying an exposed position, the suspense of waiting for an impending blow increases in tenseness as the delay continues and the expectations remain unrealized. With no inclination to be unreasonable, one even prays for the speedy delivery of the blow in the same way that the man with the aching tooth urges the dentist to speed up and have it over with.

"Why in hell don't they come back at us?" Grif-

The Night Our Guns Cut Loose

fin asks. "I've had myself all tuned up for the last twenty minutes to have a leg blown off and be thankful. I hate this waiting stuff."

"Keep your shirt on, Pete," Stanton remarks. "Give 'em a chance to get their breath and come out of their holes. That barrage drove 'em down a couple hundred feet into the ground, and they haven't any elevators to come up on. We'll hear from 'em soon enough."

We did, but it was not more than a whisper as compared with what they were receiving from our side of the line. The German artillery came into lethargic action after the American barrage had been in constant operation for thirty minutes, and then the enemy's fire was only desultory. Only an occasional shell from Kulturland[2] came our way, and even they carried a rather tired, listless buzz, as though they didn't know exactly where they were going and didn't care.

Six or eight of them hummed along a harmless orbit not far above our treetop and fell in the forest. It certainly looked as though we were shooting all the hard stuff and the German end of the fireworks party was all colored lights and Roman candles. Of the six shells that passed us, three failed to explode upon landing.

"That makes three dubs," said Guahn.

"You don't mean dubs," Stanton corrected him. "You mean duds, and even then you are wrong.

Those were gas pills. They just crack open quietly so you don't know it until you've sniffed yourself dead. Listen, you'll hear the gas alert soon."

Even as he spoke, we heard through the firing the throaty gurgling of the sirens. The alarm started on our right and spread from station to station through the woods. We adjusted the respirators and turned our muffled faces toward the firing line. Through the moisture-fogged glasses of my mask, I looked first upon my companions on this rustic scaffold above the forest.

War's demands had removed our appearances far from the human. Our heads were topped with uncomfortable steel casques [helmets], harder than the backs of turtles. Our eyes were large, flat, round glazed surfaces, unblinking and owl-like. Our faces were shapeless folds of black rubber cloth. Our lungs sucked air through tubes from a canvas bag under our chins, and we were inhabiting a treetop like a family of apes. It really required imagination to make it seem real.

"Looks like the party is over," came the muffled remark from the masked figure beside me. The cannonading was dying down appreciably. The blinking line of lights in front of us grew less.

From the German lines an increased number of flares shot skyward, and as the cannon cracks ceased, save for isolated booms, the enemy machine guns could be heard at work, riveting the night with

The Night Our Guns Cut Loose

sprays of lead and sounding for all the world like a scourge of hungry woodpeckers.

I descended the tree, leaving my companions to wait for the orders necessary for their departure. Unfamiliar with the unmarked paths of the forest and guided only as to general directions, I made my way through the trees some distance in search of the road back from the front.

A number of mud- and water-filled shell holes intervened to make the exertion greater and consequently the demand upon lungs for air greater. After floundering several kilometers through a strange forest with a gas mask on, one begins to appreciate the temptation that comes to tear off the stifling nose bag and risk asphyxiation for just one breath of fresh air.

A babel of voices in the darkness to one side guided me to a log cabin, where I learned from a sentry that the gas scare had just been called off. Continuing on the road, I collided head-on in the darkness with a walking horse. Its rider swore, and so did I, with slightly the advantage over him as his head was still encased. I told him the gas alarm was off, and he tore away the mask with a sigh of relief. I left him while he was removing the horse's gas mask.

A light snow was beginning to fall as I said good night to the battalion commander in front of his roadside shack. A party of mounted runners was passing on the way to their quarters. With an admirable lack of dignity quite becoming a national guard cavalry major in command of regular army artillery, he said: "Good night, men. We licked hell out of them."

Notes

1. Broockon: Gibbons might be referring to a massive explosion at a shoe factory in Brockton, Massachusetts, in 1905.
2. Kulturland: Kulture is a German concept with many meanings but roughly connoting to Germans the superior elements of their culture such as hard work, loyalty, and refinement.

Into Picardy to Meet the German Push

Toward the end of March 1918, just at the time when the American Expeditionary Forces were approaching the desired degree of military effectiveness, the fate of civilization was suddenly imperiled by the materialization of the long-expected German offensive.

This push, the greatest the enemy had ever attempted, began on March 21, and the place that Hindenburg[1] selected for the drive was Picardy, the valley of the Somme, the ancient cockpit of Europe. On that day the German hordes, scores upon scores of divisions, hurled themselves against the British line between Arras and Noyon.

Before that tremendous weight of manpower, the Allied line was forced to give, and one of the holding British armies, the Fifth, gave ground on the right flank, and with its left as a hinge, swung back like a gate, opening the way for the Germans toward Paris.

Upon the heels of the German successes in Picardy, developments followed fast. Principal among these was the materialization of a unified command of all the armies of the Allies. General Ferdinand Foch[2] was selected and placed in supreme command of every fighting man under the Allied flags.

The action met with the unqualified endorsement of every officer and man in the American forces. From that minute on, the American slogan in France was "Let's go," and every regiment began to hope that it would be among the American organizations selected to do battle with the German in Picardy.

Particularly were there cheers when the news spread through the ranks of the First United States Division, then on duty on the line in front of Toul, that it had been the first American division chosen to go into Picardy. I was fortunate enough to make arrangements to go with them.

I rode out from old positions with the guns and boarded the troop train, which took our battery by devious routes to changes of scenery, gratifying both to vision and spirit. We lived in our cars on tinned meat and hard bread, washed down with swallows of *vin ordinaire* [cheap table wine], hurriedly purchased at station *buvettes*. The horses rode well.

Officers and men, none of us cared for train schedules simply because none of us knew where we were going, and little time was wasted in conjecture. Soldierly curiosity was satisfied with the knowledge that we were on our way, and with this satisfaction, the hours passed easily. In fact, the blackjack game in the officers' compartment had reached the point

U.S. Marines on a troop train in France

where the battery commander had garnered almost all of the French paper money in sight, when our train passed slowly through the environs of Paris.

Other American troop trains had preceded us, because where the railroad embankment ran close and parallel to the street of some nameless *faubourg* [suburb], our appearance was met with cheers and cries from a welcoming regiment of Paris street gamins, who trotted in the street beside the slow-moving troop train and shouted and threw their hats and wooden shoes in the air. *Sous* and fifty centime pieces and franc pieces showered from the side doors of the horses' cars as American soldiers, with typical disregard for the value of money, pitched coin after coin to the scrambling mob of children. At least a hundred francs must have been cast out upon those happy, romping waves of childish faces and upstretched dirty hands.

"A soldier would give his shirt away," said a platoon commander, leaning out of the window and watching the spectacle, and surreptitiously pitching a few coins himself. "Hope we get out of this place before the men pitch out a gun or a horse to that bunch. Happy little devils, aren't they? It's great to think we are on our way up to meet their daddies."

Unnumbered hours more passed merrily in the troop train before we were shunted into the siding of a little town. Work of unloading was started and completed within an hour. Guns and wagons were

Into Picardy to Meet the German Push

unloaded on the quay, while the animals were removed from the cars on movable runways or ramps. As each gun or wagon reached the ground, its drivers hitched in the horses and moved it away. Five minutes later we rode out of the yards and down the main street of the town.

Broad steel tires on the carriages of the heavies bumped and rumbled over the clean cobbles, and the horses pranced spryly to get the kinks out of their legs, long fatigued from vibrations of the train. Women, old and young, lined the curbs, smiling and throwing kisses, waving handkerchiefs and aprons, and begging for souvenirs. If every request for a button had been complied with, our battery would have reached the front with a shocking shortage of safety pins.

Darkness came on and with it a fine rain as we cleared the town and halted on a level plain between soft fields of tender new wheat, which the horses sensed and snorted to get at. In twenty minutes, Mess Sergeant Kelly, from his high altar on the rolling kitchen, announced that the last of hot coffee had been dispensed. Somewhere up ahead in the darkness, battery bugle notes conveyed orders to prepare to mount. With the rattle of equipment and the application of endearing epithets, which horses unfortunately don't understand, we moved off at the sound of "forward."

Midnight passed, and we were still wheeling our

Gibbons's Locations in the Picardy Region

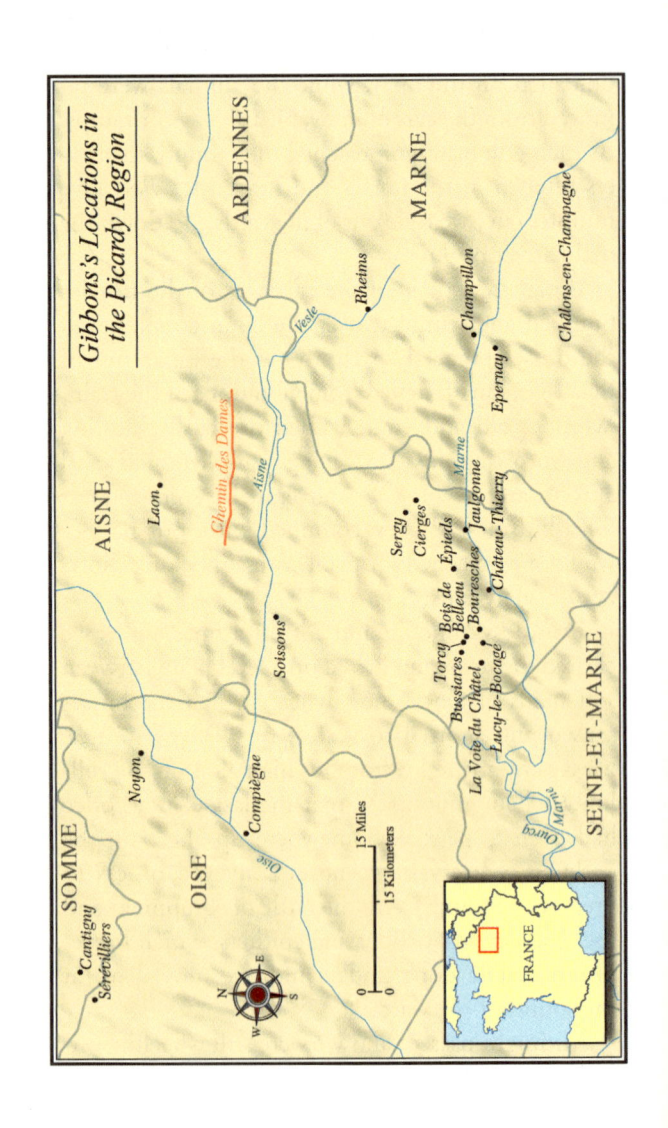

SOMME
• Cantigny
• Sereviliers

ARDENNES

AISNE
• Laon
Chemin des Dames
• Rheims
Vesle
Aisne

MARNE
• Champillon
• Epernay
• Châlons-en-Champagne

• Soissons
• Sergy
• Clerges
• Épieds
Torcy • Bois de Belleau
Bussiares • Bouresches • Jaulgonne
La Voie du Châtel • Château-Thierry
• Lucy-le-Bocage
Marne

OISE
• Noyon
• Compiègne

SEINE-ET-MARNE
Ourcq

15 Miles
15 Kilometers

FRANCE

Into Picardy to Meet the German Push

way through sleeping villages, consulting maps under rays of flashlights, gathering directions some of the time from mileposts and wall signs, and at other times gaining knowledge of roads and turns and hills from sleepy heads in curl wrappers that protruded from bedroom chambers and were overgenerous in advice.

The animals were tired. Rain soaked the cigarettes and made them draw badly. Above was drizzle and below was mud. There were a few grumbles, but no man in our column would have traded places with a brother back home even if offered a farm to boot.

It was after three in the morning when we parked the guns in front of a château, brought forward some lagging combat wagons, and discovered the rolling kitchen had gone astray. In another hour the animals had been unhitched but not unharnessed, fed and watered in darkness, and the men, in utter weariness, prepared to lie down and sleep anywhere. At this juncture, word was passed through the sections that the battery would get ready to move immediately. Orders were to clear the village by six o'clock. Neither men nor horses were rested, but we moved out on time and breakfasted on the road.

During the afternoon, a veterinarian turned over two horses to a French peasant. One was exhausted and unable to proceed, and the other suffered a bad hoof, which would require weeks for healing. News that both animals were not going to be shot was received with joy by two men who had ridden them.

An hour later, a young cannoneer gave in to fatigue and ignored orders to the extent of reclining on the gun trail and falling asleep. A rut in the road made a stiff jolt, he rolled off, and one ponderous wheel of the gun carriage passed over him. One leg, one arm, and two ribs were broken and his feet crushed was the doctor's verdict as the victim was carried away in an ambulance.

"He'll get better all right," said the medico, "but he's finished his bit in the army."

The column halted for lunch outside of a small town, and I climbed on foot to the hilltop castle where medieval and modern were mixed in mute mélange. A drawbridge crossed a long, dry moat to cracked walls of rock covered with ivy. For all its well-preserved signs of artistic ruin, it was occupied and well fitted within. From the topmost parapet of one rickety-looking tower, a wire stretched out through the air to an old, ruined mill which was surmounted by a modern wind motor, the tail of which incongruously advertised the words "Ideal power," with the typical conspicuity of American salesmanship.

Near the base of the old mill was another jumble of moss-covered rocks, now used as a summer house, but open on all sides. At a table in the center of this open structure sat a blond-haired young

Into Picardy to Meet the German Push

American soldier with black receivers clamped to either ear. I approached and watched him jotting down words on a paper pad before him. After several minutes of intent silence, he removed the harness from his head and told me that he belonged to the wireless outfit with the artillery and this station had been in operation since the day before.

"Seems so peaceful here with the sun streaming down over these old walls," he said.

"What do you hear out of the air?" I asked.

"Oh, we pick up a lot of junk," he replied. "I'm waiting for the German communiqué now. Here's some Spanish stuff I just picked up and some more junk in French. The English stations haven't started this afternoon. A few minutes ago I heard a German airplane signaling by wireless to a German battery and directing its fire. I could tell every time the gun was ordered to fire and every time the aviator said the shot was short or over. It's kinder funny to sit back here in quiet and listen in the war, isn't it?" I agreed it was weird, and it was.

In darkness again at the end of a hard day on the road, we parked the guns that night in a little village which was headquarters for our regiment and where I spent the night writing by an old oil lamp in the mayor's office. A former Chicago bellhop who spoke better Italian than English and naturally should was sleeping on a blanket roll on the floor near me. On the walls of the room were posted nu-

And They Thought We Wouldn't Fight

U.S. soldiers relaxing in their billet in a stable in France

merous flag-decked proclamations, some now yellow with the time that had passed over them since their issue back in 1914. They pertained to the mobilization of the men of the village, men whose names remain now only as a memory.

But in their place was the new khaki-clad Chicago bellhop snoring there on the floor and several thousand more as sturdy and ready as he, all billeted within a stone's throw of that room. They were here to finish the fight begun by those village peasants who had marched away four years before when the mayor of the town posted that bulletin. These Americans stood ready to go down to honored graves beside them.

* * *

Into Picardy to Meet the German Push

On the day before our departure for the front from the concentration area in Picardy, every officer in the division, and they numbered almost a thousand, was summoned to the temporary divisional headquarters, where General Pershing addressed to them remarks which have since become known as the commander's "farewell to the First." We had passed out from his command, and from then on our orders were to come from the commander of the French army to which the division was to be attached.

General Pershing stood on a mound at the rear of a beautiful château of Norman architecture, the Château du Jard, located on the edge of the town of Chaumont-en-Vexin. The officers ranged themselves in informal rows on the grass. Birds were singing somewhere above in the dense, green foliage, and sunlight was filtering through the leaves of the giant trees.

The American commander spoke of the traditions which every American soldier should remember in the coming trials. He referred to the opportunity then present for us, whose fathers established liberty in the New World, now to assist the Old World in throwing off its yoke of tyranny. Throughout this touching farewell to the men he had trained—to his men then leaving for scenes from which some of them would never return—the commander's voice never betrayed the depth of feeling behind it.

That night we made final arrangements for the morrow's move. I traveled with the artillery, where orders were received for the reduction of all packs to the lightest possible, as all men would be dismounted and the baggage wagons would be reserved for food, ammunition, and officers' luggage only. Officers' packs, by the same order, had to shrink from 150 pounds to twenty.

There were many misgivings that night as owners were forced to discard cherished belongings. Cumbersome camp paraphernalia, rubber bathtubs, pneumatic mattresses, extra blankets, socks, sweaters, etc., all parted company from erstwhile owners. That order caused many a heartbreak and the abandonment of thousands of dollars' worth of personal equipment in our area.

I have no doubt that some of the village maidens were surprised at the remarkable generosity of officers and men who presented them with expensive toilet sets. Marie at the village *estaminet* received five of them, all fitted in neat leather rolls and inscribed with as many different sets of initials. The old men of the town gloried in the sweaters, woolen socks, and underwear.

There was no chance to fudge on the slim baggage order. An officer, bound by duty, weighed each officer's kit as it reached the baggage wagons, and those tipping the scales at more than the prescribed twenty pounds were thrown out entirely. I hap-

Into Picardy to Meet the German Push

pened to be watching the loading when it came turn for the regimental band to stow away its encased instruments in one wagon. It must be remembered that musicians at the front are stretcher bearers. The baggage judge lifted the case containing the bass horn.

"No horn in the world ever weighed that much," he said. "Open it up" was the terse command. The case was opened and the base horn pulled out. The baggage officer began operations on the funnel. I watched him remove from the horn's interior two spare blankets, four pairs of socks, an extra pair of pants, and a carton of cigarettes. He then inserted his arm up to the shoulder in the instrument's innards and brought forth two apples, a small tin of blackberry jam, and an egg wrapped in an undershirt.

The man who played the "umpah umpah" in the band was heartbroken. The clarinet player, who had watched the operation and whose case followed for inspection, saved the inspector trouble by removing an easily hidden chain of sausage. I noticed one musician who was observing the ruthless pillage, but, strangely, his countenance was the opposite of the others. He was actually smiling. I inquired the cause of his mirth.

"When we packed up, those guys with the big hollow instruments all had the laugh on me," he said. "Now I've got it on them. I play the piccolo."

Three Soldiers with a Horse *by George Harding*

Into Picardy to Meet the German Push

All the mounted men under the rank of battery commanders were dismounted in order to save the horses for any possibilities in the war of movement. A dismounted artilleryman carrying a pack and also armed with a rifle is a most disconsolate subject to view just prior to setting out for a long tramp. In his opinion, he has been reduced too near the status of the despised doughboy.

We were on the march early in the morning, but not without some initial confusion by reason of the inevitable higher orders which always come at the last minute to change programs. On parallel roads through that zone of unmarred beauty which the Normans knew, our columns swung along the dusty highroads.

It takes a hard march to test the morale of soldiers. When the feet are road-sore, when the legs ache from the endless pounding of hobnails on hard macadam, when the pack straps cut and burn to the shoulder blades, and the tin hat weighs down like a crown of thorns, then keep your ear open for a jest, and if your hearing is rewarded, you will know that you march with men.

Many times that first day, those jests came to enliven dejected spirits and put smiles on sweat-rinsed faces. I recall our battery as it negotiated the steep hills. When the eight horses attached to the gun carriages were struggling to pull them up the incline, a certain subaltern [junior officer] with a voice slow, but damnably insistent, would sing out, "Cannoneers, to the wheels." This reiterated command at every grade forced aching shoulders already weary with their own burdens to strain behind the heavy carriages and ease the pull on the animals.

Once on a downgrade, our way crossed the tracks of a narrow-gauge railroad. Not far from the crossing could be seen a dinky engine puffing and snorting furiously in terrific effort to move up the hill its attached train of loaded ammunition cars. The engine was having a hard fight, when some lighthearted weary one in our column gave voice to something which brought up the smile.

"Cannoneers, to the wheel!" was the shout, and even the dignified subaltern whose pet command was the butt of the exclamation joined in the wave of laughs that went down the line.

An imposing château of the Second Empire now presided over by an American heiress, the wife of a French officer, was regimental headquarters that night. Its barns and outbuildings were the cleanest in France according to individuals who had slept in so many barns that they feel qualified to judge.

"Painfully sanitary," said a young lieutenant, who remarked that the tile floor might make a stable smell sweeter, but it hardly offered the slumbering possibilities of a straw shakedown. While the men arranged their blankets in those quarters, the horses grazed and rolled in green paddocks fenced with

Into Picardy to Meet the German Push

white painted rails. The cooks got busy with the evening meal, and the men off duty started exploring the two nearby villages.

For the American soldier, financial deals were always a part of these explorations. It was seldom more than an hour after his arrival in a populated village before the stock market and board of trade were in full operation. The dealings were not in bushels of wheat or shares in oils or rails. Delicacies were the bartered commodities, and of these, eggs were the strongest. The German intelligence service could have found no surer way to trace the peregrinations of American troops about France than to follow up the string of eggless villages they left behind them.

As soon as billets were located, those without extra duty began the egg canvass of the town. There was success for those who made the earliest start and struck the section with the most prolific hens. Eggs were bought at various prices before news of the American arrivals had caused peasants to set up a new scale of charges. The usual late starter and the victim of arrangements was the officer's striker [servant], who lost valuable time by having to take care of his officer's luggage and get the latter established in billets. It was then his duty to procure eggs for the officer's mess.

By that time, all natural egg sources had been obliterated, and the only available supply was cornered by the soldiers' board of trade. The desired breakfast food could be obtained in that place only. It was the last and only resort of the striker, who is euphoniously known as a dog robber. In the board of trade he would find soldiers with helmets full of eggs which could be bought at anywhere from two to three times their original price. It was only by the payment of such prices that the officer was able to get anything that could possibly leave a trace of yellow on his chin. If there was a surplus, the soldiers themselves had ample belt room to accommodate it.

In one village tavern, I saw one soldier eat fourteen eggs which he ordered Madame to fry in succession. I can believe it because I saw it. Madame saw it also, but I feel that she did not believe her eyes. A captain of the judge advocate's office also witnessed the gastronomic feat.

"Every one of those eggs was bought and paid for," he said. "Our department handles claims for all stolen or destroyed property, and we have yet to receive the first claim from this town. Of course everyone knows that a hungry man will steal to eat, and there are those who hold that theft for the purpose of satisfying demands of the stomach is not theft. But our records show that the American soldier in France is ready to, willing to, and capable of buying what he needs outside of his ration allowance.

Into Picardy to Meet the German Push

"There was one case, though, in which Uncle Sam paid the bill himself, and maybe if you could send the story back home, the citizens who paid it would get a laugh worth the money. It happened during a recent cold spell when some of our troops were coming from seaboard to the interior. They traveled in semi-opened horse cars, and it was cold, damn cold.

"One of the trains stopped in front of a small railroad station, and six soldiers with cold hands and feet jumped from the car and entered the waiting room, in the center of which was a large square coal stove with red-hot sides. One man stood on another one's shoulders and disjointed the stove pipe. At the same time, two others placed poles under the bottom of the stove, lifted it off the floor and walked out of the room with it.

"They placed it in the horse car, stuck the pipe out of one door, and were warm for the remainder of the trip. It was the first time in the history of that little village that anybody had ever stolen a red-hot stove. The French government, owning the railroads, made claim against us for four hundred francs for the stove and eleven francs' worth of coal in it. Uncle Sam paid the bill and was glad to do it."

There was one thing, however, that men on the move found it most difficult to steal, and that was sleep. So at least it seemed the next morning when we swung into the road at daybreak and continued our march into the north.

* * *

In billets that night, in a village not far from Beauvais, the singing contest for the prize of fifty dollars offered by the battalion commander Major Robert R. McCormick[3] was resumed with intense rivalry between the tenors and basses of batteries A and B. A B-Battery man was croaking "Annie Laurie," when an A-Battery booster in the audience remarked audibly, "Good Lord, I'd rather hear first call." First call is the bugle note that disturbs sleep and starts the men on the next day's work.

The third and fourth day's march brought us into regions nearer the front, where the movement of refugees on the roads seemed greater, where the roll of the guns came constantly from the north, where enemy motors droned through the air on missions of frightfulness.

At one o'clock one morning, orders reached the battalion for reconnaissance detail, each battery to be ready to take road by daylight. We were off at break of day in motor trucks with a reel cart of telephone wire hitched on behind. Thirty minutes later we rumbled along roads under range of German field pieces and arrived in a village designated as battalion headquarters to find that we were first to

Into Picardy to Meet the German Push

reach the sector allotted for American occupation. The name of the town was Sérévillers.

Our ears did not delude us about the activity of the sector, but I found that officers and men of the detail were inclined to accept the heavy shelling in a noncommittal manner until a French interpreter attached to us remarked that artillery action in the sector was as intense as any he had experienced at Verdun.

If the ever-present crash of shells reminded us that we were opposite the peak of the German push, there was plenty of work to engage minds that might otherwise have paid too much attention to the dangers of their location. A chalk cellar with a vaulted ceiling and ventilators, unfortunately opening on the enemy side of the upper structure, was selected as the battalion command post. The men went to work immediately to remove piles of dirty billeting straw under which was found glass, china, silverware, and family portraits, all of which had been hurriedly buried by the owners of the house not two weeks before.

While linemen planned communications and battery officers surveyed gun positions, the battalion commander and two orienting officers went forward to the frontal zone to get the first look at our future targets and establish observation posts from which our firing could be directed. I accompanied the small party, which was led by a French officer familiar with the sector. It was upon his advice that we left the roads and took cuts across fields, avoiding the path and road intersections and taking advantage of any shelter offered by the ground.

Virgin fields on our way bore the enormous craters left by the explosion of poorly directed German shells of heavy caliber. Orders were to throw ourselves face downward upon the ground upon the sound of each approaching missile. There is no textbook logic on judging from the sound of a shell whether it has your address written on it, but it is surprising how quick that education may be obtained by experience. Several hours of walking and dropping to the ground resulted in an attuning of the ears, which made it possible to judge approximately whether that oncoming, whining, unseen thing from above would land dangerously near or ineffectively far from us. The knowledge was common to all of us, and all of our ears were keenly tuned for the sounds. Time after time the collective judgment and consequent prostration of the entire party was proven well timed by the arrival of a shell uncomfortably close.

We gained a wooded hillside that bristled with busy French Seventy-fives, which the German tried in vain to locate with his howitzer fire. We mounted a forest plateau, in the center of which a beautiful white château still held out against the enemy's best

Into Picardy to Meet the German Push

efforts to locate it with his guns. One shell addressed in this special direction fortunately announced its coming with such unmistakable vehemence that our party all landed in the same shell hole at once.

Every head was down when the explosion came. Branches and pieces of tree trunk were whirled upward, and the air became populated with deadly bumble bees and hummingbirds, for such is the sound that the shell splinters make. When I essayed our shell hole afterward, I couldn't fathom how five of us had managed to accommodate ourselves in it, but in the rush of necessity, no difficulty had been found.

Passing from the woods forward, one by one, over a bald field, we skirted a village that was being heavily shelled and reached a trench on the side of the hill in direct view of the German positions. The enemy partially occupied the ruined village of Cantigny, not eight hundred yards away, but our glasses were unable to pick up the trace of a single person in the debris. French shells, arriving endlessly in the village, shot geysers of dust and wreckage skyward. It was from this village, several days later, that our infantry patrols brought in several prisoners, all of whom were suffering from shell shock.[4] But our men in the village opposite underwent the same treatment at the hands of the German artillery.

It was true of this sector that what corresponded

to the infantry front line was a much safer place to be in than in the reserve positions, or about the gun pits in villages or along roads in our back area. Front-line activity was something of minor consideration, as both sides seemed to have greater interests at other points, and, in addition to that, the men of both sides were busy digging trenches and shelters. There were numerous machine-gun posts which swept with lead the indeterminate region between the lines, and at night, patrols from both sides explored as far as possible the holdings of the other side.

Returning to the battalion headquarters that night by a route apparently as popular to German artillery as was the one we used in the forenoon, we found a telephone switchboard in full operation in the subcellar, and mess headquarters established in a clean kitchen above the ground. Food was served in the kitchen, and we noticed that one door had suffered some damage, which had caused it to be boarded up, and that the plaster ceiling of the room was full of fresh holes and rents in a dozen places. At every shock to the earth, a little stream of oats would come through the holes from the attic above. These falling down on the officer's neck in the midst of a meal would have no effect other than causing him to call for his helmet to ward off the cereal rain.

We learned more about the sinister meaning of

Into Picardy to Meet the German Push

that broken door and the ceiling holes when it became necessary later in the evening to move mess to a safer location. The kitchen was located just thirty yards back of the town crossroads, and an unhealthy percentage of German shells that missed the intersection caused too much interruption in our cook's work.

We found that the mess room was vacant by reason of the fact that it had become too unpleasant for French officers, who had relinquished it the day before. We followed their suit and were not surprised when an infantry battalion mess followed us into the kitchen and just one day later, to the hour, followed us out of it.

Lying on the floor in that chalk cellar that night and listening to the pound of arriving shells on nearby crossroads and battery positions, we estimated how long it would be before this little village would be completely leveled to the ground. Already gables were disappearing from houses, sturdy chimneys were toppling, and stone walls were showing jagged gaps. One whole wall of the village school had crumbled before one blast, so that now the wooden desks and benches of the pupils and their books and papers were exposed to view from the street. On the blackboard was a penmanship model which read: "Let no day pass without having saved something."

An officer came down the dark stone steps into

the cellar, kicked off his boots, and lay down on some blankets in one corner.

"I just heard some shells come in that didn't explode," I remarked. "Do you know whether they were gas or duds?"

"I don't know whether they were gas or not," he said, "but I do know that that horse out in the yard is certainly getting ripe."

The defunct animal referred to occupied an uncovered grave adjoining our ventilator. Sleeping in a gas mask was not the most unpleasant form of slumber.

Notes

1. Paul von Hindenburg (1847–1934), German field marshal and second president of the Weimar Republic (1925–34). He appointed Hitler chancellor in 1933.

2. Ferdinand Foch (1851–1929), French army officer. After the war, he played a major role in the Paris Peace Conference.

3. Robert R. McCormick (1880–1955), editor and publisher of the *Chicago Tribune* (Gibbons's employer). McCormick was later promoted to a colonel.

4. Shell shock: a psychological malady, similar to post-traumatic stress disorder, resulting from prolonged exposure to combat.

Before Cantigny

It is strange how sleep can come at the front in surroundings not unlike the interior of a boiler factory, but it does. I heard of no man who slept in the cellars beneath the ruins of Sérévillers that night being disturbed by the pounding of the shells and the jar of the ground, both of which were ever present through our dormant senses. Stranger still was the fact that at midnight when the shelling almost ceased, for small intervals, almost every sleeper there present was aroused by the sudden silence. When the shelling was resumed, sleep returned.

"When I get back on the farm outside of Chicago," said one officer, "I don't believe I will be able to sleep unless I get somebody to stand under my window and shake a thunder sheet all night."

It is also remarkable how the tired human, under such conditions, can turn off the switch on an energetic imagination and resign himself completely to fate. In those cellars that night, every man knew that one direct hit of a "two-ten" [210mm] German shell on his particular cellar wall would mean taps for everybody in the cave. Such a possibility demands consideration in the slowest-moving minds.

Mentalities and morale of varying caliber cogitate upon this matter at varying lengths, but I doubt in the end if there is much difference in the conclusion arrived at. Such reflections produce the inevitable decision that if one particular shell is coming into your particular abode, there is nothing you can do to keep it out, so "What the hell!" You might just as well go to sleep and forget it, because if it gets you, you most probably will never know anything about it anyway. I believe such is the philosophy of the shelled.

By daylight, I explored the town, noting the havoc wrought by the shells that had arrived in the night. I had thought, in seeing refugees moving southward along the roads, that there was little variety of articles related to human existence that they failed to carry away with them. But one inspection of the abandoned abodes of the unfortunate peasants of Sérévillers was enough to convince me of the greater variety of things that had to be left behind. Old people have saving habits, and the French peasants pride themselves upon never throwing anything away.

The cottage rooms were littered with the discarded clothing of all ages, discarded but saved. Old shoes and dresses, ceremonial high hats and frock coats, brought forth only for weddings or funerals, were mixed on the floor with children's toys, prayer books, and broken china. Shutters and doors hung aslant by single hinges. In the village *estaminet* much mud had been tracked in by exploring feet, and the red-tiled floor was littered with straw and pewter measuring mugs, dear to the heart of the antiquary.

The ivory balls were gone from the dust-covered billiard table, but the six American soldiers billeted in the cellar beneath had overcome this discrepancy. They enjoyed after-dinner billiards just the same, with three large wooden balls from a croquet court in the garden. A croquet ball is a romping substitute when it hits the green cushions.

That afternoon we laid more wire across fields to the next town to the north. Men who do this job are, in my opinion, the most daring in any organization that depends for efficiency upon uninterrupted telephone communication. For them, there is no shelter when a deluge of shells pours upon a field across which their wire is laid. Without protection of any kind from the flying steel splinters, they must go to that spot to repair the cut wires and restore communication. During one of these shelling spells, I reached cover of the roadside *abri* and prepared to await clearer weather.

When the strafing subsided, I reached the next deserted town without incident. It was almost the vesper hour, or what had been the allotted time for that rite in those parts, when I entered the yard of the village church, located in an exposed position at a crossroads on the edge of the town. A sudden unmistakable whirr sounded above, and I threw myself on the ground just as the high-velocity, small-caliber

German shell registered a direct hit on the side of the nave where roof and wall met.

While steel splinters whistled through the air, an avalanche of slate tiles slid down the slanting surface of the roof and fell in a clattering cascade on the graves in the yard below. I sought speedy shelter in the lee of a tombstone. Several other shells had struck the churchyard, and one of them had landed on the final resting place of the family of Roger La Porte. The massive marble slab which had sealed the top of the sunken vault had been heaved aside, and one wall was shattered, leaving open to the gaze a cross-section view of eight heavy caskets lying in an orderly row.

Nearby were fresh mounds of yellow earth, surmounted by now unpainted wooden crosses on which were inscribed in pencil the names of French soldiers with dates, indicating that their last sacrifice for the tri-color of la Patria had been made ten days prior. In the soil at the head of each grave, an ordinary beer bottle had been planted neck downward, and through the glass one could see the paper scroll on which the name, rank, and record of the dead man was preserved. While I wondered at this prosaic method of identification, an American soldier came around the corner of the church, lighted a cigarette, and sat down on an old tombstone.

"Stick around if you want to hear something good," he said. "That is if that last shell didn't bust

Before Cantigny

A French poilu, *or footsoldier, by H. Delaspre*

the organ. There's a French *poilu* who has come up here every afternoon at five o'clock for the last three days, and he plays the sweetest music on the organ. It certainly is great. Reminds me of when I was an altar boy, back in St. Paul."

We waited, and soon there came from the rickety old organ loft the soothing tones of an organ. The ancient pipes, sweetened by the benedictions of ages, poured forth melody to the touch of one whose playing was simple, but of the soul. We sat silently among the graves as the rays of the dying sun brought to life new coloring in the leaded windows of stained glass behind which a soldier of France swayed at the ivory keyboard and with heavenly harmony ignored those things of death and destruction that might arrive through the air any minute.

My companion informed me that the *poilu* at the organ wore a uniform of horizon blue which marked him as casual to this village, whose French garrisons were Moroccans, with the distinctive khaki worn by all French colonials in service. The sign of the golden crescent on their collar tabs identified them as children of Mahomet, and one would have known as much anyway upon seeing the use to which the large crucifix standing in what was the marketplace had been put.

So as not to impede traffic through the place, it had become necessary to elevate the field telephone wires from the ground and send them across the road overhead. The crucifix in the center of the place had presented itself as excellent support for this wire, and the sons of the prophet had utilized it with no intention of disrespect. The uplifted right knee of the figure on the cross was insulated and wired. War, the modernizer and mocker of Christ, seemed to

Before Cantigny

have devised new pain for the Teacher of Peace. The crucifixion had become the electrocution.

At the foot of the cross had been nailed a rudely made sign conveying to all who passed the French warning that this was an exposed crossing and should be negotiated rapidly. Fifty yards away another board bore the red letters R.A.S., and by following the direction indicated by arrows, one arrived at the cellar in which the American doctor had established a Relief Aid Station. The medico had furnished his subterranean apartments with furniture removed from the house above.

Across the street an American battalion headquarters had been established on the first floor and in the basement of the house, which appeared the most pretentious in the village. Telephone wires now entered the building through broken window panes, and within, maps had been tacked to plaster walls and the furniture submitted to the hard usage demanded by war. An old man conspicuous by his civilian clothes wandered about the yard here and there, picking up some stray implement or knickknack, hanging it up on a wall or placing it carefully aside.

"There's a tragedy," the battalion commander told me. "That man is mayor of this town. He was forced to flee with the rest of the civilians. He returned today to look over the ruins. This is his house we occupy. I explained that much of it is as

A first aid station

Before Cantigny

we found it, but that we undoubtedly have broken some things. I could see that every broken chair and window and plate meant a heartthrob to him, but he only looked up at me with his wrinkled old face and smiled as he said, 'It is all right, monsieur. I understand. *C'est la guerre.*'"*

The old man opened one of his barn doors, revealing a floor littered with straw and a fringe of hobnailed American boots. A night-working detail was asleep in blankets. A sleepy voice growled out something about closing the door again, and the old man with a polite, "*Pardonnez-moi, messieurs,*" swung the wooden portal softly shut. His home—his house—his barn—his straw—*c'est la guerre.*

An evening meal of "corn willy" [canned corned beef], served on some of the mayor's remaining chinaware, was concluded by a final course of fresh spring onions. These came from the mayor's own garden just outside the door. As the cook affirmed, it was no difficulty to gather them.

"Every night Germans drop shells in the garden," he said. "I don't even have to pull 'em. Just go out in the morning and pick 'em up off the ground."

I spent part of the night in gun pits along the roadside, bordering the town. This particular battery of heavies was engaged on a night-long program of interdiction fire laid down with irregular

---

* Tr: *C'est la guerre.* Such is war.

intensity on crossroads and communication points in the enemy's back areas. Under screens of camouflage netting, these howitzers with mottled bores squatting frog-like on their carriages, intermittently vomited flame, red, green, and orange. The detonations were ear-splitting, and cannoneers relieved the recurring shocks by clapping their hands to the sides of their head and balancing on the toes each time the lanyard was pulled.

Infantry reserves were swinging along in the road directly in back of the guns. They were moving up to forward positions, and they sang in an undertone as they moved in open order.

Glor—ree—us, Glor—ree—us!
One keg of beer for the four of us.
Glory be to Mike there are no more of us,
For four of us can drink it all alone.

A train of ammunition trucks, timed to arrive at the moment when the road was unoccupied, put in appearance as the end of the infantry column passed, and the captain in charge urged the men on to speedy unloading and fumed over delays by reason of darkness. The men received big shells in their arms and carried them to the roadside dumps, where they were piled in readiness for the guns. The road was in an exposed position, and this active battery was liable to draw enemy fire at any time, so

Before Cantigny

the ammunition train captain was anxious to get his charges away in a hurry.

His fears were not without foundation, because in the midst of the unloading, one German missile arrived in a nearby field and sprayed the roadway with steel just as everyone flattened out on the ground. Five ammunition hustlers arose with minor cuts, and one driver was swearing at the shell fragment which had gone through the radiator of his truck and liberated the water contents. The unloading was completed with all speed, and the ammunition train moved off, towing a disabled truck. With some of the gunners who had helped in unloading, I crawled into the chalk dugout to share sleeping quarters in the straw.

* * *

Our positions were located in a country almost as new to war as were the fields of Flanders in the fall of '14. A little over a month before, it had all been peaceful farming land, far behind the belligerent lines. Upon our arrival, its sprouting fields of late wheat and oats were untended and bearing their first harvest of shell craters.

The abandoned villages now occupied by troops told once more the mute tales of the homeless. The villagers, old men, old women, and children, had fled, driving before them their cows and farm animals, even as they themselves had been driven back by the train of German shells. In their deserted cottages remained the fresh traces of their departure and the ruthless rupturing of home ties, generations-old.

On every hand were evidences of the reborn war of semi-movement. One day I would see a battery of light guns swing into position by a roadside, see an observing officer mount by ladder to a treetop and direct the firing of numberless rounds into the rumbling east. By the next morning, they would have changed position, rumbled off to other parts, leaving beside the road only the marks of their cannon wheels and mounds of empty shell cases.

Between our infantry lines and those of the German, there was yet to grow the complete web of woven wire entanglements that marred the landscapes on the long-established fronts. Still standing, silent sentinels over some of our front-line positions were trees, church steeples, dwellings, and barns that as yet had not been leveled to the ground. Dugouts had begun to show their entrances in the surface of the ground, and crossroads had started to sprout with rudely constructed shelters. Fat sandbags were just taking the places of potted geraniums on the sills of first-floor windows. War's toll was being exacted daily, but the country had yet to pay the full price. It was going through that process of degeneration toward the stripped and barren, but it still held much of its erstwhile beauty.

Before Cantigny

Those days before Cantigny were marked by particularly heavy artillery fire. The ordnance duel was unrelenting, and the daily exchange of shells reached an aggregate far in excess of anything that the First Division had ever experienced before.

The small nameless village that we occupied almost opposite the German position in Cantigny seemed to receive particular attention from the enemy artillery. In retaliation, our guns almost leveled Cantigny and a nearby village which the enemy occupied. Every hour, under the rain of death, the work of digging was continued, and the men doing it needed no urging from their officers. There was something sinister and emphatic about the whine of a "two-ten German H[igh] E[xplosive]" that inspired one with a desire to start for the antipodes by the shortest and most direct route.

This taste of the war of semi-movement was appreciated by the American soldier. It had in it a dash of novelty, lacking in the position warfare to which he had become accustomed in the mud and marsh of the Moselle and the Meuse. For one thing, there were better and cleaner billets than had ever been encountered before by our men. Fresh, unthrashed oats and fragrant hay had been found in the hurriedly abandoned lofts back of the line and in the caves and cellars nearer the front.

In many places the men were sleeping on feather mattresses in old-fashioned wooden bedsteads that had been removed from jeopardy above ground to comparative safety below. Whole caves were furnished, and not badly furnished, by this salvage of furniture, much of which would have brought fancy prices in any collection of antiques.

Beyond the villages, our riflemen found protection in quickly scraped holes in the ground. There were some trenches, but they were not contiguous. "No man's land" was an area of uncertain boundary. Our gunners had quarters burrowed into the chalk not far from their gun pits. All communication and the bringing up of shells and food were conducted under cover of darkness. Under such conditions, we lived and waited for the order to go forward.

Our sector in that battle of the Somme was so situated that the opposing lines ran north and south. The enemy was between us and the rising sun. Behind our rear echelons was the main road between Amiens and Beauvais. Amiens, the objective of the German drive, was thirty-five kilometers away on our left; Beauvais was the same distance on our right and two hours by train from Paris.

We were eager for the fight. The graves of our dead dotted new fields in France. We were holding with the French on the Picardy line. We were between the Germans and the sea. We were before Cantigny.

The Rush of the Raiders

While the First U.S. Division was executing in Picardy, a small, planned operation which resulted in the capture of the German fortified positions in the town of Cantigny, other American divisions at other parts along the line were indulging in that most common of frontal diversions—the raid.

I was a party to one of these affairs on the Toul front. The 26th Division, composed of National Guard troops from New England, made the raid. On Memorial Day, I had seen those men of the Yankee Division decorating the graves of their dead in a little cemetery back of the line. By the dawning light of the next morning, I saw them come trooping back across no man's land after successfully decorating the enemy positions with German graves.

It was evening when we dismissed our motor in the ruined village of Hammondville and came into first contact with the American soldiers that had been selected for the raid. Their engineers were at work in the street connecting sections of long dynamite-loaded pipes which were to be used to blast an ingress through the enemy's wire. In interested circles about them were men who were to make the dash through the break even before the smoke cleared and the debris ceased falling. They were to be distinguished from the village garrison by the fact that the helmets worn by the raiders were covered with burlap and some of them had their faces blackened.

In the failing evening light, we walked on through several heaps of stone and rafters that had once been villages and were stopped by a military policeman who inquired in broad Irish brogue for our passes. These meeting with his satisfaction, he advised us to avoid the road ahead with its dangerous twist, known as "Dead Man's Curve," for the reason that the enemy was at that minute placing his evening contribution of shells in that vicinity. Acting on the policeman's suggestion, we took a shortcut across fields rich with shell holes. Old craters were grown over with the grass and mustard flowers with which this country abounds at this time of year. Newer punctures showed as wounds in the yellow soil and contained pools of evil-smelling water, green with scum.

Under the protection of a ridge, which at least screened us from direct enemy observation, we advanced toward the jagged skyline of a ruined village on the crest. The odor of open graves befouled the sheltered slope, indicating that enemy shells had penetrated its small protection and disturbed the final dugouts of the fallen.

Once in the village of Beaumont, we followed the winding duckboards and were led by small signs painted on wood to the colonel's headquarters. We descended the stone steps beneath a rickety-looking ruin and entered.

"Guests for our party" was the colonel's greeting. The command post had a long, narrow interior which was well lighted but poorly ventilated, the walls and floor were of wood, and a low-beamed ceiling was supported by timbers. "Well, I think it will be a good show."

"We are sending over a little party of new boys just for practice and a 'look-see' in Hunland.[1] We have two companies in this regiment which feel they've sorter been left out on most of the fun to date, so this affair has been arranged for them. We put the plans together last week and pushed the boys through three days of training for it back of the lines. They're fit as fiddlers tonight, and it looks like there'll be no interruption to their pleasure.

"No one man in the world, be he correspondent or soldier, could see every angle of even so small a thing as a little raid like this," the colonel explained. "What you can't see, you have got to imagine. I'm suggesting that you stay right in here for the show. That telephone on my adjutant's desk is the web center of all things occurring in this sector tonight, and the closer you are to it, the more you can see and learn. Lieutenant Warren will take you up the road first and give you a look out of the observatory so you'll know in what part of Germany our tourists are going to explore."

And They Thought We Wouldn't Fight

Darkness had fallen when we emerged, but there were sufficient stars out to show up the outline of the gaping walls on either side of our way. We passed a number of sentries and entered a black hole in the wall of a ruin. After stumbling over the uneven floor in a darkened passage for some minutes, we entered a small room where several officers were gathered around a table on which two burning candles were stuck in bottles. Our guide, stepping to one end of the room, pulled aside a blanket curtain and passed through a narrow doorway. We followed.

Up a narrow, steep wooden stairway between two walls of solid masonry, not over two feet apart, we passed, and arrived on a none-too-stable wooded runway with a guide rail on either side. Looking up through the ragged remains of the wooden roof frame, now almost nude of tiles, we could see the starry sky. Proceeding along the runway, we arrived, somewhere in that cluster of ruins, in a darkened chamber whose interior blackness was relieved by a lighter slit, an opening facing the enemy.

Against the starry skyline, we could see the black outline of a flat tableland in the left distance which we knew to be that part of the heights of Meuse for whose commanding ridge there have been so many violent contests between the close-locked lines in the forest of Apremont. More to the center of the picture stood Mont Sec, detached from the range and pushing its summit up through the lowland

The Rush of the Raiders

mist like the dorsal fin of a porpoise in a calm sea. On the right the lowland extended to indistinct distances, where it blended with the horizon.

In all that expanse of quiet night, there was not a single flicker of light, and at that time not a sound to indicate that unmentionable numbers of our men were facing one another in parallel ditches across the silent moor.

"See that clump of trees way out there?" said the lieutenant, directing our vision with his arm. "Now then, hold your hand at arm's length in front of you, straight along a line from your eyes along the left edge of your hand to that clump of trees. Now then, look right along the right edge of your hand, and you will be looking at Richecourt. The Boche[2] hold it. We go in on the right of that tonight."

We looked as per instructions and saw nothing. As far as we were concerned, Richecourt was a daylight view, but these owls of the lookout knew its location as well as they knew the streets of their native towns back in New England. We returned to the colonel's command post, where cots were provided, and we turned in for a few hours' sleep on the promise of being called in time.

It was 2 A.M. when we were summoned to command post for the colonel's explanation of the night's plans. The regimental commander, smoking a long pipe with a curved stem, sat in front of a map on which he conducted the exposition.

"Here," he said, placing his finger on a section of the line marking the American trenches, "is the point of departure. That's the jumping-off place. These X marks running between the lines is the enemy wire, and here, and here, and here are where we blow it up. We reach the German trenches at these points and clean up. Then the men follow the enemy communicating trenches, penetrate three hundred meters to the east edge of Richecourt, and return.

"Zero hour is 2:30. It's now 2:10. Our raiders have left their trenches already. They are out in no man's land now. The engineers are with them carrying explosives for the wire. There are stretcher bearers in the party to bring back our wounded and also signalmen right behind them with wire and one telephone. The reports from that wire are relayed here, and we will also be kept informed by runners. The whole party has thirty minutes in which to crawl forward and place explosives under the wire. They will have things in readiness by 2:30, and then the show begins."

Five minutes before the hour, I stepped out of the dugout and looked at the silent sky toward the front. Not even a star shell disturbed the blue-black starlight. The guns were quiet. Five minutes more, and all this was to change into an inferno of sound and light, flash and crash. There is always that minute of uncertainty before the raiding hour when the tensity of the situation becomes almost painful. Has

The Rush of the Raiders

the enemy happened to become aware of the plans? Have our men been deprived of the needed element of surprise? But for the thousands of meters behind us, we know that in black battery pits anxious crews are standing beside their loaded pieces waiting to greet the tick of 2:30 with the jerk of the lanyard.

Suddenly the earth trembles. Through the dugout window facing back from the lines, I see the night sky burst livid with light. A second later and the crash reaches our ears. It is deafening. Now we hear the whine of shells as they burn the air overhead. The telephone bell rings.

"Yes, this is Boston," the adjutant speaks into the receiver. We listen breathlessly. Has something gone wrong at the last minute?

"Right, I have it," said the adjutant, hanging up the receiver and turning to the colonel; "X-4 reports barrage dropped on schedule."

"Good," said the colonel. "Gentlemen, here's what's happening. Our shells are this minute falling all along the German front line, in front of the part selected for the raid and on both flanks. Now then, this section of the enemy's position is confined in a box barrage which is pounding in his front and is placing a curtain of fire on his left and his right and another in his rear. Any German within the confines of that box trying to get out will have a damn hard time, and so will any who try to come through it to help him."

Over the Top, *soldiers charging from a trench, stereo card*

The Rush of the Raiders

"Boston talking," the adjutant is making answer over the telephone. He repeats the message. "233, all the wire blown up, right."

"Fine," says the colonel. "Now they are advancing and right in front of them is another rolling barrage of shells which is creeping forward on the German lines at the same pace our men are walking. They are walking in extended order behind it. At the same time our artillery has taken care of the enemy's guns by this time so that no German barrage will be able to come down on our raiders. Our guns for the last three minutes have been dumping gas and high explosives on every battery position behind the German lines. That's called 'neutralization.'"

2:45. "Boston talking." The adjutant turns to the colonel and repeats, "Pittsburgh wants to know if there's much coming in here."

"Tell them nothing to amount to anything," replies the colonel, and the adjutant repeats the message over the wire. As he finished, one German shell did land so close to the dugout that the door blew open. The officer stepped to the opening and called out into the darkness.

"Gas guard. Smell anything?"

"Nothing, sir. Think they are only high explosives."

2:47. "Boston talking. Enemy sent up one red, one green rocket and then three green rockets from B-14," the adjutant repeats.

"Where is that report from?" asks the colonel.

"The operator at Jamestown, sir," replies the adjutant.

"Be ready for some gas, gentlemen," says the colonel. "I think that's Fritzie's order for the stink. Orderly, put down gas covers on the doors and windows."

I watched the man unroll the chemically dampened blankets over the doors and windows.

3:02. "Storming party reports unhindered progress. No enemy encountered yet."

This was the first message back from the raiders. It had been sent over the wire and the instruments they carried with them, and then relayed to the colonel's command post.

3:05. "Boston talking. Hello, yes, nothing coming in here to amount to anything. Just had a gas warning, but none arrived yet."

3:07. "Boston talking—Yes, all right" (turning to colonel); "operator just received message from storming party 'so far so good.'"

"Not so bad for thirty-seven minutes after opening of the operation," remarks the colonel.

With gas mask at alert, I walked out for a breath of fresh air. The atmosphere in a crowded dugout is stifling. From guns still roaring in the rear and from in front came the trampling sound of shells arriving on German positions. The first hints of dawn were in the sky. I returned in time to note the hour and hear:

The Rush of the Raiders

3:21. "Boston talking—23 reports that the barrage called for in their sector was because the enemy had advanced within two hundred yards of his first position. Evidently they wanted to start something, but the barrage nipped them, and they fell back fast."

3:33. "Boston talking—white stars reported from Richecourt."

"They must be on their way back by this time," says the colonel, looking at his watch.

3:42. "Boston talking—signalman with the party reports everything O.K."

"We don't know yet whether they have had any losses or got any prisoners," the colonel remarks. "But the mechanism seems to have functioned just as well as it did in the last raid. We didn't get a prisoner that time, but I sorter feel that the boys will bring back a couple with them tonight."

3:49. "Boston talking—G-9 reports some of the raiding party has returned and passed that point."

"Came back pretty quick, don't you think so, Major?" said the colonel with some pride. "Must have returned over the top."

It is 3:55 when we hear fast footsteps on the stone stairs leading down to the dugout entrance. There is a sharp rap on the door followed by the colonel's command, "Come in."

A medium-height private of stocky build, with shoulders heaving from labored breathing and face wet with sweat, enters. He removes his helmet, revealing disordered blond hair. He faces the colonel and salutes.

"Sir, Sergeant Ransom reports with message from liaison officer. All groups reached the objectives. No enemy encountered on the right, but a party on the left is believed to be returning with prisoners. We blew up their dugouts and left their front line in flames."

"Good work, boy," says the colonel, rising and shaking the runner's hand. "You got here damn quick. Did you come by the Lincoln trench?"

"No, sir, I came over the top from the battalion post. Would have been here quicker, but two of us had to carry back one boy to that point before I could get relieved."

"Wounded?"

"No, sir—dead."

"Who was it?" asks the young lieutenant.

"Private Kater, sir, my squad mate."

As the sergeant raised his hand in parting salute, all of us saw suspended from his right wrist a most formidable weapon, apparently of his own construction. It was a pick handle with a heavy iron knob on one end and the same end cushioned with a mass of barbed wire rolled up like a ball of yarn. He smiled as he noticed our gaze.

"It's the persuader, sir," he said. "We all carried them."

The Rush of the Raiders

He had hardly quitted the door when another heavily breathing figure with shirt half torn off by barbed wire appeared.

"K Company got there, sir; beg pardon, sir. I mean sir, Sergeant Wiltur reports, sir, with message from liaison officer. All groups reached the objectives. They left their dugouts blazing and brought back one machine gun and three prisoners."

"Very good, Sergeant," said the colonel. "Orderly, get some coffee for these runners."

"I'd like to see the doctor first, sir," said the runner with the torn shirt. "Got my hand and arm cut in the wire."

"Very well," said the colonel, turning to the rest of the party, "I knew my boys would bring back bacon."

More footsteps on the entrance stairway, and two men entered carrying something between them. Sweat had streaked through the charcoal coating on their faces, leaving striped zebra-like countenances.

"Lieutenant Burlon's compliments, sir," said the first man. "Here's one of their machine guns."

"Who got it?" inquired the colonel.

"Me and him, sir."

"How did you get it?"

"We just rolled 'em off it and took it."

"Rolled who off of it?"

"Two Germans, sir."

"What were they doing all that time?"

U.S. Infantry charging an enemy line

The Rush of the Raiders

"Why, sir, they weren't doing anything. They were dead."

"Oh, very well, then," said the colonel. "How did you happen to find the machine gun?"

"We knew where it was before we went over, sir," said the man simply. "We were assigned to get it and bring it back. We expected we'd have to fight for it, but I guess our barrage laid out the crew. Anyhow we rushed to the position and found them dead."

"All right," said the colonel. "Return to your platoon. Leave the gun here. It will be returned to you later and will be your property."

I went out with the machine-gun captors and walked with them to the road. There was the hum of motors high overhead, and we knew that American planes were above, going forward to observe and photograph German positions before the effects of our bombardments could be repaired. A line of flame and smoke pouring up from the enemy's front line showed where their dugouts and shelters were still burning.

Daylight was pouring down on a ruined village street, up which marched the returning raiders without thought of order. They were a happy, gleeful party, with helmets tipped back from their young faces, wet and dirty, with rifles swung over their shoulders and the persuaders dangling from their wrists. Their wrap puttees were mostly in tatters from the contact with the entanglements through which they had penetrated.

As they approached, I saw the cause for some of the jocularity. It was a chubby little boyish figure, who sat perched up on the right shoulder of a tall, husky Irish sergeant. The figure steadied itself by grasping the sergeant's helmet with his left hand. The sergeant steadied him by holding one right arm around his legs.

But there was no smile on the face of the thus transformed object. His chubby countenance was one of easily understood concern. He was not a day over sixteen years, and this was quite some experience for him. He was one of the German prisoners, and these happy youngsters from across the seas were bringing him in almost with as much importance as though he had been a football hero. He was unhurt, and it was unnecessary to carry him, but this tribute was voluntarily added, not only as an indication of extreme interest, but to reassure the juvenile captive of the kindly intentions of his captors.

"Jiggers, here's the colonel's dugout," one voice shouted. "Put him down to walk, now."

The big sergeant acted on the suggestion, and the little Fritz was lowered to the ground. He immediately caught step with the big sergeant and took up the latter's long stride with his short legs and feet encased in clumsy German boots. His

The Rush of the Raiders

soiled uniform had been the German field gray-green. His helmet was gone, but he wore well back on his head the flat round cloth cap. With his fat cheeks he looked like a typical baker's boy, and one almost expected to see him carrying a tray of rolls on his head.

"For the luva Mike, Tim," shouted an ambulance man, "do you call that a prisoner?"

"Sure he does look like a half portion," replied Sergeant Tim with a smile. "We got two hundred francs for a whole one. I don't know what we can cash this one in for."

"He ought to be worth more," someone said; "that barrage cost a million dollars. He's the million-dollar baby of the raid."

"Sergeant, I'm not kidding," came one serious voice. "Why turn him in as a prisoner? I like the kid's looks. Why can't we keep him for the company mascot?"

The discussion ended when the sergeant and his small charge disappeared into the colonel's quarters for the inevitable questioning that all prisoners must go through. Several wounded were lying on the stretchers in front of the first-aid dugout waiting for returning ambulances and passing the time meanwhile by smoking cigarettes and explaining how close each of them had been to the shell that exploded and "got 'em."

But little of the talk was devoted to themselves.

And They Thought We Wouldn't Fight

They were all praise for the little chaplain from New England who, without arms, went over the top with "his boys" and came back with them. It was their opinion that their regiment had some sky pilot. And it was mine, also.

NOTES

1. Hunland: Germany. "Hun" was a propaganda term used by the British and Americans to compare German soldiers to the barbaric tribes who invaded Europe in the fourth century.

2. Boche: a disparaging French term for German soldiers.

On Leave in Paris

"So this—is paris,"—this observation spoken in mock seriousness, in a George Cohan nasal drawl and accompanied by a stiff and stagy wave of the arm, was the customary facetious password with which American soldiers on leave or on mission announced their presence in the capital of France.

Paris, the beautiful—Paris, the gay—Paris, the historical—Paris, the artistic—Paris, the only Paris, opened her arms to the American soldier and proceeded toward his enlightenment and entertainment on the sole policy that nothing was too good for him.

I saw the first American soldiers under arms reach Paris. It was early in the morning of July 3, 1917, when this first American troop train pulled into the Gare d'Austerlitz. It was early in the morning, yet Paris was there to give them a welcome. The streets outside the station were jammed with crowds. They had seen Pershing; they had seen our staff officers and headquarters details, but now they wanted to see the type of our actual fighting men— they wanted to see the American *poilus*—the men who were to carry the Stars and Stripes over the top.

The men left the cars and lined up in the station yard. It had been a long fifteen-hour night ride, and the cramped quarters of the troop train had permitted but little sleep. There was no opportunity for them to breakfast or wash before they were put on exhibition. Naturally, they were somewhat nervous.

The standing line was ordered to produce its mess cups and hold them forward. Down the line came a bevy of pretty French girls, wearing the uniform of Red Cross nurses. They carried canisters of black coffee and baskets of cigarettes. They ladled out steaming cupfuls of the black liquid to the men. The incident gave our men their first surprise.

Rum or alcohol has never been a part of the United States army ration. In the memory of the oldest old-timers in the ranks of our old regular army, "joy water" had never been issued. On the other hand, its use had always been strictly forbidden in the company messes. Our men never expected it. Thus it was that, with no other idea occurring to them, they extended their mess cups to be filled with what they thought was simply strong hot coffee. Not one of them had the slightest suspicion that the French cooks who had prepared that coffee for their new American brothers in arms had put a stick in it—had added just that portion of cognac which they had considered necessary to open a man's eyes and make him pick up his heels after a long night in a troop train.

I watched one old-timer in the ranks as he lifted the tin cup to his lips and took the initial gulp. Then he lowered the cup. Across his face there

Souvenir postcard of Paris sent by a soldier to his sweetheart in Ohio

dawned first an expression of curious suspicion, then a look of satisfied recognition, and then a smile of pleased surprise, which he followed with an audible smacking of the lips. He finished the cup and allowed quite casually that he could stand another.

"So this is Paris,"—well, it wasn't half bad to start with. With that "coffee" under their belts, the men responded snappily to the march order, and in column of four, they swung into line and moved out of the station yard, at the heels of their own band, which played a stirring marching air.

Paris claimed them for her own. All that the war had left of Paris's gay life, all the lights that still burned, all the music that still played, all the pretty smiles that had never been reduced in their quality or quantity, all that Paris had to make one carefree and glad to be alive—all belonged that day to that pioneer band of American infantrymen.

The women kissed them on the street. Gray-headed men removed their hats to them and shook their hands, and street boys followed in groups at their heels making the air ring with shrill "*vive*"s. There were not many of them, only three companies. The men looked trim and clean-cut. They were tall and husky-looking, and the snap with which they walked was good to the eyes of old Paris that loves verve.

With a thirty-two-inch stride that made their following admirers stretch their legs, the boys in khaki marched from the Austerlitz station to the

On Leave in Paris

Neuilly barracks over a mile away, where they went into quarters. Paris was in gala attire. In preparation for the celebration of the following day, the shop windows and building fronts were decked with American flags.

Along the line of march, traffic piled up at the street intersections, and the gendarmes were unable to prevent the crowds from overflowing the sidewalks and pressing out into the streets, where they could smile their greetings and throw flowers at closer range. A sergeant flanking a column stopped involuntarily when a woman on the curb reached out, grabbed his free hand, and kissed it. A snicker ran through the platoon as the sergeant, with face red beneath the tan, withdrew his hand and recaught his step. He gave the snickering squads a stern, "Eyes front!" and tried to look at ease.

How the bands played that day! How the crowds cheered! How the flags and handkerchiefs and hats waved in the air, and how thousands of throats volleyed the "*vive*"s! This was the reception of our first fighting men. But on the following day they received even a greater demonstration when they marched through the streets of the city on parade and participated in the first Parisian celebration of American Independence Day.

Parisians said that never before had Paris shown so many flags, not even during the days three years before when the sons of France had marched away to keep the Germans out of Paris. It seemed that the customary clusters of Allied flags had been almost entirely replaced for the day by groups composed solely of the French tri-color and the Stars and Stripes. Taxis and fiacres [small hired carriages] flew flags and bunting from all attachable places. Flag venders did wholesale business on the crowded streets. Street singers sang patriotic parodies, eulogizing Uncle Sam and his nephews, and garnered harvests of *sous* for their efforts.

The three companies of our regulars marched with a regiment of French colonials, all veterans of the war and many of them incapacitated for front service through wounds and age. French soldiers on leave from the trenches and still bearing the mud stains of the battlefront life cheered from the sidewalks. Bevies of midinettes [salesgirls] waved their aprons from the windows of millinery shops. Some of them shouted, "*Vive les Teddies!*" America—the great, good America—the sister republic from across the seas was spoken of and shouted all day long. Paris capitulated unconditionally to three companies of American infantry.

From that day on, every American soldier visiting Paris has been made to feel himself at home. And the unrestricted hospitality did not seem to be the result of an initial wave of enthusiasm. It was continuous. For months afterward, anyone wearing an American uniform along the boulevards could

On Leave in Paris

hear behind him dulcet whispers that carried the words *très gentil* [very kind].

At first, our enlisted men on leave in Paris or detailed for work in the city were quartered in the old Pipincerie Barracks, where other soldiers from all of the Allied armies in the world were quartered. Our men mingled with British Tommies, swarthy Italians and Portuguese, tall, blond Russians, French *poilus*, Canadians, Australians, and New Zealanders. At considerable expense to these comrades in arms, our men instructed them in the all-American art of plain and fancy dice rolling.

Later, when our numbers in Paris increased, other arrangements for housing were made. The American policing of Paris, under the direction of the Expeditionary provost general, Brigadier General Hillaire, was turned over to the marines. Whether it was that our men conducted themselves in Paris with the orderliness of a guest at the home of his host, or whether it was that the marines with their remarkable discipline suppressed from all view any too hearty outbursts of American exuberance, it must be said that the appearance and the bearing of American soldiers in Paris were always above reproach.

I have never heard of one being seen intoxicated in Paris, in spite of the fact that more opportunities presented themselves for drinking than had ever before been presented to an American army. The privilege of sitting at a table in front of a sidewalk

Le Théâtre Français, postcard sent by "sailors mail" to New Jersey. "Having the time of my life in this, one of the most wonderful cities of the world."

On Leave in Paris

café on a busy boulevard and drinking a small glass of beer unmolested was one that our men did not take advantage of. It was against the law to serve any of the stronger liqueurs to men in uniform, but beer and light wines were obtainable all the time. All cafés closed at 9:30. In spite of the ever-present opportunity to obtain beverages of the above character, there was many and many an American soldier who tramped the boulevards and canvassed the cafés, drug stores, and delicatessen shops in search of a much-desired, inexistent ice-cream soda.

Many of our men spent their days most seriously and most studiously, learning the mysteries of transportation on the buses and the Paris underground system, while they pored over their guidebooks and digested pages of information concerning the points of interest that Paris had to offer. Holidays found them shuffling through the tiled corridors of the Invalides or looking down into the deep crypt at the granite tomb of the great Napoleon. In the galleries of the Louvre, the gardens of the Tuilleries, or at the Luxembourg, the American uniform was ever present. At least one day out of every ten-day leave was spent in the palace and the grounds at Versailles.

The theaters of Paris offered a continual change of amusement. One of the most popular among these was the Folies Bergère. Some of our men didn't realize until after they entered the place that it was a French theater. Due to the French pronunciation of the name, some of the American soldiers got the idea that it was a saloon run by an Irishman by the name of Foley. "Bergère" to some was unpronounceable, so the Folies Bergère was most popularly known in our ranks as "Foley's place."

Another popular amusement place was the Casino de Paris, where an echo from America was supplied by an American Negro jazz band, which dispensed its questionable music in the *promenoir* [huge lobby] during the intermission. There were five Negroes in the orchestra, and each one of them seemed to have an ardent dislike for the remaining four. Individually they manifested their mutual contempt by turning their backs on one another while they played. Strange as it may seem, a most fascinating type of harmony resulted, producing much swaying of shoulders, nodding of heads, and snapping of fingers among the American soldiers in the crowd. French men and women, with their old-world musical taste, would consider the musical gymnastics of the demented drummer in the orchestra, then survey the swaying Americans, and come to the conclusion that the world had gone plumb to hell.[1]

NOTES

1. Jazz became very popular in France during and after the war. Many African American musicians, most notably Josephine Baker, became famous in France.

Château-Thierry
and the Bois de Belleau

I HAVE ENDEAVORED to show in preceding chapters the development of the young American army in France from a mere handful of new troops up to the creation of units capable of independent action on the front. Only that intense and thorough training made it possible for our oversea forces to play the veteran part they did play in the great Second Battle of the Marne.

The battle developed as a third phase of the enemy's western front offensives of the year. The increasing strength of the American forces overseas forced Germany to put forth her utmost efforts in the forlorn hope of gaining a decision in the field before the Allied lines could have the advantage of America's weight.

On March 21, the Germans had launched their first powerful offensive on a front of fifty miles from Arras to Noyon in Picardy and had advanced their lines from St. Quentin to the outskirts of Amiens.

On April 9, the German hordes struck again in Flanders on a front of twenty miles from Lens northward to the River Lys and had cut into the Allied front as far as Armentières.

There followed what was considered an abnormal delay in the third act of the demonstration. It was known that the Germans were engaged in making elaborate arrangements for this midsummer push. It was the enemy hope in this great offensive to strike a final effective blow against the hard-pressed Allied line before America's rising power could be thrown into the fight.

The blow fell on the morning of May 27. The front selected for the assault was twenty-five miles in width, extending from the Ailette near Vauxaillon to the Aisne-Marne Canal near Brimont. The Prussian crown prince was the titular chief of the group of armies used in the assault. One of these forces was the army of General von Boehm, which before the attack had numbered only nine divisions and had extended from the Oise at Noyon to east of Craponne. The other army was that of General Fritz von Bülow, previously composed of eight divisions and supporting a front that extended from Craponne across the Rheims front to Suippes, near Auberive. On the day of the attack, these armies had been strengthened to twice their normal number of divisions, and subsequently captured German plans revealed that the enemy expected to use forty-five divisions or practically half a million men in the onslaught.

The battle began at dawn. It was directed against the weakly held French positions on the Chemin des Dames. It was preceded by a three-hour bom-

Château-Thierry and the Bois de Belleau

bardment of terrific intensity. The French defenders were outnumbered four to one. The Germans put down a rolling barrage that was two miles deep. It destroyed all wire communications and flooded battery emplacements and machine gun posts with every brand of poison gas known to German *kultur*. Dust and artificial smoke clouds separated the defenders into small groups and screened the attacking waves until they had actually penetrated the French positions.

The French fought hard to resist the enemy flood across the Chemin des Dames with its ground sacred with tragic memories,[1] but a withdrawal was necessary. The French command was forced to order a retreat to the Aisne. Hard-fighting French divisions and some units of the British Fifth Army, which had been badly hit in Picardy in March, made an orderly withdrawal southward.

On the second day of the fight, the enemy made a strong thrust toward Soissons, and after keeping the city under continual bombardment, succeeded in overcoming all resistance and occupying the city on May 29. On the first day of the attack alone, twelve thousand explosive, incendiary, and poison gas shells were hurled in among the hospitals in Soissons. American ambulance units did heroic work in the removal of the wounded.

The Germans forced a crossing on the Aisne. On the following day, May 30, they had crossed the

And They Thought We Wouldn't Fight

Vesle River and had captured Fère-en-Tardenois. On the following day their victorious hordes had reached the Marne and were closing in on Château-Thierry.

Some idea of the terrific strength of the enemy offensive may be gained from a recapitulation which would show that in five days the Germans had pushed through five successive lines of Allied defense and had penetrated more than twenty-five miles. On the first day, they had captured the Chemin des Dames; on the second day, they had overcome all resistance on the Aisne; on the third day, their forces, pushing southward, had crossed the Vesle River; on the fourth day, they had destroyed the lines of resistance along the Ourcq; on the fifth day, they had reached the Marne.

It was a crisis. The battle front formed a vast triangle, with the apex pointing southward toward Paris. The west side of the triangle extended fifty miles northward from the Marne to the Oise near Noyon. The east side of the triangle ran northeastward thirty miles to Rheims. The point of this new thrust at Paris rested on the north bank of the Marne at Château-Thierry. The enemy had advanced to within forty miles of the capital of France; the fate of the Allied world hung in the balance.

Undoubtedly I am prejudiced, but I like to feel that I know the real reason why the German hordes stopped at Château-Thierry on the north bank of

Château-Thierry and the Bois de Belleau

the Marne. To me that reason will always be this—because on the south bank of the Marne stood the Americans.

On that day and in that event, there materialized the German fears which had urged them on to such great speed and violence. In the eleventh hour, there at the peak of the German thrust, there at the climax of Germany's triumphant advances, there at the point where a military decision for the enemy seemed almost within grasp, there and then the American soldier stepped into the breach to save the democracy of the world.

The Marne River makes a loop at this place, and Château-Thierry lies on both banks. The Marne there is called a river, but it would hardly come up to the American understanding of the word. The waterway is more like a canal with banks built up with stone blocks. There are streets on either bank, and these, being the principal streets of the town, are bordered with comparatively high buildings.

While the Germans were on the outskirts of the city, American forces had made brilliant counterattacks on both sides. To the west of Château-Thierry, the German advance forces, seeking to penetrate Neuilly Wood, had been hurled back by our young troops. To the east of Château-Thierry, the enemy had succeeded in crossing the Marne in the vicinity of Jaulgonne.

This operation was carried out by the German

And They Thought We Wouldn't Fight

36th Division. On the night of May 30, at a point where the Marne looped northward eight miles to the east of Château-Thierry, the enemy succeeded in putting a few men across the river.

Along the south bank of the river at that place, the Paris-Châlons [rail line] ran through a number of deep cuts and one tunnel. The enemy took shelter in these natural protections. They suffered serious losses from the Allied artillery, which also destroyed some of their pontoons across the river, but in spite of this, the Germans succeeded in re-enforcing the units on the south bank to the strength of about a battalion.

Almost at the same time, the French defenders at this place received re-enforcements from the Americans. Units of the 3rd United States Regular Division and the 28th U.S. Division, comprised largely of Pennsylvania National Guardsmen, were rushed forward from training areas, miles back of the line, where they were engaged in fitting themselves for line duty. These incompletely trained American units abandoned their bayonet-stabbing of gunny-sacks and make-believe warfare to rush forward into the real thing.

On June 2, these Americans, under command of French officers, began the counterattack to sweep the Germans back from the south bank. By that time, the enemy had succeeded in putting twenty-two light bridges across the Marne and had estab-

Château-Thierry and the Bois de Belleau

lished a strong bridgehead position with a number of machine guns and a strong force of men in the railway station on the south bank of the river opposite Jaulgonne.

This position was attacked frontally by the Americans and French. Our novices in battle were guilty of numerous so-called strategical blunders, but in the main purpose of killing the enemy, they proved irresistible. The Germans broke and ran. At the same time, the French artillery lowered a terrific barrage on the bridges crossing the river, with the result that many of the fleeing enemy were killed and more drowned. Only thirty or forty escaped by swimming. One hundred of them threw down their arms and surrendered. The remainder of the battalion was wiped out. At the close of the engagement, the Americans and the French were in full command of the south bank.

But it was in Château-Thierry itself that the Germans made their most determined effort to cross the river and get a footing on the south bank, and it was there, again, that their efforts were frustrated by our forces. On May 31, American machine-gun units, then in training seventy-five kilometers south of the Marne, were hurriedly bundled into motor lorries [trucks] and rushed northward into Château-Thierry.

The Germans were advancing their patrols into the north side of the city. They were pouring down the streets in large numbers, with the evident purpose of crossing the bridges and establishing themselves on the south bank.

It was four o'clock in the afternoon of May 31 that those American machine gunners got their first glimpse of real war. That night while the German artillery raked the south bank of the river with high explosive shells, those Americans, shouldering their machine guns, marched into the city and took up defensive positions on the south bank of the river.

During the night, many houses were turned into ruins. Shells striking the railroad station had caused it to burn. In the red glare our men saw the houses about them collapse under clouds of dust and debris. Under cover of darkness, the Germans filtered through the streets on the north side of the river. The American machine gunners went into position in the windows of houses on the south bank and in gardens between the houses, and from these positions it was possible to command all of the bridge approaches and streets leading to the river on the opposite side.

With the coming of dawn, the Germans began to make their rushes for the bridges. Small compact forces would dart forward carrying light machine guns and ammunition with them. They encountered a terrific burst of American fire and wilted in front of it. Those that survived crawled back to the shelter of protecting walls, where they were re-

Château-Thierry and the Bois de Belleau

enforced with fresh units, and again the massed formations charged down the streets toward the bridges. The slaughter of Germans increased until the approaches were dotted with bodies of the enemy slain.

On June 1, the Germans having consolidated positions on the hills commanding the city from the north, they directed a terrific artillery and machine-gun fire into our exposed positions on the south bank.

On the following day, the Germans were in occupation of all the houses facing the north bank of the river and could be seen from time to time darting from one shelter to another. Throughout the day their artillery maintained a terrific downpour of shells on the positions held by our men on the south bank. So intense was the rifle fire and activity of snipers, that it meant death to appear in the open. The Americans manned their guns throughout the day but refrained from indulging in machine-gun fire because it was not desired to reveal the locations of the guns. Nightfall approached with a quiet that was deadly ominous of impending events.

At nine o'clock the enemy formations lunged forward to the attack. Their dense masses charged down the streets leading toward the river. They sang as they advanced. The orders, as revealed in documents captured later, came straight from the high

Women walking through the rubble of Château-Thierry

Château-Thierry and the Bois de Belleau

command and demanded the acquisition of a foothold on the south bank at all costs. They paid the costs but never reached the south bank.

Our machine gunners turned the northern bank of the river into a no man's land. Their vigilance was unrelenting, and every enemy attempt to elude it met with disaster. There were serious American casualties during that terrific fire, but they were nothing in comparison with the thousand or more German dead that dotted the streets and clogged the runways of the big bridge in piles. The last night of the fight, enormous charges of explosive were placed beneath the bridge and discharged.

The bridge was destroyed. High into the air were blown bits of stone, steel, timber, debris, wreckage, and the bodies of German dead, all to fall back into the river and go bobbing up and down in the waters of the Marne.

Thus did the Americans save the day at Château-Thierry, but it became immediately necessary for the French high command to call upon our young forces for another great effort. In response to this call, the Second United States Division, including one brigade of the United States Marines, the 5th and 6th Regiments, started for the front. The division was then occupying support positions in the vicinity of Gisors behind the Picardy line. At four o'clock on the morning of May 31, the marine brigade and regiments of United States Infantry, the

9th and the 23rd Regulars, boarded camions [trucks], twenty to thirty men and their equipment in each vehicle.

They were bound eastward to the valley of the Marne. The road took them through the string of pretty villages fifteen miles to the north of Paris. The trucks loaded with United States troops soon became part of the endless traffic of war that was pouring northward and eastward toward the raging front. Our men soon became coated with the dust of the road. The French people in the villages through which they passed at top speed cheered them and threw flowers into the lorries.

The Second Division was bound for the line to the northwest of Château-Thierry. On June 1, the 6th Marines relieved the French on the support lines. The sector of the 6th Regiment joined on the left the sector held by two battalions of the 5th. The line on the right was held by the French. As the French withdrew to the rear, hard pressed by the enemy, the marines held the new first line.

The regimental headquarters of the 6th was located in a stone farmhouse at a crossroads called La Voie du Châtel, situated between the villages of Champillon and Lucy-le-Bocage. There was clear observation from that point toward the north. At five o'clock in the afternoon on that day of clear visibility, the Germans renewed their attacks from

Château-Thierry and the Bois de Belleau

the north and northeast toward a position called Hill 165, which was defended by the 5th Regiment.

The Germans advanced in two solid columns across a field of golden wheat. More than half of the two columns had left the cover of the trees and were moving in perfect order across the field, when the shrapnel fire from the American artillery in the rear got range on the target. Burst after burst of white smoke suddenly appeared in the air over the column, and under each burst the ground was marked with a circle of German dead. It was not barrage fire: it was individual firing against two individual moving targets, and its success spoke well for the training which that brigade of American artillery had received.

French aviators from above directed the fire of our guns, and from high in the air signaled down their "bravos" in congratulation on the excellent work. At the same time, the machine gunners of the 5th covered the ravines and wooded clumps with a hot fire to prevent small bodies of the enemy from infiltrating through our lines. The French marveled at the deliberateness and accuracy of our riflemen.

The Germans, unaware that a change had taken place in the personnel that faced them, reeled back demoralized and unable to understand how such a sudden show of resistance had been presented by the weakened French troops which they had been driving before them for a week. The enemy's advance had been made openly and confidently in the mistaken flush of victory. Their triumphant advances of the previous week had more than supported the statements of the German officers, who had told their men that they were on the road to Paris—the end of the war and peace. It was in this mood of victory that the enemy encountered the marines' stone wall and reeled back in surprise.

That engagement, in addition to lowering the enemy morale, deprived them of their offensive spirit and placed them on the defensive. The next few days were spent in advancing small strong points and the strengthening of positions. In broad daylight one group of marines rushed a German machine-gun pit in the open, killed or wounded every man in the crew, disabled the gun, and got back to their lines in safety.

It was at five o'clock on the bright afternoon of June 6 that the United States Marines began to carve their way into history in the battle of the Bois de Belleau. Major General Harbord,[2] former chief of staff to General Pershing, was in command of the marine brigade. Orders were received for a general advance on the brigade front. The main objectives were the eastern edge of the Bois de Belleau and the towns of Bussiares, Torcy, and Bouresches.

Owing to the difficulty of liaison in the thickets of the wood, and because of the almost impossible

Château-Thierry and the Bois de Belleau

task of directing it in conjunction with the advancing lines, the artillery preparation for the attack was necessarily brief. At five o'clock to the dot the marines moved out from the woods in perfect order and started across the wheat fields in four long waves. It was a beautiful sight, these men of ours going across those flat fields toward the tree clusters beyond from which the Germans poured a murderous machine-gun fire.

The woods were impregnated with nests of machine guns, but our advance proved irresistible. Many of our men fell, but those that survived pushed on through the woods, bayoneting right and left and firing as they charged. So sweeping was the advance that in some places small isolated units of our men found themselves with Germans both before and behind them.

The enemy put up a stubborn resistance on the left, and it was not until later in the evening that this part of the line reached the northeast edge of the woods, after it had completely surrounded a most populous machine-gun nest which was located on a rocky hill

On the right Lieutenant Robertson, with twenty survivors out of his entire platoon, emerged from the terrific enemy barrage and took the town of Bouresches at the point of the bayonet. Captain Duncan, receiving word that one marine company, with a determination to engage the enemy in hand-to-hand combat, had gone two hundred yards in advance, raced forward on the double-quick with the 96th Marine Company, and was met by a terrific machine-gun barrage from both sides of Bouresches.

Lieutenant Robertson, looking back, saw Duncan and the rest of his company going down like flies as they charged through the barrage. He saw Lieutenant Bowling get up from the ground, his face white with pain, and go stumbling ahead with a bullet in his shoulder. Duncan, carrying a stick and with his pipe in his mouth, was mowed down in the rain of lead. Robertson saw Dental Surgeon Osborne pick Duncan up. With the aid of a Hospital Corps man, they had just gained the shelter of some trees, when a shell wiped all three of them out.

In the street fighting that ensued in Bouresches, Lieutenant Robertson's orderly, Private Dunlavy, who was later killed in the defense of the town, captured one of the enemy's own machine guns and turned it against them.

In the dense woods the Germans showed their mastery of machine-gun manipulation and the method of infiltration by which they would place strong units in our rear and pour in a deadly fire. Many of these guns were located on rocky ridges, from which they could fire to all points. These marines worked with reckless courage against heavy odds, and the Germans exacted a heavy toll for

Château-Thierry and the Bois de Belleau

every machine gun that was captured or disabled, but in spite of losses, the marine advance continued.

Lieutenant Overton, commanding the 76th Company, made a brilliant charge against a strong German position at the top of a rocky hill. He and his men captured all of the guns and all of their crews. Overton was hit later when the Germans retaliated by a concentration of fire against the captured position for forty-eight hours.

Lieutenant Robertson, according to the report brought back by a regimental runner, was last seen flat on a rock not twenty yards away from one enemy gun, at which he kept shooting with an automatic in each hand. He was hit three times before he consented to let his men carry him to the rear.

In such fashion did the marines go through the Bois de Belleau. Their losses were heavy, but they did the work. The sacrifice was necessary. Paris was in danger. The marines constituted the thin line between the enemy and Paris. The marines not only held that line—they pushed it forward.

The fighting was terrific. In one battalion alone the casualties numbered 64 percent officers and 64 percent men. Several companies came out of the fighting under command of their first sergeants, all of the officers having been killed or wounded.

I witnessed some of that fighting. I was with the marines at the opening of the battle. I never saw men charge to their death with finer spirit. I am sorry that wounds prevented me from witnessing the victorious conclusion of the engagement. In view of my subsequent absence from the fight, I wish to give credit and thanks at this place to Major Frank E. Evans, who, as adjutant of the 6th Regiment of Marines, provided me with much of the foregoing material which occurred while I was in the hospital.

The bravery of that marine brigade in the Bois de Belleau fight will ever remain a bright chapter in the records of the American army. For the performance of deeds of exceptional valor, more than a hundred marines were awarded Distinguished Service Crosses.

* * *

Since the days I read Hugo's chapters on the Battle of Waterloo in *Les Misérables*,[3] I always considered as an ideal of fighting capacity and the military spirit of sacrifice the old sergeant of Napoleon's Old Guard. Hugo made me vividly see that old sergeant standing on a field with a meager remnant of the Old Guard gathered around him. Unable to resist further, but unwilling to accept surrender, he and his followers faced the British cannon. The British, respecting this admirable demonstration of courage, ceased firing and called out to them, "Brave Frenchmen, surrender."

Château-Thierry and the Bois de Belleau

The old sergeant, who was about to die, refused to accept this offer of his life from the enemy. Into the very muzzles of the British cannon the sergeant hurled back the offer of his life with one word. That word was the vilest epithet in the French language. The cannons roared, and the old sergeant and his survivors died with the word on their lips. Hugo wisely devoted an entire chapter to that single word.

But I have a new ideal today. I found it in the Bois de Belleau. A small platoon line of marines lay on their faces and bellies under the trees at the edge of a wheat field. Two hundred yards across that flat field the enemy was located in trees. I peered into the trees but could see nothing, yet I knew that every leaf in the foliage screened scores of German machine guns that swept the field with lead. The bullets nipped the tops of the young wheat and ripped the bark from the trunks of the trees three feet from the ground on which the marines lay. The minute for the marine advance was approaching. An old gunnery sergeant[4] commanded the platoon in the absence of the lieutenant, who had been shot and was out of the fight. This old sergeant was a marine veteran. His cheeks were bronzed with the wind and sun of the seven seas. The service bar across his left breast showed that he had fought in the Philippines, in Santo Domingo, at the walls of Pekin, and in the streets of Vera Cruz. I make no apologies for his language. Even if Hugo were not my precedent, I would make no apologies. To me his words were classic, if not sacred.

As the minute for the advance arrived, he arose from the trees first and jumped out onto the exposed edge of that field that ran with lead, across which he and his men were to charge. Then he turned to give the charge order to the men of his platoon—his mates—the men he loved. He said:

"COME ON, YOU SONS-O'-BITCHES! DO YOU WANT TO LIVE FOREVER?"

Notes

1. This was the third bloody battle of the war fought at this location.
2. John Guthrie Harbord (1866–1947), U.S. Army officer. Served in Cuba and the Philippines. Accompanied General Pershing to France as chief of staff. In 1918, took command of the Second Division. After the armistice, served as chief of the Military Mission to Armenia. After retirement from the army was chairman of the board of the Radio Corporation of America (RCA).
3. *Les Misérables:* a novel by the French author Victor Hugo (1802–65), published in 1862. The well-known musical version (1985) does not contain this episode.
4. Daniel Daly (1873–1937), sergeant major, U.S. Marine Corps. Daly was one of the corps' most decorated soldiers, twice receiving the Medal of Honor. He was later wounded at Verdun.

Wounded—How It Feels to Be Shot

Just how does it feel to be shot on the field of battle? Just what is the exact sensation when a bullet burns its way through your flesh or crashes through your bones?

I always wanted to know. As a police reporter I "covered" scores of shooting cases, but I could never learn from the victims what the precise feeling was as the piece of lead struck. For long years I had cherished an inordinate curiosity to know that sensation, if possible, without experiencing it. I was curious and eager for enlightenment, just as I am still anxious to know how it is that some people willingly drink buttermilk when it isn't compulsory.

I am still in the dark concerning the inexplicable taste for the sour, clotted product of a sweet, well-meaning cow and the buttery, but I have found out how it feels to be shot. I know it now by experience.

Three Germans bullets that violated my person left me as many scars and at the same time completely satisfied my curiosity. I think now if I can ever muster up enough courage to drink a glass of buttermilk, I shall have bereft myself of my last inquisitiveness.

It happened on June 6 just to the northwest of Château-Thierry in the Bois de Belleau. On the morning of that day, I left Paris by motor for a rush to the front. The Germans were on that day within forty miles of the capital of France. On the night before, the citizens of Paris, in their homes and hotels, had heard the roll of the guns drawing ever nearer. Many had left the city.

But American divisions were in the line between the enemy and their goal, and the operation of these divisions was my object in hustling to the front. On the broad paved highway from Paris to Meaux, my car passed miles and miles of loaded motor trucks bound frontward. Long lines of these carried thousands of Americans. Other long lines were loaded down with shells and cartridge boxes. On the right side of the road, bound for Paris and points back of the line, was an endless stream of ambulances and other motor trucks bringing back wounded. Dense clouds of dust hung like a pall over the length of the road. The day was hot; the dust was stifling.

From Meaux we proceeded along the straight highway that borders the south banks of the Marne to La Ferté-sous-Juarre, at which place we crossed the river and turned north to Montreuil-aux-Lions, which was the newly occupied headquarters of the Second United States Army Division, General Omar Bundy commanding. On the day before, the two infantry brigades of that division, one composed of the 5th and 6th U.S. Marines, under command of Brigadier General Harbord, the other composed of the 9th and 23rd U.S. Infantry, had been thrown into the line which was just four miles to the north and east.

The fight had been hot during the morning. The marines on the left flank of the divisional sector had been pushing their lines forward through triangle woods and the village of Lucy-le-Bocage. The information of their advances was given to me by the Divisional Intelligence officer, who occupied a large room in the rear of the building that was used as Divisional Headquarters. The building was the village *mairie* [town hall], which also included the village schoolhouse. Now the desks of the school children were being used by our staff officers, and the walls and blackboards were covered with maps.

I was accompanied by Lieutenant Oscar Hartzell,[1] formerly of the *New York Times* staff. We learned that orders from the French High Command called for a continuation of the marine advance during the afternoon and evening, and this information made it possible for us to make our plans. Although the Germans were shelling roads immediately behind the front, Lieutenant Hartzell and I agreed to proceed by motor from Montreuil a mile or so to a place called La Voie du Châtel, which was the headquarters of Colonel Neville[2] of the 5th Marines. Reaching that place around four o'clock, we turned a dispatch over to the driver of our staff car with instructions that he proceed with all haste to Paris and there submit it to the U.S. Press Bureau.

Lieutenant Hartzell and I announced our intentions of proceeding at once to the front line to Colonel Neville.

"Go wherever you like," said the regimental commander, looking up from the outspread maps on the kitchen table in the low-ceilinged stone farmhouse that he had adopted as headquarters. "Go as far as you like, but I want to tell you it's damn hot up there."

An hour later found us in the woods to the west of the village of Lucy-le-Bocage, in which German shells were continually falling. To the west and north another nameless cluster of farm dwellings was in flames. Huge clouds of smoke rolled up like a smudge against the background of blue sky.

The ground under the trees in the wood was covered with small bits of white paper. I could not account for their presence until I examined several of them and found that these were letters from American mothers and wives and sweethearts—letters—whole packages of them, which the tired, dog-weary marines had been forced to remove from their packs and destroy in order to ease the straps that cut into aching grooves in their shoulders. Circumstances also forced the abandonment of much other material and equipment.

Occasional shells were dropping in the woods, which were also within range from a long-distance, indirect machine-gun fire from the enemy. Bits of lead, wobbling in their flight at the end of their long trajectory, sung through the air above our heads and clipped leaves and twigs from the branches. On the edge of the woods, we came upon a hastily dug out pit in which there were two American machine guns and their crews.

The field in front of the woods sloped gently down some two hundred yards to another cluster of trees. This cluster was almost as big as the one we were in. Part of it was occupied by the Germans. Our machine gunners maintained a continual fire into that part held by the enemy.

Five minutes before five o'clock, the order for the advance reached our pit. It was brought there by a second lieutenant, a platoon commander. "What are you doing here?" he asked, looking at the green brassard and red "C" on my left arm.[3]

"Looking for the big story," I said.

"If I were you, I'd be about forty miles south of this place," said the lieutenant, "but if you want to see the fun, stick around. We are going forward in five minutes."

That was the last I saw of him until days later, when both of us, wounded, met in the hospital. Of course, the first thing he said was, "I told you so."

We hurriedly finished the contents of the can of cold "corn willy" which one of the machine gunners and I were eating. The machine guns were taken down, and the barrels, cradles, and tripods were handed over to the members of the crew whose duties it was to carry them.

And then we went over. There are really no heroics about it. There is no bugle call, no sword waving, no dramatic enunciation of catchy commands, no theatricalism—it's just plain get up and go over. And it is done just the same as one would walk across a peaceful wheat field out in Iowa.

But with the appearance of our first line, as it stepped from the shelter of the woods into the open exposure of the flat field, the woods opposite began to cackle and rattle with the enemy machine-gun fire. Our men advanced in open order, ten and twelve feet between men. Sometimes a squad would run forward fifty feet and drop. And as its members flattened on the ground for safety, another squad would rise from the ground and make another rush.

They gained the woods. Then we could hear shouting. Then we knew that work was being done with the bayonet. The machine-gun fire continued in intensity and then died down completely. The wood had been won. Our men consolidated the position by moving forward in groups ever on the watch-out for snipers in the trees. A number of these were brought down by our crack pistol shots.

At different times during the advance, runners had come through the woods inquiring for Major John Berry, the battalion commander. One of these runners attached himself to Lieutenant Hartzell and

Wounded—How It Feels to Be Shot

myself, and together the three of us located the major coming through the woods. He granted permission for Lieutenant Hartzell and me to accompany him, and we started forward, in all, a party of some fifteen, including ten runners attached to the battalion commander.

Owing to the continual evidences of German snipers in the trees, everyone in our party carried a revolver ready in his hand, with the exception of myself. Correspondents, you will remember, are noncombatants and must be unarmed. I carried a notebook, but it was loaded. We made our way down the slope of the wooded hillside.

Midway down the slope, the hill was bisected by a sunken road which turned forward on the left. Lying in the road were a number of French bodies and several of our men who had been brought down but five minutes before. We crossed that road hurriedly, knowing that it was covered from the left by German machine guns.

At the bottom of the slope, there was a V-shaped field. The apex of the V was on the left. From left to right the field was some two hundred yards in width. The point where we came out of the woods was about one hundred yards from the apex. At that point the field was about one hundred yards across. It was perfectly flat and was covered with a young crop of oats between ten and fifteen inches high.

This V-shaped oat field was bordered on all sides

by dense clusters of trees. In the trees on the side opposite the side on which we stood were German machine guns. We could hear them. We could not see them, but we knew that every leaf and piece of greenery there vibrated from their fire, and the tops of the young oats waved and swayed with the streams of lead that swept across.

Major Berry gave orders for us to follow him at intervals of ten or fifteen yards. Then he started across the field alone at the head of the party. I followed. Behind me came Hartzell. Then the woods about us began to rattle fiercely. It was unusually close range. That lead traveled so fast that we could not hear it as it passed. We soon had visual demonstration of the hot place we were in when we began to see the dust puffs that the bullets kicked up in the dirt around our feet.

Major Berry had advanced well beyond the center of the field, when I saw him turn toward me and heard him shout:

"Get down everybody."

We all fell on our faces. And then it began to come hot and fast. Perfectly withering volleys of lead swept the tops of the oats just over us. For some reason it did not seem to be coming from the trees hardly a hundred yards in front of us. It was coming from a new direction—from the left.

I was busily engaged flattening myself on the ground. Then I heard a shout in front of me. It

Wounded—How It Feels to Be Shot

came from Major Berry. I lifted my head cautiously and looked forward. The major was making an effort to get to his feet. With his right hand he was savagely grasping his left wrist.

"My hand's gone," he shouted. One of the streams of lead from the left had found him. A ball had entered his left arm at the elbow, had traveled down the side of the bone, tearing away muscles and nerves of the forearm and lodging itself in the palm of his hand. His pain was excruciating.

"Get down. Flatten out, Major," I shouted, and he dropped to the ground. I did not know the extent of his injuries at that time, but I did know that he was courting death every minute he stood up.

"We've got to get out of here," said the major. "We've got to get forward. They'll start shelling this open field in a few minutes."

I lifted my head for another cautious look. I judged that I was lying about thirty yards from the edge of the trees in front of us. The major was about ten yards in front of me.

"You are twenty yards from the trees," I shouted to the major. "I am crawling over to you now. Wait until I get there, and I'll help you. Then we'll get up and make a dash for it."

"All right," replied the major; "hurry along."

I started forward, keeping as flat on the ground as it was possible to do so and at the same time move. As far as was feasible, I pushed forward by digging in with my toes and elbows extended in front of me. It was my object to make as little movement in the oats as possible. I was not mistaken about the intensity of fire that swept the field. It was terrific.

And then it happened. The lighted end of a cigarette touched me in the fleshy part of my upper left arm. That was all. It just felt like a sudden burn and nothing worse. The burned part did not seem to be any larger in area than that part which could be burned by the lighted end of a cigarette.

At the time there was no feeling within the arm, that is, no feeling as to aches or pain. There was nothing to indicate that the bullet, as I learned several days later, had gone through the bicep muscle of the upper arm and had come out on the other side. The only sensation perceptible at the time was the burning touch at the spot where the bullet entered.

I glanced down at the sleeve of my uniformed coat and could not even see the hole where the bullet had entered. Neither was there any sudden flow of blood. At the time there was no stiffness or discomfort in the arm, and I continued to use it to work my way forward.

Then the second one hit. It nicked the top of my left shoulder. And again came the burning sensation, only this time the area affected seemed larger. Hitting as it did in the meaty cap of the shoulder, I

Wounded—How It Feels to Be Shot

feared that there would be no further use for the arm until it had received attention, but again I was surprised when I found upon experiment that I could still use it. The bone seemed to be affected in no way.

Again there was no sudden flow of blood, nor stiffness. It seemed hard for me to believe at the time, but I had been shot twice, penetrated through by two bullets and was experiencing not any more pain than I had experienced once when I dropped a lighted cigarette on the back of my hand. I am certain that the pain in no way approached that sensation which the dentist provides when he drills into a tooth with a live nerve in it.

So I continued to move toward the major. Occasionally I would shout something to him, although, at this time, I am unable to remember what it was. I only wanted to let him know I was coming. I had fears, based on the one look that I had obtained of his pain-distorted face, that he had been mortally shot in the body.

And then the third one struck me. In order to keep as close to the ground as possible, I had swung my chin to the right so that I was pushing forward with my left cheek flat against the ground, and in order to accommodate this position of the head, I had moved my steel helmet over so that it covered part of my face on the right.

Then there came a crash. It sounded to me like

someone had dropped a glass bottle into a porcelain bathtub. A barrel of whitewash tipped over, and it seemed that everything in the world turned white. That was the sensation. I did not recognize it because I have often been led to believe and often heard it said that when one receives a blow on the head everything turns black.

Maybe I am contrarily constructed, but in my case everything became pure white. I remember this distinctly because my years of newspaper training had been in but one direction—to sense and remember. So it was that, even without knowing it, my mind was making mental notes on every impression that my senses registered.

I did not know yet where I had been hit or what the bullet had done. I knew that I was still knowing things. I did not know whether I was alive or dead, but I did know that my mind was still working. I was still mentally taking notes on every second.

The first recess in that note-taking came when I asked myself the following question:

"Am I dead?"

I didn't laugh or didn't even smile when I asked myself the question without putting it in words. I wanted to know. And wanting to know, I undertook to find out. I am not aware now that there was any appreciable passage of time during this mental progress. I feel certain, however, that I never lost consciousness.

Wounded—How It Feels to Be Shot

How was I to find out if I was dead? The shock had lifted my head off the ground, but I had immediately replaced it as close to the soil as possible. My twice punctured left arm was lying alongside my body. I decided to try and move my fingers on my left hand. I did so, and they moved. I next moved my left foot. Then I knew I was alive.

Then I brought my right hand up toward my face and placed it to the left of my nose. My fingers rested on something soft and wet. I withdrew the hand and looked at it. It was covered with blood. As I looked at it, I was not aware that my entire vision was confined to my right eye, although there was considerable pain in the entire left side of my face.

This was sufficient to send me on another mental investigation. I closed my right eye and—all was dark. My first thought following this experiment was that my left eye was closed. So I again counseled with myself and tried to open my left eye—that is, tried to give the mental command that would cause the muscles of the left eye to open the lid and close it again.

I did this but could not feel or verify in any way whether the eyelid responded or not. I only knew that it remained dark on that side. This brought me to another conclusion and not a pessimistic one at that. I simply believed, in spite of the pain, that something had struck me in the eye and had closed it.

I did not know then, as I know now, that a bullet

And They Thought We Wouldn't Fight

Gibbons's helmet with shrapnel damage

striking the ground immediately under my left cheek bone had ricocheted upward, going completely through the left eye and then crashing out through my forehead, leaving the eyeball and upper eyelid completely halved, the lower eyelid torn away, and a compound fracture of the skull.

Further progress toward the major was impossible. I must confess that I became so intensely interested in the weird sensations and subjective research, that I even neglected to call out and tell the wounded officer that I would not be able to continue to his assistance. I held this view in spite of the fact that my original intentions were strong. Lying there with my left cheek flat on the ground, I was able to observe some minutes later the wounded major rise to his feet and in a perfect hail of lead rush forward and out of my line of vision.

It was several days later, in the hospital, that I learned that he reached the shelter of the woods beyond without being hit again, and in that place, although suffering intense pain, was able to shout back orders which resulted in the subsequent wiping out of the machine-gun nest that had been our undoing. For this supreme effort, General Pershing decorated him with the Distinguished Service Cross.

I began to make plans to get out of the exposed position in which I was lying. Whereas the field when I started across it had seemed perfectly flat, now it impressed me as being convex, and I was further impressed with the belief that I was lying on the very uppermost and most exposed curvature of it. There is no doubt that the continued stream of machine-gun lead that swept the field superinduced this belief. I got as close to the ground as a piece of paper on top of a table. I remember regretting sincerely that the war had reached the stage of open movement and one consequence of which was that there wasn't a shell hole anywhere to crawl into.

This did not, however, eliminate the dangerous possibility of shelling. With the fatalism that one acquires along the fronts, I was ready to take my chances with the casual German shell that one

Americans advancing past German wounded at Belleau Wood, postcard

might have expected, but I devoted much thought to a consideration of the French and American artillery some miles behind me. I considered the possibility of word having been sent back that our advancing waves at this point had been cut down by enemy machine gunners who were still in position, preventing all progress at this place. I knew that such information, if sent back, would immediately be forwarded to our guns, and then a devastating concentration of shells would be directed toward the location of the machine-gun nests.

I knew that I was lying one hundred yards from one of those nests, and I knew that I was well within the fatal bursting radius of any shells our gunners might direct against that German target. My fear was that myself and other American wounded lying in that field would die by American guns. That is what would have happened if that information had reached our artillery, and it is what should have happened.

The lives of the wounded in that field were as nothing compared with the importance of wiping out that machine-gun nest on our left which was holding up the entire advance.

I wanted to see what time it was, and my watch was attached to my left wrist. In endeavoring to get a look at it, I found out that my left arm was stiff and racked with pain. Hartzell, I knew, had a watch, but I did not know where he was lying, so I called out.

He answered me from some distance away, but I could not tell how far or in what direction. I could see dimly but only at the expense of great pain. When he answered, I shouted back to him:

"Are you hit?"

"No, are you?" he asked.

"Yes, what time is it?" I said.

"Are you hit badly?" he asked in reply.

"No, I don't think so," I said. "I think I'm all right."

"Where are you hit?" he asked.

"In the head," I said; "I think something hit my eye."

"In the head, you damn fool," he shouted louder with just a bit of anger and surprise in his voice. "How the hell can you be all right if you are hit in the head? Are you bleeding much?"

"No," I said. "What time is it? Will you tell me?"

"I'm coming over to get you," shouted Hartzell.

"Don't move, you damn fool, you want to kill both of us?" I hastened to shout back. "If you start moving, don't move near me. I think they think I'm dead."

"Well you can't lie there and bleed to death," Hartzell replied. "We've got to do something to get the hell out of here. What'll we do?"

"Tell me what time it is and how long it will be before it's dark," I asked.

"It's six o'clock now," Hartzell said, "and it won't

Wounded—How It Feels to Be Shot

be dark 'til nine; this is June. Do you think you can stick it out?"

I told him that I thought I could, and we were silent for some time. Both of us had the feeling that other ears—ears working in conjunction with eyes trained along the barrels of those machine guns a hundred yards on our left—would be aroused to better marksmanship if we continued to talk.

I began to take stock of my condition. During my year or more along the fronts, I had been through many hospitals, and from my observations in those institutions, I had cultivated a keen distaste for one thing—gas gangrene. I had learned from doctors its fatal and horrible results, and I also had learned from them that it was caused by germs which exist in large quantities in any ground that has been under artificial cultivation for a long period.

Such was the character of the very field I was lying in, and I came to the realization that the wound in the left side of my face and head was resting flatly on the soil. With my right hand I drew up my British box respirator, or gas mask, and placed this under my head. Thus I rested with more confidence, although the machine-gun lead continued to pass in sheets through the tops of the oats not two or three inches above my head.

All of it was coming from the left—coming from the German nests located in the trees at the apex of the V-shaped field. Those guns were not a hundred yards away, and they seemed to have an inexhaustible supply of ammunition. Twenty feet away on my left a wounded marine was lying. Occasionally I would open my right eye for a painful look in his direction.

He was wounded and apparently unconscious. His pack, "the khaki doll," was still strapped between his shoulders. Unconsciously he was doing that which all wounded men do—that is, to assume the position that is the most comfortable. He was trying to roll over on his back.

But the pack was on his back, and every time he would roll over on this, it would elevate his body into full view of the German gunners. Then a withering hail of lead would sweep the field. It so happened that I was lying immediately in line between those German guns and this unconscious moving target. As the marine would roll over on top of the pack, his chest would be exposed to the fire.

I could see the buttons fly from his tunic and one of the shoulder straps of the back pack part as the sprays of lead struck him. He would limply roll off the pack over on his side. I found myself wishing that he would lie still, as every movement of his brought those streams of bullets closer and closer to my head. I even considered the thickness of the box respirator on which I had elevated my head off the ground. It was about two inches thick.

Wounded—How It Feels to Be Shot

I remembered my French gas mask hanging from my shoulder and recalled immediately that it was much flatter, being hardly half an inch in thickness. I forthwith drew up the French mask to my head, extracted the British one and rested my cheek closer to the ground on the French one. Thus, I lowered my head about an inch and a half—an inch and a half that represented worlds of satisfaction and some optimism to me.

Sometimes there were lulls in the firing. During those periods of comparative quiet, I could hear the occasional moan of other wounded on that field. Very few of them cried out, and it seemed to me that those who did were unconscious when they did it. One man in particular had a long, low groan. I could not see him, yet I felt he was lying somewhere close to me. In the quiet intervals, his unconscious expression of pain reminded me of the sound I had once heard made by a calf which had been tied by a short rope to a tree. The animal had strayed round and round the tree until its entanglements in the rope had left it a helpless prisoner. The groan of that unseen, unconscious wounded American who laid near me on the field that evening sounded exactly like the pitiful bawl of that calf.

Those three hours were long in passing. With the successive volleys that swept the field, I sometimes lost hope that I could ever survive it. It seemed to me that if three German bullets had found me within the space of fifteen minutes, I could hardly expect to spend three hours without receiving the fatal one. With such thoughts on my mind, I re-opened conversation with Hartzell.

"How's it coming, old man?" I shouted.

"They're coming damn close," he said; "how is it with you? Are you losing much blood?"

"No, I'm all right as far as that goes," I replied, "but I want you to communicate with my wife, if its 'west' for me."

"What's her address?" said Hartzell.

"It's a long one," I said. "Are you ready to take it?"

"Shoot," said Hartzell.

"'Mrs. Floyd Gibbons, No. 12 Bis, Rue de la Chevalier de la Barre, Dijon, Côte d'Or, France.'" I said slowly.

"My God," said Hartzell, "say it again."

Back and forth we repeated the address correctly and incorrectly some ten or twelve times until Hartzell informed me that he knew it well enough to sing it. He also gave me his wife's address. Then just to make conversation, he would shout over, every fifteen minutes, and tell me that there was just that much less time that we would have to lie there.

I thought that hour between seven and eight o'clock dragged the most, but the one between eight and nine seemed interminable. The hours were so long, particularly when we considered that a Ger-

Wounded—How It Feels to Be Shot

man machine gun could fire three hundred shots a minute. Dusk approached slowly. And finally Hartzell called over:

"I don't think they can see us now," he said; "let's start to crawl back."

"Which way shall we crawl?" I asked.

"Into the woods," said Hartzell.

"Which woods?" I asked.

"The woods we came out of, you damn fool," he replied.

"Which direction are they in?" I said, "I've been moving around, and I don't know which way I am heading. Are you on my left or on my right?"

"I can't tell whether I'm on your left or your right," he replied. "How are you lying, on your face or on your back?"

"On my face," I said, "and your voice sounds like it comes from in back of me and on the left."

"If that's the case," said Hartzell, "your head is lying toward the wrong woods. Work around in a half circle, and you'll be facing the right direction."

I did so and then heard Hartzell's voice on my right. I started moving toward him. Against my better judgment and expressed wishes, he crawled out toward me and met me halfway. His voice close in front of me surprised me.

"Hold your head up a little," he said. "I want to see where it hit you."

"I don't think it looks very nice," I replied, lifting

And They Thought We Wouldn't Fight

my head. I wanted to know how it looked myself, so I painfully opened the right eye and looked through the oats eighteen inches into Hartzell's face. I saw the look of horror on it as he looked into mine.

Twenty minutes later, after crawling painfully through the interminable yards of young oats, we reached the edge of the woods and safety.

That's how it feels to be shot.

NOTES

1. Lieutenant Oscar Hartzell (Gibbons gave an incorrect first name.): Arthur E. Hartzell (1891–1940), journalist and advertising executive. Pre-war, with the *New York Times* and on the cable desk of the *New York Sun*. Commissioned a lieutenant in 1917 and assigned to G-2-D, which handled censorship and press matters. At Château-Thierry, accompanied the *Tribune* vehicle. Later promoted to captain and information officer. After the war worked with the J. Walter Thompson Agency.
2. Wendell C. Neville (1870–1930), U.S. Marine Corps officer who commanded both the 4th and 5th Marine Regiments in World War I. Later promoted to major general and commandant of the Marine Corps.
3. In World War I, a war correspondent wore an army officer's uniform without insignia or rank and a green brassard (armband) with the letter "C" in red.

"Good Morning, Nurse"

Weakness from the loss of blood began to grow on me as Lieutenant Hartzell and I made our way through the deepening shadows of the wooded hillside in the rear of the field on which I had been shot. In an upright position of walking, the pains in my head seemed to increase. We stopped for a minute, and, neither of us having first aid kits with us, I resurrected a somewhat soiled silk handkerchief with which Hartzell bound up my head in a manner that applied supporting pressure over my left eye and brought a degree of relief.

Hartzell told me later that I was staggering slightly when we reached a small relief dugout about a mile back of the wood. There a medical corps man removed the handkerchief and bound my head with a white gauze bandage. I was anxious to have the wound cleaned, but he told me there was no water. He said they had been forced to turn it over to the men to drink. This seemed to me to be as it should be because my thirst was terrific, yet there was no water left.

We stumbled rearward another half mile and, in the darkness, came upon the edge of another wooded area. A considerable number of our wounded were lying on stretchers on the ground. The Germans were keeping up a continual fire of shrapnel and high explosive shell in the woods, apparently to prevent the mobilization of reserves, but the doctors, taking care of the wounded, proceeded with their work without notice to the whine of the shells passing overhead or the bursting of those that landed nearby. They went at their work just as though they were caring for injured men on a football field.

Hartzell stretched me out on the ground and soon had a doctor bending over me. The doctor removed the eye bandage, took one look at what was beneath it, and then replaced it. I remember this distinctly because at the time I made the mental note that the doctor apparently considered my head wound beyond anything he could repair. He next turned his attention to my arm and shoulder. He inserted his scissors into my left sleeve at the wrist and ripped it up to the shoulder. He followed this operation by cutting through my heavy khaki tunic from the shoulder to the collar. A few more snips of the nickel-plated blades, and my shirt and undershirt were cut away. He located the three bullet holes, two in the arm and one across the top of the shoulder, and bound them up with bandages.

"We're awful shy on ambulances," he said; "you will have to lie here a while."

"I feel that I can walk all right if there is no reason why I shouldn't," I replied.

"You ought to be in an ambulance," said the doc-

"Good Morning, Nurse"

tor, "but if you feel that you can make it, you might take a try at it."

Then turning to Lieutenant Hartzell, he said, "Keep right with him, and if he begins to get groggy, make him lie down."

So Hartzell and I resumed our rearward plodding or staggering. He walked at my right side and slightly in front of me, holding my right arm over his right shoulder and thereby giving me considerable support. We had not proceeded far before we heard the racing motor of an automobile coming from behind us. An occasional shell was dropping along the road we were now on.

A stick struck my legs from behind in the darkness. And then an apologetic voice said: "Beg your pardon, sir, just feeling along the road for shell holes. Ambulance right behind me, sir. Would you mind stepping to one side? Come on, Bill," to the driver of the ambulance; "it looks all clear through here."

The automobile with the racing motor turned out to be a light ambulance of a popular Detroit make. Its speeding engine was pure camouflage for its slow progress. It bubbled and steamed at the radiator cap as it pushed along at almost a snail's pace.

"All full?" Hartzell shouted into the darkness of the driver's seat.

"To the brim," responded the driver. "Are you wounded?"

"No, but I have a wounded man with me," said

And They Thought We Wouldn't Fight

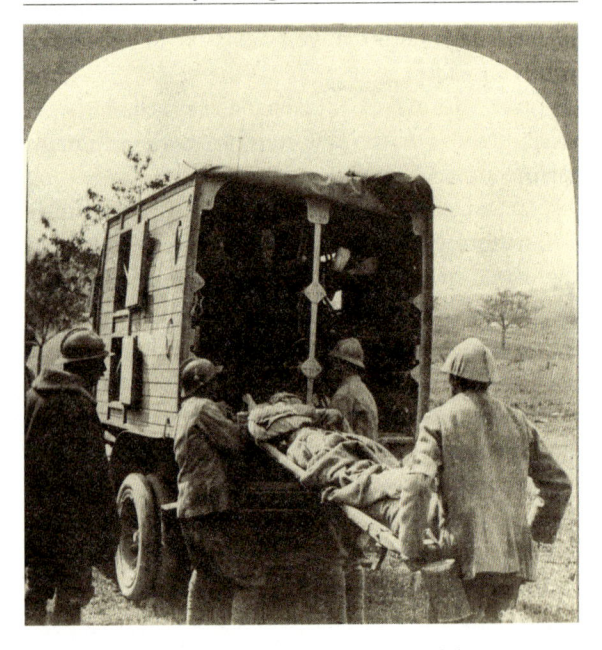

An ambulance taking away the wounded

Hartzell. "He can sit beside you on the seat if you have room."

"Get right in," said the driver, and Hartzell boosted me into the front seat. We pushed along slowly, Hartzell walking beside the car and the driver's assistant proceeding ahead of us, searching the dark road with his cane for new shell craters.

Occasionally, when our wheels would strike in

"Good Morning, Nurse"

one of these, groans would come from the ambulance proper.

"Take it easy" would come a voice through pain-pressed lips; "for Christ's sake, do you think you are driving a truck?"

I heard the driver tell Hartzell that he had three men with bullet-splintered legs in the ambulance. Every jolt of the car caused their broken bones to jolt and increased the pounding of their wearied nerves to an extremity of agony. The fourth occupant of the ambulance, he said, had been shot through the lungs.

Some distance along, there came a knock on the wooden partition behind my back—the partition that separates the driver's seat from the ambulance proper. The car stopped, and the driver and Hartzell went to the rear door and opened it. The man with the shot through the lungs was half sitting up on his stretcher. He had one hand to his mouth and his lips, as revealed in the rays of the driver's flashlight, were red wet.

"Quick—get me—to a doctor," the man said between gulps and gurgles.

The driver considered. He knew we were ten miles from the closest doctor. Then he addressed himself to the other three stretcher-cases—the men with the torture-torn legs.

"If I go fast, you guys are going to suffer the agonies of hell," he said, "and if I go slow, this guy with the hemorrhage will croak before we get there. How do you want me to drive?"

There was not a minute's silence. The three broken-leg cases responded almost in unison. "Go as fast as you can," they said.

And we did. With Hartzell riding the running board beside me and the crater finder clinging to the mud guards on the other side, we sped through the darkness regardless of the ruts and shell holes. The jolting was severe, but never once did there come another complaint from the occupants of the ambulance.

In this manner did we arrive in time at the first medical clearing station. I learned later that the life of the man with the hemorrhage was saved, and he is alive today.

The clearing station was located in an old church on the outskirts of a little village. Four times during this war the flow and ebb of battle had passed about this old edifice. Hartzell half carried me off the ambulance seat and into the church. As I felt my feet scrape on the flagstoned flooring underneath the Gothic entrance arch, I opened my right eye for a painful survey of the interior.

The walls, gray with age, appeared yellow in the light of the candles and lanterns that were used for illumination. Blankets and bits of canvas and carpet had been tacked over the apertures where once stained glass windows and huge oaken doors had

"Good Morning, Nurse"

An army field hospital inside the ruins of a church

been. These precautions were necessary to prevent the lights from shining outside the building and betraying our location to the hospital-loving eyes of German bombing planes, whose motors we could hear even at that minute, humming in the black sky above us.

Our American wounded were lying on stretchers all over the floor. Near the door, where I entered, a number of pews had been pushed to one side, and on these our walking wounded were seated. They were smoking cigarettes and talking and passing observations on every fresh case that came through the door. They all seemed to be looking at me.

My appearance must have been sufficient to have shocked them. I was hatless, and my hair was matted with blood. The red-stained bandage around my forehead and extending down over my left cheek did not hide the rest of my face, which was unwashed, and consequently red with fresh blood.

On my left side I was completely bare from the shoulder to the waist with the exception of the strips of white cloth about my arm and shoulder. My chest was splashed with red from the two body wounds. Such was my entrance. I must have looked somewhat gruesome because I happened to catch an involuntary shudder as it passed over the face of one of my observers among the walking wounded, and I heard him remark to the man next to him: "My God, look what they're bringing in."

Hartzell placed me on a stretcher on the floor and went for water, which I sorely needed. I heard someone stop beside my stretcher and bend over me, while a kindly voice said: "Would you like a cigarette, old man?"

"Yes," I replied. He lighted one in his own lips and placed it in my mouth. I wanted to know my benefactor. I asked him for his name and organization.

"I am not a soldier," he said; "I am a noncombatant, the same as you. My name is Slater, and I'm from the YMCA.

That cigarette tasted mighty good. If you who

"Good Morning, Nurse"

read this are one of those whose contributions to the YMCA made that distribution possible, I wish to herewith express to you my gratefulness and the gratefulness of the other men who enjoyed your generosity that night.

In front of what had been the altar in the church, there had been erected a rudely constructed operation table. The table was surrounded with tall candelabrum of brass and gilded wood. These ornate accessories had been removed from the altar for the purpose of providing better light for the surgeons who busied themselves about the table in their long gowns of white—stained with red.

I was placed on that table for an examination, and I heard a peculiar conversation going on about me. One doctor said, "We haven't any more of it." Then another doctor said, "But I thought we had plenty." The first voice replied, "Yes, but we didn't expect so many wounded. We have used up all we had." Then the second voice said, "Well, we certainly need it now. I don't know what we're going to do without it."

From their further conversation I learned that the subject under discussion was anti-tetanus serum—the all-important inoculation that prevents lockjaw and is also an antidote for the germs of gas gangrene. You may be sure I became more than mildly interested in the absence of this valuable boon, but there was nothing I could say that would help the case, so I remained quiet. In several minutes my composure was rewarded. I heard hurried footsteps across the flagstoned flooring and a minute later felt a steel needle penetrating my abdomen. Then a cheery voice said: "It's all right, now; we've got plenty of it. We've got just piles of it. The Red Cross just shot it out from Paris in limousines."

After the injection, Hartzell informed me that the doctors could do nothing for me at that place and that I was to be moved further to the rear. He said ambulances were scarce, but he had found a place for me in a returning ammunition truck. I was carried out of the church and somewhere in the outer darkness was lifted up into the body of the truck and laid down on some straw in the bottom. There were some fifteen or twenty other men lying there beside me.

The jolting in this springless vehicle was severe, but its severity was relieved in some of our cases by the quieting injections we had received. The effects of these narcotics had worn off in some of the men, and they suffered the worse for it. One of them continually called out to the truck driver to go slower and make less jolting. To each request the driver responded that he was going as slow as he could. As the jolting continued, the man with the complaining nerves finally yelled out a new request. He said: "Well, if you can't make it easier by going slow, then for God's sake throw her into high and go as fast as you can. Let's get it over as quick as we can."

Lying on my back in the truck with a raincoat as a pillow, I began to wonder where we were bound for. I opened my eye once and looked up toward the roof of the leafy tunnel which covered the road. Soon we passed out from beneath the trees bordering the roadside, and I could see the sky above. The moon was out, and there were lots of stars. They gave one something to think about. After all, how insignificant was one little life.

Sometime during the dark hours of the early morning, we stopped in the courtyard of a hospital, and I was taken into another examination room illuminated with painfully brilliant lights. I was placed on a table for an examination, which seemed rather hurried, and then the table was rolled away some distance down a corridor. I never understood that move until some weeks later when a lieutenant medical officer told me that it was he who had examined me at that place.

"You're looking pretty fit, now," he said, "but that night when I saw you I ticketed you for the dead pile. You didn't look like you could live till morning."

His statement gave me some satisfaction. There is always joy in fooling the doctor.

Hartzell, who still accompanied me, apparently rescued me from the "dead pile," and we started on another motor trip, this time on a stretcher in a large, easier-riding ambulance. In this I arrived shortly after dawn at the United States Military Base Hospital at Neuilly-sur-Seine, on the outskirts of Paris.

There were more hurried examinations, and soon I was rolled down a corridor on a wheeled table, into an elevator that started upward. Then the wheeled table raced down another long corridor, and I began to feel that my journeyings were endless. We stopped finally in a room where I distinctly caught the odor of ether. Someone began removing my boots and clothes. As that someone worked. he talked to me.

"I know you, Mr. Gibbons," he said. "I'm from Chicago also. I am Sergeant Stephen Hayes. I used to go to Hyde Park High School. We're going to fix you up right away."

I learned from Hayes that I was lying in a room adjoining the operating chamber and was being prepared for the operating table. Some information concerning the extent of my injuries and the purpose of the operation would have been comforting and would have relieved the sensation of utter helpless childishness that I was experiencing.

I knew I was about to go under the influence of the anesthetic and that something was going to be done to me. I had every confidence that whatever was done would be for the best, but it was perfectly

"Good Morning, Nurse"

natural that I should be curious about it. Was the operation to be a serious one or a minor one? Would they have to remove my eye? Would they have to operate on my skull? How about the arm? Would there be an amputation? How about the other eye? Would I ever see again? It must be remembered that in spite of all the examinations, I had not been informed and consequently had no knowledge concerning the extent of my injuries. The only information I had received had been included in vague remarks intended as soothing, such as "You're all right, old man." "You'll pull through fine." "You're coming along nicely." But all of it had seemed too professionally optimistic to satisfy me, and my doubts still remained.

They were relieved, however, by the pressure of a hand and the sound of a voice. In the words spoken and in the pressure of the hand, there was hardly anything different from similar hand pressures and similar spoken phrases that had come to me during the night, yet there was everything different. This voice and this hand carried supreme confidence. I could believe in both of them. I felt the hand pressure on my right shoulder, and the mild kindly voice said: "Son, I am going to operate on you. I have examined you, and you are all right. You are going to come through fine. Don't worry about anything."

"Thank you, very much," I said. "I like your

voice. It sounds like my father's. Will you tell me your name?"

"I am Major Powers," the kindly voice said. "Now just take it easy, and I will talk to you again in a couple of hours when you feel better."

The speaker, as I learned later, was Major Charles Powers, of Denver, Colorado, one of the best-known and best-loved surgeons in the West. A man far advanced in his profession and well advanced in his years, a man whose life has not been one of continual health, a man who, upon America's entry of the war, sacrificed the safety of the beneficial air rarity of his native Denver to answer the country's call, to go to France at great personal risk to his health—a risk only appreciated by those who know him well. It was Major Powers who operated upon the compound fracture in my skull that morning.

My mental note-taking continued as the anesthetist worked over me with the ether. As I began breathing the fumes, I remember that my senses were keenly making observations on every sensation I experienced. The thought even went through my mind that it would be rather an unusual thing to report completely the impressions of coma. This suggestion became a determination, and I became keyed up to everything going on about me.

The conversation of the young doctor who was administering the anesthetic interested me unusually. He was very busy and businesslike, and al-

"Good Morning, Nurse"

though I considered myself an important and most interested party in the entire proceedings, his conversation ignored me entirely. He not only did not talk to me, but he was not even talking about me. As he continued to apply the ether, he kept up a running fire of entirely extraneous remarks with some other person near the table. I did not appreciate then, as I do now, that I was only one of very, very many that he had anesthetized that morning and the night before, but at the time his seeming lack of all interest in me as me, piqued me considerably.

"You will pardon me for manifesting a mild interest in what you are doing to me," I said, "but you see I know that something is going to be done to my right eye, and inasmuch as that is the only eye I've got on that side, I can't help being concerned."

"Now, you just forget it and take deep breaths."

"I'll take deep breaths if you'll loosen the straps over my chest," I said, getting madder each minute. "How can I take a full breath when you've got my lungs strapped down?"

"Well, how's that?" responded the conversational anesthetist, as he loosened one of the straps. "Now, take one breath of fresh air—one deep, long breath, now."

I turned my head to one side to escape the fumes from the stifling towel over my face and made a frenzied gulp for fresh air. As I did so, one large drop of ether fell on the table right in front of my nose, and the deep long breath I got had very little air in it. I felt I had been tricked.

I was completely ignored, and the table started moving. As I started riding the table down the runway, I began to see that I was descending an inclined tube which seemed to be filled with yellow vapor. Some distance down, the table slowed up, and we came to a stop in front of a circular bulkhead in the tunnel.

"You're all right, now," said a sweet voice; "just try to take a little nap and you'll feel better."

Then I knew it was all over, that is, the operation was over, or something was over. Anyhow my mind was working, and I was in a position where I wanted to know things again. I recall now, with a smile, that the first things that passed through my mind were the threadbare bromides so often quoted "Where am I?" I recall feeling the urge to say something at least original, so I enquired: "What place is this, and will you please tell me what day and time it is?"

"This is the Military Base Hospital at Neuilly-sur-Seine just on the outskirts of Paris, and it is about eleven o'clock in the morning and today is Friday, June the seventh."

Then I went back to sleep with an etherized taste in my mouth like a motorman's glove.

Groans, Laughs, and Sobs in the Hospital

There were fourteen wounded American soldiers in my ward—all men from the ranks and representing almost as many nationalistic extractions. There was an Irishman, a Swede, an Italian, a Jew, a Pole, one man of German parentage, and one man of Russian extraction. All of them had been wounded at the front, and all of them now had something nearer and dearer to them than any traditions that might have been handed down to them from a mother country—they had fought and bled and suffered for a new country, *their* new country.

Here in this ward was the new melting pot of America. Not the melting pot of our great American cities where nationalistic quarters still exist, but a greater fusion process from which these men had emerged with unquestionable Americanism. They are the real and the new Americans—born in the hell of battle.

One night as we lay there, we heard an automobile racing through a street in this sleepy, warm little *faubourg* of Paris. The motor was sounding on its siren a call that was familiar to all of us. It was the alarm of a night attack from the air. It meant that German planes had crossed the front line and were on their way with death and destruction for Paris.

A nurse entered the room and drew the curtains of the tall windows to keep from our eyes the flash and the glitter of the shells that soon began to burst in the sky above us as the aerial defenses located on the outer circle of the city began to erect a wall of bursting steel around the French capital. We could hear the guns barking close by and occasionally the louder boom that told us one of the German bombs had landed. Particles of shrapnel began falling in the garden beneath the windows of our ward, and we could hear the rattle of the pieces on the slate roof of a pavilion there. It is most unpleasant, it goes without saying, to lie helpless on one's back and grapple with the realization that directly over your head—right straight above your eyes and face—is an enemy airplane loaded with bombs. Many of us knew that those bombs contained, some of them, more than two hundred pounds of melinite,[1] and some of us had witnessed the terrific havoc they wrought when they landed on a building. All of us knew, as the world knows, the particular attraction that hospitals have for German bombs.

The aerial bombardment subsided after some ten or fifteen minutes, and soon we heard the motor racing back through the streets while a musician in the car sounded on a bugle the "prologue," or the

Groans, Laughs, and Sobs in the Hospital

signal that the raid was over. The invaders had been driven back. All of us in the ward tried to sleep. But nerves tingled from this more or less uncomfortable experience, and wounds ached and burned. Sleep was almost out of the question, and in the darkened ward I soon noticed the red glow of cigarette after cigarette from bed to bed as the men sought to woo relief with tobacco smoke.

We began to discuss a subject very near and very dear to all wounded men. That is, what they are going to do as soon as they get out of the hospital. It is known, of course, that the first consideration usually is to return to the front, but in many instances in our ward, this was entirely out of the question.

So it was with Dan Bailey, who occupied a bed two beds on my right. His left leg was off above the knee. He lost it going over the top at Cantigny.

"I know what I'm going to do when I get home," he said. "I am going to get a job as an instructor in a roller-skating rink."

In a bed on the other side of the ward was a young man with his right arm off. His name was Johnson, and he had been a musician. In time of battle, musicians lay aside their trombones and cornets and go over the top with the men, only they carry stretchers instead of rifles. Johnson had done this. Something had exploded quite close to him, and his entire recollection of the battle was that he had awakened being carried back on his own stretcher.

"I know where I can sure get work," he said, glancing down at the stump of his lost arm. "I am going to sign up as a pitcher with the St. Louis Nationals."[2]

But concerning after-the-war occupations, I endeavored that night to contribute something in a similar vein to the general discussion, and I suggested the possibility that I might return to give lessons on the monocle.

The prize prospect, however, was submitted by a man who occupied a bed far over in one corner of the room. He was the possessor of a polysyllabic name—a name sprinkled with *k*'s, *s*'s, and *z*'s, with a scarcity of vowels—a name that we could not pronounce, much less remember. On account of his size, we called him "Big Boy." His was a peculiar story.

He had been captured by three Germans who were marching him back to their line. In telling me the story, Big Boy said, "Mr. Gibbons, I made up my mind as I walked back with them that I might just as well be dead as to spend the rest of the war studying German."

So he had struck the man on the right and the one on the left and had downed both of them, but the German in back of him got him with the bayonet. A nerve center in his back was severed by the

Groans, Laughs, and Sobs in the Hospital

slash of the steel that extended almost from one shoulder to the other, and Big Boy had fallen to the ground, his arms and legs powerless. Then the German with the bayonet robbed him. Big Boy enumerated the loss to me—fifty-three dollars and his girl's picture.

Although paralyzed and helpless, there was nothing down in the mouth about Big Boy—indeed, he provided most of the fun in the ward. He had an idea all of his own about what he was going to do after the war, and he let us know about it that night.

"All of you guys have told what you're going to do," he said. "Now I'm going to tell you the truth. I'm going back to that little town of mine in Ohio and go down to the grocery store and sit there on a soap box on the porch.

"Then I'm going to gather all the little boys in the neighborhood round about me, and then I'm going to outlie the GAR."[3]

There was one thing in that ward that nobody could lie about, and that was the twitches of pain we suffered in the mornings when the old dressings of the day before were changed and new ones applied.

The doctor and his woman assistant who had charge of the surgical dressings on that corridor would arrive in the ward shortly after breakfast. They would be wheeling in front of them a rubber-tired, white-enameled vehicle on which were piled the jars of antiseptic gauze and trays of nickel-plated instruments, which both the doctor and his assistant would handle with rubber-gloved hands. In our ward that vehicle was known as the "Agony Cart," and every time it stopped at the foot of a bed, you would be pretty sure to hear a groan or a stifled wail in a few minutes.

We had various ways of expressing or suppressing the pain. You who have had a particularly vicious mustard plaster jerked off that tender spot in the back, right between the shoulders, have some small conception of the delicate sensation that accompanies the removal of old gauze from a healing wound.

Some of the men would grit their teeth and grunt; others would put their wrists in their mouths and bite themselves during the operation. Some others would try to keep talking to the doctor or the nurse while the ordeal was in progress, and others would just simply shout. There was little satisfaction to be gained from these expressions of pain because while one man was yelling, the other thirteen in the ward were shouting with glee and chaffing him, and as soon as his wounds had been redressed, he would join in the laughs at the expense of those who followed him.

Messages were usually carried by a young American woman who had a particular interest in our ward. Not strange to say, she had donned a Red Cross nursing uniform on the same day that most

Groans, Laughs, and Sobs in the Hospital

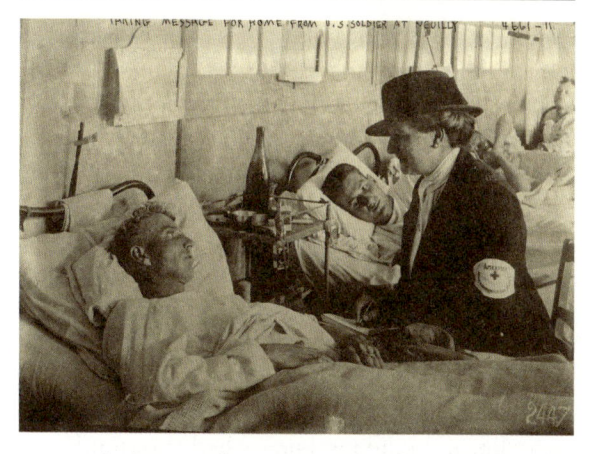

An American volunteer writing a letter for a wounded soldier at the hospital in Neuilly

of us arrived in that ward. She was one of the American women who brought us fruit, ice cream, candy, and cigarettes. She wrote letters for us to our mothers. She worked long hours, night and day, for us. In her absence, one day, the ward went into session and voted her its guardian angel. Out of modesty, I was forced to answer "Present" instead of "Aye" to the roll call. The Angel was and is my wife.

As Official Ward Angel, it was among the wife's duties to handle the matter of visitors, of which there were many. It seemed, during those early days in June, that every American woman in France dropped whatever war work she was doing and rushed to the American hospitals to be of whatever service she could. And it was not easy work these women accomplished. There was very little "forehead-rubbing" or "moving-picture nursing." Much of it was tile corridor scrubbing and pan cleaning. They stopped at no tasks they were called upon to perform. Many of them worked themselves sick during the long hours of that rush period.

During the first four or five days I was an inmate of the ward, I was most interested in all the voices I heard because I lay in total darkness. The bandages extended down from the top of my head to my upper lip, and I did not know whether or not I ever would see again. I would listen carefully to all remarks within ear shot, whether they be from doctors, nurses, or patients. I listened in the hope that from them I might learn whether or not there was a possibility of my regaining vision. But all of their remarks with regard to my condition were ambiguous and unsatisfactory. But from this I gained a listening habit, and that was how I became particularly interested in the very gruff voice that came from the corner on my left.

Other patients directing remarks into that corner would address them to a man whom they would call by the name "Red Shannahan." I was quick to connect the gruff voice and the name "Red Shannahan," and as I had lots of time and nothing else to do, I built up in my mind's eye a picture of a tall,

Groans, Laughs, and Sobs in the Hospital

husky, rough and ready, tough Irishman, with red hair—a man of whom it would be conceivable that he had wiped out some two or three German regiments before they got him. To find out more about this character, I called over to him one day. "Red Shannahan, are you there?" I said.

"Yes, Mr. Gibbons, I'm here" came the reply, and I was immensely surprised because it was not the gruff voice at all. It was the mild, unchanged voice of a boy, a boy whose tones were still in the upper register. The reply seemed almost girlish in comparison with the gruffer tones of the other patients, and I marveled that the owner of this polite, mannerly, high-pitched voice could be known by any such name as "Red Shannahan," I determined upon further investigation.

"Red Shannahan, what work did you do before you became a United States soldier?" I asked.

"Mr. Gibbons," came the reply, almost girlishly, "I am from Baltimore. I drove the wagon for Mr. Bishop, the canary bird and goldfish man."

All that had happened to this canary-bird fancier and goldfish tamer was that he had killed two Germans and captured three before they got him.

Among those who came to visit us in that ward, there appeared one day a man I had not seen in many years. When I knew him last, he had been a sport-loving fellow-student of mine at college and one of the fastest, hardest-fighting ends our varsity football squad ever had. Knowing this disposition of the man, I was quite surprised to see on the sleeve of his khaki service uniform the red shield and insignia of the Knights of Columbus.

I was well aware of the very valuable work done by this institution wherever American soldiers are in France, but I could not imagine this former college chum of mine being engaged in such work instead of being in the service. He noticed my silence, and he said, "Gib, do you remember that game with the Indians on Thanksgiving Day?"

"Yes," I replied, "they hurt your leg that day."

"Yes," replied my old college mate, whom we might as well call MacDougal inasmuch as that was not his name. "Yes, they took that leg away from me three years later."

I knew then why MacDougal was with the KC, and I wondered what service he would perform in our ward in the name of his organization. I soon found out. Without introduction, MacDougal proceeded to the bedside of Dan Bailey, the infantryman with one leg off, who was lying in a bed on my right. MacDougal walked back and forth two or three times past the foot of Bailey's bed. "How does that look?" he said to Bailey. "Do I walk all right?"

"Looks all right to me," replied Bailey; "what's the matter with you?"

MacDougal then began jumping, skipping, and hopping up and down and across the floor at the

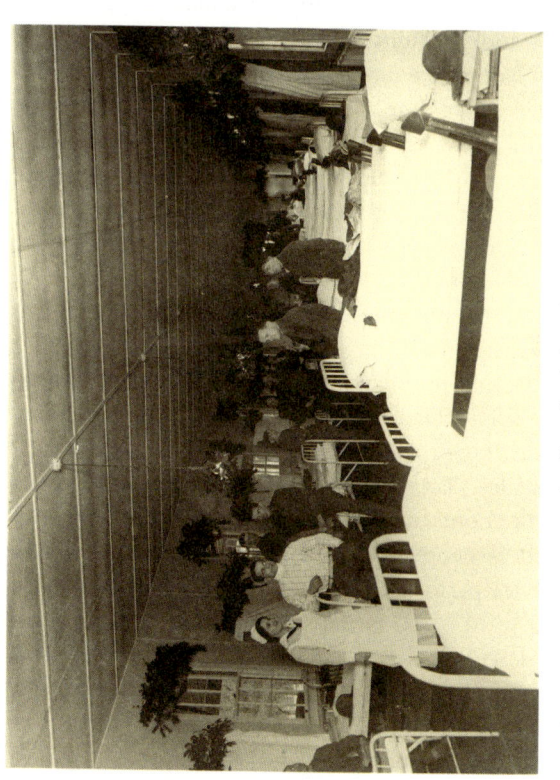

A military hospital ward

foot of Bailey's bed. Finishing these exercises breathlessly, he again addressed himself to the sufferer with one leg. "How did that look?" he said. "Did that look all right?"

"I don't see anything the matter with you," replied Bailey, "unless it is that you're in the wrong ward."

Then MacDougal stood close by Bailey's bedside where the boy with one leg could watch him closely. MacDougal took his cane and struck his own right leg a resounding whack. And we all knew by the sound of the blow that the leg he struck was wooden.

In that peculiar way did MacDougal bring into the life of Dan Bailey new interest and new prospects. He proved to Dan Bailey that for the rest of his life, Dan Bailey with an artificial limb could walk about and jump and skip and hop almost as well as people with two good legs. That was the service performed by the Knights of Columbus in our ward.

There was one other organization in that hospital that deserves mention. It was the most exclusive little clique and rather inclined toward snobbishness. I was a member of it. We used to look down on the ordinary wounded cases that had two eyes. We enjoyed, either rightly or wrongly, a feeling of superiority. Death comes mighty close when it nicks an eye out of your head. All of the one-eyed cases

Groans, Laughs, and Sobs in the Hospital

and some of the no-eyed cases received attention in one certain ward, and it was to this ward after my release from the hospital that I used to go every day for fresh dressings for my wounds. Every time I entered the ward, a delegation of one-eyed would greet me as a comrade and present me with a petition. In this petition I was asked and urged to betake myself to the hospital library, to probe the depths of the encyclopedias and from their wordy innards tear out one name for the organization of the one-eyed. This was to be our lifelong club, they said, and the insistence was that the name above all should be a "classy" name. So it came to pass that after much research and debate, one name was accepted, and from that time on we became known as the Cyclops Club.[4]

A wonderful Philadelphia surgeon was in charge of the work in that ward. Hundreds of American soldiers for long years after the war will thank him for seeing. I thank him for my sight now. His name is Dr. Fewell. The greatest excitement in the ward prevailed one day when one of the doctor's assistants entered carrying several flat, hard wood cases, each of them about a yard square. The cases opened like a book and were laid flat on the table. Their interiors were lined with green velvet, and there on the shallow receptacles in the green velvet were just dozens of eyes, gleaming unblinkingly up at us.

A shout went up and down the ward, and the

Cyclopians gathered around the table. There was a grand grab right and left. Everybody tried to get a handful. There was some difficulty reassorting the grabs. Of course, it happened that fellows that really needed blue or gray ones managed to get hold of black ones or brown ones, and some confusion existed while they traded back and forth to match up proper colors, shades, and sizes.

One Cyclopian was not in on the grab. In addition to having lost one eye, he had received about a pound and a half of assorted hardware in his back, and these flesh wounds confined him to his bed. He had been sleeping, and he suddenly awoke during the distribution of the glassware. He apparently became alarmed with the thought that he was going to be left out of consideration. I saw him sit bolt upright in bed as he shouted clear across the ward: "Hey, Doc, pass the grapes."

When it became possible for me to leave that hospital, I went to another one three blocks away. This was a remarkable institution that had been maintained by wealthy Americans living in France before the war. I was assigned to a room on the third floor—a room adjoining a sun parlor, overlooking a beautiful Old World garden with a lagoon, rustic bridges, trees, and shrubbery.

In early June, when that flood of American wounded had come back from the Marne, it had become necessary to erect hospital ward tents in the

Groans, Laughs, and Sobs in the Hospital

garden, and there a number of our wounded were cared for. I used to notice that every day two orderlies would carry out from one of the small tents a small white cot on which there lay an American soldier. They would place the cot on the green grass where the sunlight, finding its way through the leafy branches of the tree, would shine down upon the form of this young—this very young—fighter from the U.S.A.

He was just two months over seventeen years of age. He had deliberately and patriotically lied one year on his age in order that he might go to France and fight beneath our flag.

He was wounded, but his appearance did not indicate how badly. There were no bandages about his head, arms, or body. There was nothing to suggest the severity of his injuries—nothing save his small round spot on the side of his head where the surgeons had shaved away the hair—just a small round spot that marked the place where a piece of German hand grenade had touched the skull.

This little fellow had forgotten everything. He could not remember—all had slipped his mind save for the three or four lines of one little song, which was the sole remaining memory that bridged the gap of four thousand miles between him and his home across the sea.

Over and over again he would sing it all day long as he lay there on the cot with the sunlight stream-

Gibbons recovering from his wounds in France

ing all over him. His sweet boyish voice would come up through the leafy branches to the windows of my room.

I frequently noticed my nurse standing there at the window listening to him. Then I would notice that her shoulders would shake convulsively, and she would walk out of the room, wet-eyed but silent.

Just try to picture me
Back home in Tennessee,
Right by my mother's knee.
She thinks the world of me.
She will be there to meet me
With a hug and kiss she'll greet me,
When I get back, when I get back,
To my home in Tennessee.

American doctors and American nurses, both by their skill and care and tenderness, nursed that little fellow back to complete recovery, made him remember everything, and, shortly afterward, well and cured, he started back, safe and sound, to his home in Tennessee.

Nothing I can ever say will overstate my estimation of the credit that is deserved by our American doctors and nurses for the great work they are doing. I am not alone in knowing this. I call to witness any Canadian, Englishman, or Frenchman, that, if he is wounded, when in the ambulance, he

And They Thought We Wouldn't Fight

usually voices one request, "Take me to an American hospital."

I knew of one man who entered that United States Military Base Hospital near Paris, with one bullet through the shoulder, another through an arm, an eye shot out, and a compound fracture of the skull, and those American doctors and nurses by their attention and skillfulness made it possible for him to step back into boots and breeches and walk out of the hospital in ten days.

It so happens that I am somewhat familiar with the details in that case because I am the man.

Notes

1. Melinite: a high explosive made from picric acid.
2. Refers to St. Louis's National League club. Their rival, the St. Louis Browns, played in the American League.
3. The GAR: The Grand Army of the Republic was an organization of honorably discharged veterans of the Union (Northern) armed forces of the American Civil War.
4. Cyclops: a mythological giant with a single eye in the middle of its forehead.

"July 18"—The Turn of the Tide

THROUGH THE STEADY growth of Marshal Foch's reserves, by the speedy arrival of American forces, the fourth German offensive of 1918, the personally directed effort launched by the crown prince on May 27, had been brought to a standstill. The German thrust toward Paris had been stopped by the Americans at Château-Thierry and in the Bois de Belleau.

The German offensive had succeeded in pushing forward the enemy front until it formed a loop extending southward from the Aisne to the Valley of the Marne. This salient was called the Château-Thierry pocket. The line ran southward from a point east of Soissons to Château-Thierry, where it touched the Marne, thence eastward along both sides of the river to the vicinity of Oeuilly, where it recrossed the Marne and extended northward to points beyond Rheims.

Château-Thierry was thus the peak of the German push—the apex of the triangle pointing toward Paris. The enemy supplied its forces in this peak principally by the road that ran southward from Soissons and touched the Marne at Château-Thierry. To the west of this road and just south of the city of Soissons is the forest of Villers-Cotterêts. The enemy occupied the northern and eastern limits of the forest, and the remainder of it was in the hands of the French.

This forest has always been considered one of the sentinels of Paris. It was located on the right flank of the German salient. It was a menace to that flank and offered a most attractive opportunity for an Allied counteroffensive from that direction. The Germans were not unmindful of this.

A belief existed among the German high command that an attack might be made on July 4, out of consideration to American sentiment. When the attack did not develop on that day, they then thought that the French might possibly spring the blow on July 14, in celebration of their own national fête day. And again they were disappointed in their surmises.

So, on July 14, when the Allied counteroffensive had still failed to materialize, the German forces, by the necessity for time, moved to a sudden and faulty decision. They convinced themselves that they had overestimated the Allied strength. They accepted the belief that the reason Foch had not attacked was because he did not have sufficient strength to attack. With this, then, as a basis for their plans, they immediately launched another offensive, hoping that this might be the one in which they could deliver the final blow.

This action began on Monday morning, July 15, and extended from Château-Thierry eastward along

"July 18"—The Turn of the Tide

the valley of the Marne, northward to Rheims, and thence eastward. By a remarkable coup, one small patrol of French and Americans deprived the enemy of the element of surprise in the attack. On the morning of the previous day, this patrol successfully raided the enemy lines to the east of Rheims and brought back prisoners from whom it was learned that the Germans intended striking on the following morning. The objectives of the offensive were the French cities of Épernay and Châlons [-en-Champagne].

The Germans found the Allied line prepared to receive them. Their attacking waves were mowed down with terrific machine-gun fire from French and American gunners, while at the same time heavy artillery barrages played upon the German back areas with deadly effect in the massed ranks of the reserves. The fighting was particularly vicious. It was destined to be the Germans' last action of a grand offensive nature in the entire war.

On the line east of Rheims, the German assault was particularly strong in one sector where it encountered the sturdy ranks of the Rainbow Division of United States National Guardsmen, drawn from a dozen or more different states in the Union. Regiments from Alabama and New York held the front line. Iowa and Ohio were close in support. In the support positions, sturdy youngsters from Illinois, Indiana, and Minnesota manned the American artillery.

And They Thought We Wouldn't Fight

The French general commanding the sector had not considered it possible that this comparatively small American force could withstand the first onslaught of the Germans. He had made elaborate plans for a withdrawal to high ground two or three miles southward, from which he hoped to be able to resist the enemy to greater advantage. But all day long, through the 15th and the 16th and the 17th of July, those American lines held, and the advancing waves of German storm troops melted before our guns.

And so the line held, although the French general had in preparation the plans for withdrawal. When, at the end of the third day, the American line still occupied the same position, the French general found that his labor in preparing the plans for withdrawal had been for nothing. He is reported to have thrown his hands up in the air and remarked, "There doesn't seem to be anything to do but to let the war be fought out where the New York Irish and the Alabamans want to fight it."

There was one humorous incident worthy of record in that fighting. Great rivalry existed between the New York regiment and the Alabama regiment, both of which happened to be units of the same brigade. Both the New Yorkers and the Alabamans had a mutual hatred for the German, but, in addition to that, each of them was possessed with a mutual dislike for the other. There had been frequent

"July 18"—The Turn of the Tide

clashes of a more or less sportsmanlike and fistic nature between men from both of the regiments.

On the second day of the fighting, the Germans had sent over low-flying airplanes, which skimmed the tops of our trenches and sprayed them with machine-gun fire. A man from Alabama, who had grown up from childhood with a squirrel rifle under his arm, accomplished something that had never been done before in the war. From his position in a trench, he took careful aim with his rifle and brought down one of the German planes. It was the first time in the history of the western front that a rifleman on the ground had done this.

When the colonel of the New York regiment heard this, he was wild with envy and let it be known that there would be trouble brewing unless his regiment at least equaled the feat. So, on the following day, an Irishman in the ranks stood up and brought one German plane down, to the credit of the old Sixty-ninth.

* * *

To the southwest of Rheims, Germans, who succeeded in breaking through the lines at one place on the south banks of the Marne, encountered American reinforcements and were annihilated to the number of five thousand. At no place did the enemy meet with the success desired.

The Germans had launched their attack at six

o'clock on the morning of July 15. At Vaux their demonstration was considered a feint, but along the Marne to the east of Château-Thierry, between Fossoy and Mézy [-Moulins], the assaulting waves advanced with fury and determination. At one place, twenty-five thousand of the enemy crossed the river, and the small American forces in front of them at that place were forced to retire on Condé-en-Brie. In a counterattack, we succeeded in driving fifteen thousand of them back to the north bank, the remaining ten thousand representing casualties, with the exception of fifteen hundred, who were captured.

Further eastward, the Germans established bridgehead positions on the south bank of the river, at Dormans. The enemy enjoyed a minor success in an attack on the line near Bligny to the southwest of Rheims, where Italian troops fought with remarkable valor. Everywhere else the lines held solid, and upon the close of that first night, Marshal Foch said, "I am satisfied—*Je suis content.*"

At dawn the following day, the enemy's futile efforts were resumed along the river east of Château-Thierry. The Germans suffered appalling losses in their efforts to place pontoon bridges at Gland and at Mareuil-le-Port. St. Agnan and La Chapelle-Monthodon fell into the hands of Americans on the same day.

On the 17th, the enemy's endeavors to reach Festigny on both banks of the river came to naught,

"July 18"—The Turn of the Tide

but to the southeast of Rheims, his assaulting waves reached the northern limits of Montagne Forest. The Germans were trying to pinch out the Rheims salient. This was the condition of the opposing lines on the night of July 17—the night that preceded the day on which the tide of victory turned for the Allies.

Foch was now ready to strike. The Allied commander in chief had decided to deliver his blow on the right flank of the German salient. The line chosen for the Allied assault was located between a point south of Soissons and Château-Thierry. It represented a front of some twenty-five miles extending southward from the valley of the Aisne to the Marne. Villers-Cotterêts Forest was the key position for the Allies.

It was from out that forest that the full strength of the blow was to be delivered. To make the blow effective at that most vital point, Marshal Foch needed a strong and dependable assaulting force. He needed three divisions of the hardest-fighting soldiers that he could get. He had a considerable army to select from. As commander in chief of all the Allied armies, he was in command of all of the British army, all of the French army, all of the American army, the Italian, the Belgian—all of the military forces of the Allied nations of the world. Marshal Foch's command numbered eleven million bayonets.

And They Thought We Wouldn't Fight

The commander in chief had all of these veteran fighting men from which he could select the three divisions necessary to deliver this blow upon which the civilization of the world depended.

The first division he chose was the Foreign Legion of the French army. In four years of bloody fighting, the Foreign Legion, composed of soldiers of fortune from every country in the world, had never been absent in an attack. It had lived up thoroughly to its reputation as the most fearless unit of shock troops in the French army.

And then for the other two divisions that were needed, Marshal Foch selected, from all the eleven million men under his command, the First and the Second Regular United States Army Divisions. The Second Division included the immortal Brigade of United States Marines that had covered themselves with glory in the Bois de Belleau.

It was a great distinction for those two American divisions to have thus been selected to play such a vital part in the entire war. It was an honor that every officer and man in both divisions felt keenly.

* * *

For once, at least, the elements were favorable to our cause. There was no moon. The night was very dark, and under the trees the blackness seemed impenetrable. A heavy downpour of rain began, and although it turned most of the roads into mud, the

"July 18"—The Turn of the Tide

leafy roof of the forest held much of the moisture and offered some protection to the thousands of men who spent the night beneath it. Thunder rolled as I had never heard it roll in France before. The sound drowned the occasional boom of distant cannon. At intervals, terrific crashes would be followed by blinding flashes of lightning as nature's bolts cut jagged crevices in the somber sky and vented their fury upon some splintered giant of the forest.

The immediate front was silent—comparatively silent if one considered the din of the belligerent elements. In the opposing front lines in the northern and eastern limits of the forest, German and Frenchmen alike huddled in their rude shelters to escape the rain.

Then, along every road leading through the forest to the north and to the east, streams of traffic began to pour. All of it was moving forward toward the front. No traffic bound for the rear was permitted. Every inch of available road space was vitally necessary for the forces in movement. The roads that usually accommodated one line of vehicles moving forward and one line moving to the rear now represented two streams—solid streams—moving forward. In those streams were gun carriages, caissons, limbers, ammunition carts, and grunting tractors hauling large field pieces.

In the gutters on either side of the road, long lines of American infantry plodded forward through the mud and darkness. In the occasional flash of a light, I could see that they were equipped for heavy fighting. Many of them had their coats off, their sleeves rolled up, while beads of sweat stood out on the young faces that shone eager beneath the helmets. On their backs they carried, in addition to their cumbersome packs, extra shoes and extra bandoliers of cartridges.

From their shoulders were suspended gas masks and haversacks. Their waists were girded with loaded ammunition belts, with bayonet hanging at the left side. Some of them wore grenade aprons full of explosives. Nearly all of them carried their rifles or machine-gun parts slung across their backs as they leaned forward under their burdens and plunged wearily on into the mud and darkness, the thunder and lightning, the world destiny that was before them. Their lines were interspersed with long files of plodding mules dragging small two-wheeled narrow-gauge carts loaded down with machine-gun ammunition.

Under the trees to either side of the road, there was more movement. American engineers struggled forward through the underbrush, carrying, in addition to their rifles and belts, rolls of barbed wire, steel posts, picks and shovels, and axes and saws. Beside them marched the swarthy, undersized, bearded veterans of the Foreign Legion. Further still under the trees, French cavalry, with their lances

"July 18"—The Turn of the Tide

slung slantwise across their shoulders, rode their horses in and out between the giant trunks.

At road intersections, I saw mighty metal monsters with steel-plated sides splotched with green and brown and red paint. These were the French tanks that were to take part in the attack. They groaned and grunted on their grinding gears as they maneuvered about for safer progress. In front of each tank there walked a man who bore suspended from his shoulders on his back, a white towel so that the unseen directing genius in the tank's turret could steer his way through the underbrush and crackling saplings that were crushed down under the tread of this modern juggernaut.

There was no confusion, no outward manifestations of excitement. There was no rattle of musketry, shouting of commands, or waving of swords. Officers addressed their men in whispers. There was order and quiet save for the roll of thunder and the eternal dripping of water from the wet leaves, punctuated now and then by the ear-splitting crashes that followed each nearby flash of lightning.

All night long the gathering of that sinister synod continued. I knew, all of us knew, that at the zero hour, 4:35 o'clock in the morning, all hell would land on the German line, and these men from the trees would move forward with the fate of the world in their hands.

But the enemy never knew. They never even suspected. And at the tick of 4:35 A.M. the heavens seemed to crash asunder, as tons and tons of hot metal sailed over the forest, bound for the German line.

That mighty artillery eruption came from a concentration of all the guns of all calibers of all the Allies that Foch could muster. It was a withering blast, and where it landed in that edge of the forest occupied by the Germans, the quiet of the dripping black night was suddenly turned into a roaring inferno of death.

Giant tree trunks were blown high into the air and splintered into matchwood. Heavy projectiles bearing delayed-action fuses penetrated the ground to great depth before exploding, and then, with the expansion of their powerful gases, crushed the enemy dugouts as if they were egg shells.

Then young America—your sons and your brothers and your husbands, shoulder to shoulder with the French—went over the top to victory.

The preliminary barrage moved forward, crashing the forest down about it. Behind it went the tanks ambling awkwardly but irresistibly over all obstructions. Those Germans that had not been killed in the first terrific blast came up out of their holes only to face French and American bayonets, and the "*Kamerad*" [surrender] chorus began at once.

Our assaulting waves moved forward, never hesitating, never faltering. Ahead of them were the

"July 18"—The Turn of the Tide

tanks giving special attention to enemy machine-gun nests that manifested stubbornness. We did not have to charge those death-dealing nests that morning as we did in the Bois de Belleau. The tanks were there to take care of them. One of these would move toward a nest, flirt around it several minutes, and then politely sit on it. It would never be heard from thereafter.

It was an American whirlwind of fighting fury that swept the Germans in front of it early that morning. Airplanes had been assigned to hover over the advance and make reports on all progress. A dense mist hanging over the forest made it impossible for the aviators to locate the Divisional Headquarters to which they were supposed to make the reports. These dense clouds of vapor obscured the earth from the eyes of the airmen, but with the rising sun the mists lifted.

Being but a month out of the hospital and having spent a rather strenuous night, I was receiving medical attention at daybreak in front of a dressing station not far from the headquarters of Major General Harbord, commanding the Second Division. As I lay there looking up through the trees, I saw a dark speck diving from the sky. Almost immediately I could hear the hum of its motors growing momentarily louder as it neared the earth. I thought the plane was out of control and expected to see it crash to the ground near me.

And They Thought We Wouldn't Fight

Several hundred feet above the treetops, it flattened its wings and went into an easy swoop so that its under-gear seemed barely to skim the uppermost branches. The machine pursued a course immediately above one of the roads. Something dropped from it. It was a metal cylinder that glistened in the rays of the morning sun. Attached to it was a long streamer of fluttering white material. It dropped easily to the ground nearby. I saw an American signalman, who had been following its descent, pick it up. He opened the metal container and extracted the message containing the first aerial observations of the advance of the American lines. It stated that large numbers of prisoners had been captured and were bound for the rear.

Upon receipt of this information, Division Headquarters moved forward on the jump. Prisoners were coming back in droves. I encountered one column of disarmed Germans marching four abreast with the typical attitude of a "*Kamerad*" procession. The first eight of the prisoners carried on their shoulders two rudely constructed litters made from logs and blankets. A wounded American was on one litter and a wounded Frenchman on the other.

Slightly wounded Americans came back guarding convoys of prisoners. They returned loaded with relics of the fighting. It was said that day that German prisoners had explained that in their opinion, the British were in the war because they hated

An American soldier guarding German prisoners

Germany and that the French were in the war because the war was in France, but that Americans seemed to be fighting to collect souvenirs.

* * *

The prisoners came back so fast that the Intelligence Department was flooded. The divisional intelligence officer asked me to assist in the interrogation of the captives. I questioned some three hundred of them.

An American sergeant who spoke excellent German interrogated. I sat behind a small table in a field, and the sergeant would call the prisoners forward one by one. In German he asked one captive what branch of the service he belonged to. The prisoner, wishing to display his knowledge of English and at the same time give vent to some pride, replied in English. "I am of the storm troop," he said.

"Storm troop?" replied the American sergeant. "Do you know what we are? We are from Kansas. We are Cycloners."

Another German student of English among the prisoners was represented in the person of a pompous German major, who, in spite of being a captive, maintained all the dignity of his rank. He stood proudly erect and held his head high. He wore a disgusted look on his face, as though the surroundings were painful. His uniform was well pressed; his linen was clean; his boots were well polished; he was

"July 18"—The Turn of the Tide

clean shaven. There was not a speck of dust upon him, and he did not look like a man who had gone through the hell of battle that morning. The American sergeant asked him in German to place the contents of his pockets on the table.

"I understand English," he replied superciliously, with a strong accent, as he complied with the request. I noticed, however, that he neglected to divest himself of one certain thing that caught my interest. It was a leather thong that extended around his neck and disappeared between the first and second buttons of his tunic. Curiosity forced me to reach across the table and extract the hidden terminal of that thong. I found suspended on it the one thing in all the world that exactly fitted me and that I wanted. It was a one-eyed field glass. I thanked him.

All through that glorious day of the 18th, our lines swept forward victoriously. The First Division fought it out on the left, the Foreign Legion in the center, and the Second Division with the marines pushed forward on the right. Village after village fell into our hands. We captured batteries of guns and thousands of prisoners.

On through the night the Allied assault continued. Our men fought without water or food. All road space behind the lines was devoted to the forwarding of reserves, artillery, and munitions. By the morning of the 19th, we had so far penetrated the enemy's lines that we had crossed the road running southward from Soissons to Château-Thierry, thereby disrupting the enemy's communications between his newly established base and the peak of his salient. Thus exposed to an enveloping movement that might have surrounded large numbers, there was nothing left for the Germans to do but to withdraw.

The Germans began backing off the Marne. From that day on, their movement to date has continued backward. It began July 18. Two American Divisions played glorious parts in the crisis. It was their day. It was America's day. It was the turn of the tide.

The Dawn of Victory

THE WAITED HOUR had come. The forced retreat of the German hordes had begun. Hard on their heels, the American lines started their northward push, backing the Boche off the Marne.

On the morning of July 21, I rode into Château-Thierry with the first American soldiers to enter the town. The Germans had evacuated hurriedly. Château-Thierry was reoccupied jointly by our forces and those of the French.

For seven long weeks the enemy had been in occupation of that part of the city on the north bank of the river. Now the streets were littered with debris. Although the walls of most of the buildings seemed to be in good shape, the scene was one of utter devastation.

The Germans had built barricades across the streets—particularly the streets that led down to the river—because it was those streets that were swept with the terrific fire of American machine guns. At the intersections of those streets, the Germans under cover of night had taken up the cobblestones and built parapets to protect them from the hail of lead.

Shop after shop had been looted of its contents, and the fronts of the pretty sidewalk cafés along this business thoroughfare had been reduced to shells of their former selves. Not a single living being was in sight as we marched in. Some of the old townsfolk and some young children had remained, but they were still under cover.

The town had been systematically pillaged. The German soldiers had looted from the shops much material which they had made up into packages to be mailed back to home folks in the fatherland. The church, strangely enough, was picked out as a depository for their larcenies. Nothing from the robes of the priests down to the copper faucet of a water pipe had escaped their greed.

The advancing Americans did not linger in the town—save for small squads of engineers that busied themselves with the removal of the street obstructions and the supply organizations that perfected communication for the advancing lines. These Americans were Yankees all—they comprised the 26th U.S. Division, representing the National Guard of New England.

Our lines kept pushing to the north. The Germans continued their withdrawal, and the Allied necessity was to keep contact with them. This, the Yankee Division succeeded in doing. The first obstacle encountered to the north of Château-Thierry was the stand that the Germans made at the town of Épieds.

On July 23, our infantry had proceeded up a ravine that paralleled the road into Épieds. German

The Dawn of Victory

machine guns placed on the hills about the village swept them with a terrible fire. Our men succeeded in reaching the village, but the Germans responded with such a terrific downpour of shell that our weakened ranks were forced to withdraw and the Germans re-entered the town.

On the following day we renewed the attack with the advantage of positions which we had won during the night in the Bois de Trugny and the Bois de Châtelet. We advanced from three sides and forced the Germans to evacuate. Trugny, the small village on the edge of the woods, was the scene of more bloody fighting which resulted in our favor.

Further north of Épieds, the Germans, having entrenched themselves along the roadway, had fortified the same with a number of machine guns which commanded the flat terrain in such a way as to make a frontal attack by infantry waves most costly. The security of the Germans in this position received a severe shock when ten light automobiles, each one mounting one or two machine guns, started up the road toward the enemy, firing as they sped. It was something new. The Germans wanted to surrender, but the speed of the cars obviated such a possibility. So the enemy fled before our gasoline cavalry.

The Germans were withdrawing across the river Ourcq, whose valley is parallel to that of the Marne and just to the north. The enemy retired in orderly fashion. He bitterly contested every foot of ground he was forced to give. The American troops engaged in those actions had to fight hard for every advance. The German backed out of the Marne salient as a Western "bad man" would back out of a saloon with an automatic pistol in each hand.

Those charges that our men made across the muddy flats of the Ourcq deserve a place in the martial history of America. They faced a veritable hell of machine-gun fire. They went through barrages of shrapnel and high-explosive shell. They invaded small forests that the enemy had flooded with poison gas. No specific objectives were assigned. The principal order was "Up and at 'em," and this was reinforced by every man's determination to keep the enemy on the run now that they had been started.

Even the enemy's advantage of high positions north of the river failed to hold back the men from New York, from Iowa, Alabama, Ohio, Illinois, Minnesota, and Indiana, who had relieved the hard-fighting Yankees. These new American organizations went up against fresh German divisions that had been left behind with orders to hold at all cost. But nothing the enemy could do could prevent our crossing of the Ourcq.

On July 30, the fighting had become most intense in character. The fact that the town of Sergy was captured, lost, and recaptured nine times within twenty-four hours is some criterion of the bitterness of the struggle. This performance of our men can be better understood when it is stated that the enemy opposing them there consisted of two fresh divisions of the kaiser's finest—his Prussian Guard.

After that engagement with our forces, the Fourth Prussian Guard Division went into an enforced retirement. When our men captured Sergy the last time, they did so in sufficient strength to withhold it against repeated fierce counterattacks by a Bavarian Guard Division that had replaced the wearied Prussians.

But before the crack Guard Division was withdrawn from the line, it had suffered terrible losses at our hands. Several prisoners captured said that their company had gone into the fight 150 strong, and only seven had survived. That seven were captured by our men in hand-to-hand fighting.

While our engineer forces repaired the roads and constructed bridges in the wake of our advancing lines, the enemy brought to that part of the front new squadrons of air fighters which were sent over our lines for the purpose of observation and interference with communications. They continually bombed our supply depots and ammunition dumps.

After the crossing of the Ourcq, the American advance reached the next German line of resistance, which rested on two terminal strongholds. One was in the Forêt de Nesles, and the other was in the Bois de Meunière.

The fighting about these two strong points was particularly fierce. In the Bois de Meunière and around the town of Cierges, the German resistance was most determined. About three hundred jaegers [light infantry] held Hill 200, which was located in the center of Cierges Forest, just to the south of the village of the same name. They were well provided with machine guns and ammunition. They were under explicit orders to hold, and they did.

Our men finally captured the position at the point of the bayonet. Most of its defenders fought to the death. The capture of the hill was the signal for a renewal of our attacks against the seemingly impregnable Meunière Woods. Six times our advancing waves reached the German positions in the southern edge of the woods, and six times we were driven back.

There were some American Indians in the ranks of our units attacking there—there were lumberjacks and farmer boys and bookkeepers, and they made heroic rushes against terrific barriers of hidden machine guns. But after a day of gallant fighting, they had been unable to progress.

Our efforts had by no means been exhausted. The following night our artillery concentrated on the southern end of the woods and literally turned it into an inferno with high-explosive shells. Early

The Dawn of Victory

in the morning we moved to the attack again. Two of the kaiser's most reputable divisions, the 200th Jaegers and the 216th Reserve, occupied the wood. The fighting in the wood was fierce and bloody, but it was more to the liking of our men than the rushes across fire-swept fields. Our men went to work with the bayonet. And for six hours they literally carved their way through four kilometers of the forest. Before ten o'clock the next morning, our lines lay to the north of the woods.

In consolidating the gains in the woods, our men surrounded in a small clearing some three hundred of the enemy who refused to surrender. American squads advanced with the bayonet from all sides. The Germans were fighting for their lives. Only three remained to accept the ignominy of capture.

Our forward progress continued, and by August 4 the Germans were withdrawing across the Vesle River. The immediate objective that presented itself to the Americans was the important German supply depot at Fismes. It was in and around Fismes that some of the bloodiest fighting in the Second Battle of the Marne took place.

The German line on the Vesle River fell shortly after the capture of Fismes. The enemy was forced to fall back to his next natural line of defense on the Aisne. Between the Vesle and the Aisne, the Americans assisted the French in the application of such persistent pressure that the enemy's stubborn resistance was overcome, and in many places he was forced to withdraw before he had time to destroy his depots of supply.

* * *

Through the month of August and up to the first days of September, the Americans participated in the important operations to the north of Soissons, where, on August 29, they played a big part in the capture of the Juvigny Plateau.

In this fighting, which was marked by the desperate resistance of the enemy, the Americans were incorporated in the 10th French Army under the command of General Mangin. Violent counterattacks by German shock divisions failed to stem the persistent advances of our forces.

A large hill to the north of Juvigny constituted a key and supporting position for the enemy. In spite of the large number of machine guns concealed on its slopes, the Americans succeeded in establishing a line between the hill and the town. At the same time, the American line extended itself around the other side of the hill. With the consummation of this enveloping movement, the hill was taken by assault.

On Labor Day, September 2, after bitterly engaging four German divisions for five days, the Americans advanced their lines to Terny-Sorny and the road running between Soissons and St. Quentin.

The Dawn of Victory

This achievement, which was accomplished by driving the Germans back a depth of four miles on a two-mile front, gave our forces a good position on the important plateau running to the north of the Aisne.

Our observation stations now commanded a view across the valley toward the famous Chemin des Dames, which at one time had been a part of the Hindenburg line. Before the invasion of the German hordes, France possessed no fairer countryside than the valley of the Aisne. But the Germans, retreating, left behind them only wreckage and ashes and ruin.

* * *

August 10 marked a milestone in the military effort of the United States. On that day the organization was completed of the First American Field Army. From now on, the American army was to be on a par with the French army and the British army, all three of them under the sole direction of the Allied generalissimo, Marshal Ferdinand Foch.

It might not be amiss to point out that an American division numbers thirty thousand men and that an American corps consists of six divisions and auxiliary troops, such as air squadrons, tank sections, and heavy artillery, which bring the strength of an American army corps to between 225,000 and 250,000 men. By the 1st of September, the United

African American soldiers, heavily laden, marching in France

The Dawn of Victory

States of America had five such army corps in the field, marshaling a strength of about one and one-half million bayonets. General Pershing was in command of this group of armies which comprised the First American Field Army.

It was from these forces that General Pershing selected the strong units which he personally commanded in the first major operation of the First American Field Army as an independent unit in France. That operation was the beginning of the Pershing push toward the Rhine—it was the Battle of St. Mihiel.

The important material results of the Battle of St. Mihiel are most susceptible to civilian as well as military comprehension. The St. Mihiel salient had long constituted a pet threat of the enemy. The Germans called it a dagger pointed at the heart of eastern France. For three years the enemy occupying it had successfully resisted all efforts of the Allies to oust them.

The salient was shaped like a triangle. The apex of the triangle—the point of the dagger—thrusting southward, rested on the town of St. Mihiel, on the river Meuse. The western flank of the triangle extended northward from St. Mihiel to points beyond Verdun. The eastern flank of the triangle extended in a northeasterly direction toward Pont-à-Mousson. It was the strongest position held by the Germans in Lorraine—if not on the entire front.

And They Thought We Wouldn't Fight

The geographical formation of the salient was an invitation for the application of a pincers operation. The point of leverage of the opposing jaws of the pincers was, most naturally, the apex of the triangle at St. Mihiel.

One claw of the pincers—a claw some eight-miles thick—bit into the east side of the salient near Pont-à-Mousson on the west bank of the Moselle River. The other claw of the pincers was about eight-miles thick, and it bit into the western flank of the salient in the vicinity of the little town of Haudiomont, on the heights of the Meuse and just a little distance to the east of the Meuse River.

The distance across that part of the salient through which the pincer's claws were biting was about thirty miles, and the area which would be included in the bite would be almost 175 square miles. This, indeed, was a major operation.

The battle began at one o'clock on the morning of September 12, when the concentrated ordnance of the heaviest American artillery in France opened a preparatory fire of unprecedented intensity.

At five o'clock in the dim dawn of that September morning, our infantry waves leaped from their trenches and moved forward to the assault. The claw of the pincers on the eastern flank of the salient began to bite in.

One hour later the claw of the pincers on the western flank of the salient began to move forward.

The Dawn of Victory

On the east, our men went forward on the run over ground that we had looked upon with envious eyes from the day that the first American troops reached the front. Before noon we had taken the villages of Lahayville, St. Baussant, Vilcey, and the Bois de Mort-Mare, and we were still advancing. By nightfall, our lines were still on the move beyond Essey and we were holding the important town of Thiaucourt and claimed Villers sur Penny for our own.

The seemingly impregnable fortress of Mont Sec had been surrounded, our tanks had cleared the way through Pannes, we had taken Nonsard, and the towns of Woinville and Buxières had fallen into our hands.

On the west side of the salient, the day had gone equally well for us. The western claw of the pincers had pushed due east through the towns of Spada and Lavigneville. Our men had swept on in the night through Chaillon; we had taken St. Remy and had cleared the Forêt de Montagne. By midnight their advanced patrols had reached the western part of the town of Vigneulles. In the meantime, our forces on the eastern side of the salient were pushing westward toward this same town of Vigneulles. At three o'clock in the morning, the forces from the east were occupying the eastern part of the town. The pincers had closed; the St. Mihiel salient had been pinched off.

Our forces actually met at nine o'clock on the

morning of September 13. The junction was made at the town of Heudicourt to the south of Vigneulles. We had pocketed all of the German forces to the south of that town. Our center had moved forward at nine o'clock the night before and occupied St. Mihiel on the heels of the retreating Germans. But the withdrawal was too late. Large numbers of them found themselves completely surrounded in the forests between St. Mihiel on the south and Heudicourt on the north.

We closed in during the afternoon and started to open the prize package. Located in the area, encircled by our troops, was the Bois de Versel, the Bois de Gaumont, and the Bois de Woeuvre. Each one of these little forests gave up its quota of prisoners, while much materiel and rich booty of war fell into our hands.

The principal avenue that had been opened for the Germans to make a possible withdrawal led through Vigneulles, and before our pincers had completely closed, the fleeing enemy had poured out through that gap at the rate of several thousand an hour. The roads were blocked for miles with their transportation, and when the American artillery turned its attention to these thoroughfares, crowded with confused Germans, the slaughter was terrific. For days after the battle our sanitation squads were busy at their gruesome work.

In conception and execution the entire operation

The Dawn of Victory

had been perfect. Confusion had been visited upon the method-loving enemy from the beginning. By reason of the disruption of their intercommunications, faulty liaison had resulted, and division had called to division in vain for assistance, not knowing at the time that all of them were in equally desperate straits. The enemy fought hard but to no purpose.

One entire regiment with its commander and his staff was captured. With both flanks exposed, it had suddenly been confronted by Americans on four sides. The surrender was so complete that the German commander requested that his roll should be called in order to ascertain the extent of his losses. When this was done, everyone was accounted for except one officer and one private.

As his command was so embarrassingly complete, the German commander asked permission to march it off in whatever direction desired by his captors. The request was granted, and there followed the somewhat amusing spectacle of an entire German regiment, without arms, marching off the battlefield under their own officers. The captured regiment was escorted to the rear by mounted American guards, who smilingly and leisurely rode their horses cowboy fashion as they herded their captives back to the pens.

Tons upon tons of ammunition fell into our hands in the woods. At one place twenty-two railroad cars loaded with large-caliber ammunition had to be abandoned when an American shell had torn up the track to the north of them. But if the Germans had been unable to take with them their equipment, they had succeeded in driving ahead of them on the retreat almost all of the French male civilians between sixteen and forty-five years that had been used as German slaves for more than four years.

The Americans were welcomed as deliverers by those French civilians that remained in the town. They were found to be almost entirely ignorant of the most commonly known historical events of the war. Secretary of War Baker and generals Pershing and Pétain visited the town of St. Mihiel a few hours after it was captured. They were honored with a spontaneous demonstration by the girls and aged women, who crowded about them to express thanks and pay homage for deliverance.

One of our bands began to play the "Marseillaise," and the old French civilians, who, under German domination, had not heard the national anthem for four long years, broke down and wept. The mayor of the town told how the Germans had robbed it of millions of francs. First they had demanded and received 1,500,000 francs, and later they collected 500,000 more in three installments. In addition to these robberies, they had taken by "requisition" all the furniture and mattresses and civilian comforts that they could find. They took

The Dawn of Victory

what they wanted and usually destroyed the rest. They had stripped the towns of all metal utensils, bells, statues, and water pipes.

The St. Mihiel salient thus went out of existence. The entire point in the blade of the dagger that had been thrust at the heart of France had been bitten off. Verdun with its rows upon rows of sacred dead was now liberated from the threat of envelopment from the right. The Allies were in possession of the dominating heights of the Meuse. The railroads connecting Commercy with Vigneulles, Thiaucourt, and St. Mihiel were in our hands. Our lines had advanced close to that key of victory, the Briey iron basin to the north, and the German fortress of Metz lay under American guns.

The battle only lasted twenty-seven hours. In that space of time, a German force estimated at one hundred thousand had been vanquished, if not literally cut to pieces, American soldiers had wrested 150 square miles of territory away from the Germans, captured fifteen thousand officers and men and hundreds of guns.

And while this great battle was in progress, the Allied lines were advancing everywhere. In Flanders, in Picardy, on the Marne, in Champagne, in Lorraine, in Alsace, and in the Balkans, the frontier of freedom was moving forward.

Surely the tide had turned. And surely it had been America's God-given opportunity to play the big part she did play. The German was now on the run. Suspicious whisperings of peace began to be heard in neutral countries. They had a decided German accent. Germany saw defeat staring her in the face, and, now, having failed to win in the field, she sought to win by a bluff at the peace table.

Germany was willing to make any concessions to bring about negotiations that would save her from a defeat in the field. There was one thing, however, that Germany wanted to save from the ruin she had brought down upon herself. That thing was the German army and its strong auxiliary, the German navy. Neither one of them had been destroyed. The army was in general retreat, and the navy was locked up in the Baltic, but both of them remained in existence as menaces to the future peace of the world. With these two forces of might, Germany could have given up her booty of war, offered reparation for her transgressions, and drawn back behind the Rhine to await the coming of another *Der Tag* [momentous day], when she could send them once more crashing across friendly borders and cruising the seven seas on missions of piracy.

Our army in France knew that if peace came with an unwhipped Prussian army in existence, the world would be just as unsafe for democracy as it had ever been. Our army in France wanted no compromise that would leave Germany in possession of the instruments that had made possible her crimes

U.S. 64th Regiment celebrating the armistice

against the world. Every man that had shed blood, every man that had paid the final price, every woman that had shed tears, every cherished ideal of our 140 years of national life, would have been sacrificed in vain if we had condoned Germany's high crimes against civilization and had made a compromise with the criminal.

Woodrow Wilson, president of the United States, spokesman of the Allied world, sounded the true American note when, in his reply to the insincere German peace proposals, he referred the German government to Marshal Foch, commander in chief of the Allied armies. War by the sword was to bring peace by the sword.

And as I write these lines in the last days of October 1918, unconditional surrender is the song of the dove of peace perched on our bayonets as we march into the dawn of victory.

Index

Index

Note: *Italicized* page numbers indicate illustrations. Numbers after *n* refer to notes.

African Americans: musicians, 222; soldiers, 58-59, 328
Aisne River/Valley, 225–26, 307, 325–27
Alpine Chasseurs (Blue Devils), 66, 78*n*
Amalgamation policy, xl–xli
American Expeditionary Forces (AEF), xxxix–xl; at Battle of Château-Thierry, 302–18; at Battle of the Bois de Belleau, 236–42; first all-American sector, 117–42; hospital unit, 71–72; National Guardsmen, 195, 228–229, 303, 320; in Paris, 49–50, 213–22; in Picardy region, 155–80; problems faced by, xliii–xliv; in St. Nazaire, 51, *52*, 53–64.
American neutrality, World War I and, xx–xxii
American volunteers, xli, 72
Amiens, 194, 223
Ansauville, 118–23
Apremont (forest), 198
Armentières, 223
Arras, 155, 223
Artillery batteries, 108–16; training grounds and exercises, 73–75; travel to front lines, 79–92, *84*, *87*

Bailey, Dan, 285, 292, 294
Baker, Newton D., xl, lii*n*11, 334
Baltic, 31–33
Bathelemont, 115–16
Bazin, Henri, 131, 142
Beaumont, 125, 196
Beauvais, 174, 194
Belleau, Bois de: fighting at, 236–42; casualties, xlvi, 239, 243, 252–57; Ludendorff offensives and, xlv, 301
Bernstorff, Count Johann-Heinrich von, 4, 30*n*
Berry, Maj. John, 248–51, *253*, 256–57
Besançon, 83, 85–87, *87*
Bois. *See under specific name, e.g.,* Belleau, Bois de
Bolsheviks, xxxvi
Boulogne-sur-Mare, 37, 40
Brest-Litovsk, Treaty of, xxxvi
Briey iron basin, 335
Britain: blockade policy, xxi–xxii, xlv; U.S. economic links with, xxii–xxiii; U.S. relations with, xli
Bundy, Gen. Omar, 244

Campbell, Gen. William Pitcairn, K.C.B., 33, 48*n*2

341

Index

Cantigny: American shelling and capture of, 193, 195; German occupation of, 177, 193; soldier wounded at, 285

Carranza, Venustiano, xxvi, li*n*8

Carroll, Raymond G., 109

Cedros Island, xxvii

Châlons-en-Champagne, 303

Chambrun, Marquis de (Pierre), 47, 48*n*7

Château-Thierry: battle aftermath, 319–20; *232*; fighting at/near, 226–33, 243, 302–18; location of, 227

Château-Thierry pocket, 301

Châtelet, Bois de, 321

Chaumont-en-Vexin, 165

Chemin des Dames offensive, xxxvii, xl, 224–26, 327

Chicago Tribune, xxv–xxvi, xxxi, xxxiii, li*n*6, 109

Cierges: town, 324; forest, 324

Clark, James Beauchamp, 86, 92*m*

Cohan, George M., xliii, lii*m*3, 213

Communism, democracy *vs.,* xxxvi; Wilson on, xxxv

Crillon, Hôtel de, 44, 49

Crozier, Emmet, lii*m*4

Cyclops Club, 295

Daly, Sgt. Maj. Daniel, xlvi, 242*n*4

Dear, Captain, 18, 20, 25–26

Diaz, Porfirio, xxvi

Domrémy-la-Pucelle, 66

Economic links, between U.S. and Europe, xxii–xxiii

Épernay, 303

Épieds, 320–21

Evans, Maj. Frank E., 240

Eyre, Lincoln, 130, 133, 140

Fewell, Dr. (surgeon), 295

First American Field Army, 327, 329

Flanders, 223, 335

Flirey, 117

Foch, Marshal Ferdinand, 180*n*2; Château-Thierry action and, 301–2, 306–8, 312; selected supreme commander, 155–56; First American Field Army and, 327; Wilson and, 338

Folkestone (England), 36–37

Foreign Legion (French), 308, 310, 317

Forêt. *See under specific name, e.g.,* Montagne, Forêt de

Fontaine, Hôtel de la, 98, 100–101

France: American volunteers in, xli, 72; troop mutinies, xxxvii–xxxviii; U.S. links/relations with, xxiii, xli

Frederick VIII, xxxi, 5

George V (king), 35, 48*n*3

German agents, in U.S., xxiii

German army divisions: 4th Prussian Guard, 323; 36th, 228; 216th Reserve, 325; Bavarian Guard, 323; Jaegers, 325

German-Mexican alliance, xxxi

German navy, xxi–xxii; submarine warfare, xxi, xxiii–xxv, xxix, xxxi

342

Index

German prisoners, 55-56, 61–63, 177, 205-07, 210-11, 303, 314, *315*, 316-17, 323, 332
Gibbons, Edward, li*n*5
Gibbons, Floyd: awards and honors, xlvii, l, lii*n*16; early career of, xxv–xxvi; death of, l; *Laconia* sinking and, xxxi, xxxiii; lectures in USA, xlvii; in Mexico, xxvi–xxvii; as pacifist, xlix; post-WWI career of, xlvii–xlx, *xlviii*; *The Red Napoleon*, xlix, lii*n*15; Sahara expedition, xlix:, as war correspondent, xxxiv–xxxv, xlix–l; wounded, xlvii, 243, 252-57, 278-300
Gibbons, Mrs. Floyd, 78, 264, 289
Gleaves, Rear Admiral Albert, 64, 64*n*4
Griffin, Peter, 145, 148–51
Griffiths, Maj. Richard Henry, 119, 124, 142*n*2; coded communications of, 129–30; front line tour with correspondents, 131–42
Guahn, Pat, 145, 147, 151

Haig, Sir Douglas, xxxix
Harbord, Maj. Gen. (John Guthrie), 236, 242*n*2, 244, 313
Hartzell, Lt. Arthur E. (Oscar in the text), 266*m*1; aids wounded Gibbons, 267–72, 274, 276–78; in Battle of the Bois de Belleau, 245–46, 248–50, 259–61, 264–66

Hayes, Sgt. Stephen, 278
Hillaire, Brig. Gen., 219
Hugo, Victor, 240–41, 242*n*3

Illinois National Guard, xxxiv
Infantry units, 57; at Bois de Belleau, xlvi; training grounds and exercises, 65–66, *67, 68*–69; travel to front lines, xliv, 118–33

Japanese-Mexican alliance, xxvii, xxx–xxxi
Jard, Château du, 165
Jarville-la-Malgrange, 93–95, 97
Jaulgonne, 227–29
Jeanne d'Arc, 66
Joffre, Marshal Joseph, 41, 48*n*6
Juvigny Plateau, 326

Kerensky, Alexander, xxxv–xxxvi
Knights of Columbus, 292, 294

La Ferté-sous-Juarre, 244
La Voie du Châtel, 245
Laburnum, 27
Laconia, 5–30; sinking of, xxxi, xxxiii, xxxiv, xlvi, 9–30
Lafayette, Marquis de, xlii–xliii; tomb of, 45, *46*, 47, 48*n*8
Lahayville, 143, 331
Lauder, Sir Henry, 24, 30*n*2
Les Misérables, 240–41, 242*n*3
Liverpool (England), 31–33
Lorraine Province, 104–5, 116*m*1
Louis XVI (king of France), 49
Lucy-le-Bocage, 234, 245–46

343

Index

Ludendorff offensives, xlv. *See also* Belleau, Bois de
Lunéville sector, 104–5, 117
Lusitania, sinking of, xxiii–xxiv

March, Gen. Peyton Conway, 73–74, 78*n*2, 79
Marne River/Valley, 234, 301; Château Thierry on, xlv–xlvi, 227; Château-Thierry pocket/salient along, 301; fighting along, 226–33, 303, 305–7; German retreat from, 318–19, 322; Second Battle of the, 223, 302–26; third Ludendorff offensive and, xlv–xlvi
Marshall, George, xxxv
Mary (queen), 35, 48*n*3
McCormick, Amy Irwin Adams, 77, 78*n*3
McCormick, Robert R., *xxxii,* xxxiii–xxxiv, li*n*9, 174, 180*n*3
Metz, 117, 335
Meunière, Bois de, 324–25
Meurthe River, 97
Meuse River, 198; Battle of St. Mihiel, 329–35
Mexico: Gibbons in, xxvi–xxvii; Japanese alliance, xxvii, xxx–xxxi; Mexican-American War, xxix; Revolution, xxvi–xxvii; U.S. involvement in, *xviii,* xxix–xxx; search for Pancho Villa in, xxv
Mont Sec, 198, 331
Montagne, Forêt de, 307, 331
Moselle River, 330

Nancy (city), 65
Nesles, Forêt de, 324
Neuilly-sur-Seine, American hospital at, 278, 282–300
Neuilly Wood, 227
Neutrality, American, World War I and, xx, xxi, xxii
Neville, Col. Wendell C., 245–46, 266*n*2
Nivelle, Gen. Robert, xxxvii
Noyon, 155, 223–24, 226
Nurses, 71–72, 78*n*3, 214, 284, 288–90, 299

Oise River, 224, 226
"Open warfare" system, of Pershing, xliv
Ourcq River, 226, 321–23
"Over There" (by Cohan), *xlii,* lii*m*3

Painlevé, M., 42
Paris: AEF in, 49–50, 213–22; as German goal, xlv, 226, 244, 301-2; Pershing in, 41–47, *46,* 49–50; Passchendaele offensive, xxxix, xl
Patton, George, xxxv
Pershing, Gen. John J., *xxxviii,* li*n*4; AEF and, xxxix–xl; amalgamation policy and, xl; Battle of St. Mihiel under, 329–35; at Boulogne-sur-Mare, 37; chief of staff to, 236, 242*n*2; DSC awarded by, 257; First American Field Army and, 329; at Folkestone, 36–37; at Lafayette's tomb, 45, *46,* 47; at Liverpool, 31–33; in London,

344

Index

34–35; in Mexico, xxv, xxvii, xxxi, xxxiv–xxxv; open warfare system of, xliv; in Paris, 41–47, 49–50; in Picardy Province, 165; at St. Nazaire prison camps, 63–64; train travel by, 33–34, 36, 40–41; at training grounds, 69

Pétain, Gen. Henri-Philippe, xxxvii, *xxxviii*, xxxix, xli, li*n*10–11, 334

Picpus Cemetery (Paris): Pershing's visit to, xlii–xliii, 45, *46*, 47

Pont-à-Mousson front, 117, 329–30

Powers, Maj. Charles (surgeon), 280

Queenstown (Ireland), 30

Red Napoleon, The (F. Gibbons), xlix, lii*n*15

Rheims, 224, 226, 301, 303, 305–7

Richecourt, 199–212

Roosevelt, Theodore, xxiv, xxv, li*n*2; Gibbons's meeting with, xlvii–xlviii

Royal Welsh Fusiliers, 33–35, 48*n*1

Russia, in WWI, xxxv–xxxvi

Saint-Nicolas-de-Port, 97–104

Savoy Hotel (London), 34–36

Seicheprey, 117, 128, 142

Sérévillers, 175, 181–82

Sergy, 322–23

Sharp, William, 42

Soissons: Château-Thierry pocket border and, 301; fighting near, 307, 318, 326; German capture of, 225

Somme, Battle of the, xxi, 155, 194

St. Louis Nationals (baseball club), 286, 300*m*2

St. Mihiel, 117, 329–35

St. Nazaire, 51, *52*, 53–64

St. Quentin, 223, 326

Staats-Zeitung, 63

Stanton, Col. Charles E., xliii, lii*n*12

Stanton, Mike, 145, 151–52

Stroudsburg, Penn., l

Submarine warfare, xxi, xxiii–xxv; impediment to U.S. armed forces in Europe, xliii–xliv

Suippes, 224

Supply, of U.S. armed forces, xliii

Sussex, sinking of, xxiv

Sussex Pledge, xxiv

Tampico (Mexico), U.S. troops in, xxvii, xxix

Terny-Sorny, 326–27

Thiaucourt, 331, 335

Torcy, 236

Toul, 65, 117, 156, 195

Trench *vs.* open warfare, xliv

Trugny, Bois de, 321; village, 321

United States Armed Services. *See* American Expeditionary Forces (AEF)

Index

United States Army Divisions: 1st, xxxiv, li*n*9, *102*, 165, 193, 195, 308, 317; 2nd, xliv, xlvi, 233–34, 244, 308, 313, 317; 9th, 234, 244; 23rd, 234, 244; 26th, 195, 320; 42nd (Rainbow), 303

United States First Army, xli

United States Marine Corps, 57; 2nd Div., 4th Marine Regt., 266*n*2;, 5th Regt., 233, 244-45, 266*n*2; 6th Regt., 244; at Bois de Belleau, xlv, xlvi, 236, 239–42; in Paris, 219; travel to front lines, xliv, 233–34

Unrestricted submarine warfare (USW), xxiv–xxv, xxix

Valdahon, 72–75

Veracruz (Mexico), U.S. troops in, xxvii, xxix

Verdun, xxi; American position near, 117; Daly, Sgt. Maj. Daniel at, 242*n*4; liberation of, 335; St. Mihiel salient and, 329

Vesle River, 226, 325–26

Vigneulles, 331–32, 335

Villa, Hipolito, xxvi

Villa, Pancho, xxv–xxvii, *xxviii*, xxix–xxxi, li*n*3; Gibbons's travel with, xxvi–xxvii

Villers-Cotterêts Forest, 301–2, 307

Vittel, 71–72

Viviani, René, 42

von Boehm, Gen., 224

von Bülow, Gen. Fritz, 224

von Hindenburg, Field Marshal Paul, 155, 180*m*

Vosges, 65, 72

War correspondents, xxxiv, lii*m*4, 131–42

Washington, George, xlii–xliii

Western front, xxi, xxxvi–xxxvii, xl–xli, xliv–xlv

Wilson, Woodrow, xix–xx, xxii–xxv, li*m*, 338; amalgamation policy and, xl; Gibbons's meeting with, xlvii; Pancho Villa and, xxv

Wood, Junius 140

Young Men's Christian Association (YMCA), 77, 85, 106, 274–75

Ypres offensive (third), xxxix

Zimmerman, Arthur, xxix

Zimmerman Telegram, xxix–xxx

IMAGE CREDITS

Library of Congress: ii, xxviii, xxxviii, xlviii, 19, 22, 46, 70, 84, 96, 102, 122, 129, 139, 157, 164, 185, 188, 202, 208, 232, 270, 273, 289, 293, 315, 328

Courtesy of Colonel Robert R. McCormick Research Center: xxxii

Property of the publisher: *And They Thought We Wouldn't Fight* by Floyd Gibbons (New York, George H. Doran Company, 1918) xviii, 52, 256, 298; postcards: 6, 87, 120, 146, 215, 220, 258

Courtesy of Rubenstein Library, Duke University: xlii

U.S. National Archives: 2, 67, 114, 168, 337

DESIGNED, TYPESET, PRINTED, BOUND, AND DISTRIBUTED BY
R. R. DONNELLEY & SONS COMPANY

COMPOSITION:
ALLENTOWN, PENNSYLVANIA
CHENNAI, INDIA

SCANNING AND IMAGE PROOFING:
RR DONNELLEY
PREMEDIA TECHNOLOGIES
ELGIN, ILLINOIS

COMPUTER TO PLATES, PRINTING, AND BINDING:
CRAWFORDSVILLE, INDIANA

ADDRESSING AND MAILING:
RR DONNELLEY
RESPONSE MARKETING SERVICES

WORLDWIDE DISTRIBUTION:
RR DONNELLEY LOGISTICS

BODY TYPEFACE:
11/12.85 POINT GARAMOND

CLOTH:
ARRESTOX VELLUM, LAKESIDE GREEN,
BY HOLLISTON MILLS, INC.

PAPER STOCK:
50-POUND WHITE LAKESIDE CLASSIC
FROM LINDENMYER
BY GLATFELTER

LAKESIDE CLASSICS ARE PRINTED
ON A PERMANENT PAPER
FOR ENDURING QUALITY